REVOLUTIONARY
YIDDISHLAND

REVOLUTIONARY YIDDISHLAND

A History of Jewish Radicalism

Alain Brossat and
Sylvia Klingberg

Translated by David Fernbach

VERSO
London • New York

Avec le soutien du

This work was published with the help of the French
Ministry of Culture – Centre national du livre
Ouvrage publié avec le concours du Ministère français
chargé de la culture – Centre national du livre

First published in English by Verso Books 2016
First published by Balland in 1983 as *Le Yiddishland révolutionnaire*.
This English translation is from the second edition published by Éditions Syllepse
in 2009, which was revised by David Forest with the addition of new editorial
notes and references
© Balland 1983
© Éditions Syllepse 2009
Translation © David Fernbach 2016

1 3 5 7 9 10 8 6 4 2

Verso
UK: 6 Meard Street, London W1F 0EG
US: 20 Jay Street, Suite 1010, Brooklyn, NY 11201
versobooks.com

Verso is the imprint of New Left Books

ISBN-13: 978-1-78478-606-9 (HB)
ISBN-13: 978-1-78478-608-3 (US EBK)
ISBN-13: 978-1-78478-609-0 (UK EBK)

British Library Cataloguing in Publication Data
A catalogue record for this book is available from the British Library

Library of Congress Cataloging-in-Publication Data

Names: Brossat, Alain, author. | Klingberg, Sylvia, author. | Fernbach,
David, translator.
Title: Revolutionary Yiddishland : a history of Jewish radicalism / Alain
Brossat and Sylvia Klingberg ; translated by David Fernbach.
Other titles: Yiddishland râevolutionnaire. English
Description: First edition. | New York : Verso, 2016.
Identifiers: LCCN 2016023967 | ISBN 9781784786069 (hardback)
Subjects: LCSH: Jewish radicals – Europe, Eastern. | Holocaust, Jewish
(1939-1945) | Jews – Soviet Union – History. | Soviet Union – Ethnic
relations.
Classification: LCC DS135.E8 B7613 2016 | DDC 320.53092/3924047 – dc23
LC record available at https://lccn.loc.gov/2016023967

Typeset in Minion Pro by MJ&N Gavan, Truro, Cornwall
Printed and bound by
CPI Group (UK) Ltd, Croydon, CR0 4YY

For Ian

Contents

Preface to the 2009 Edition

In the quarter of a century since this book was written, most of the faces who appear in it are no more. This fading of individual memory comes on top of the weaknesses of collective memory – the 'black hole' that swallowed up revolutionary Yiddishland, a world that is more than lost, being actually denied, even unpronounceable today with the new policing of discourse. As Kurt Tucholsky sarcastically noted, any revolutionary energy that does not find the means to inflect and alter the course of history is condemned to be 'realized' in culture, finding here retroactively a form of domesticated inscription. Having failed to achieve its hopes, its utopias, its political programmes and strategies, broken on the rocks of twentieth-century European history, Yiddishland survives, in the account of the past, as a culture, a lost treasure entrusted to antiquarian remembrance. The history of the victors has done the rest, by imposing its retrospective certainties: if all those whose testimonies are gathered in this book belong to the camp of the vanquished, this is because, in the common sense of a certain 'historicism' referred to by Walter Benjamin, they were politically misled; they had linked their fate to the grand narrative of working-class emancipation, fraternity between peoples, socialist egalitarianism – rather than to that of a Jewish state solidly established on its ethnic foundations, territorial conquests and realpolitik alliances.

On more than one count, therefore, a new edition of this book goes against the current. In the twenty-five years since its first publication, its features of 'untimeliness' have only become more pronounced.

In 1983, it was still conceivable to write a book on the Jewish world of Eastern Europe in the twentieth century, focused on its historical condition, and organized around the major theme of *revolution* rather than *Shoah* – which in no way implies that the mass exterminations carried out by the Nazis hold a secondary place here, as will be abundantly clear. In 1983 it was still possible, with memory not yet governed by disciplinary regulations and a speech police established at the heart of the media and close to the executive and judicial powers, to write a book of this kind from a point of view decidedly different from any form of Zionist teleology. In 1983, a book whose guiding thread was basically the notion of 'terrorist' history (to refer here to Kojève); whose collective characters were revolutionary parties, mass organizations, workers' councils; whose striking scenes were workers' insurrections, civil wars, movements of armed struggle, still spoke a language intelligible to a section of its potential readership, and described events whose experience was capable of arousing empathy.

Since this time, a dense layer of ash (ideological, discursive, as you prefer) has covered up the systems of self-evidence or connivance that this book appeals to in the very way it is written. Today, as soon as such subjects are tackled, historical reason is expressed only in declarations of principle concerning the unassailable character of the state of Israel; more generally, any account of this history of molten lava that places at its heart such figures as that of the revolutionary militant, the worker resisting and struggling, arms in hand, is immediately revoked by those newly sanctified as morally correct – the human rights campaigner, the humanitarian firefighter, the tireless and non-violent promoter of democratic values and forms …

In this sense, rereading this book today requires, for its authors above all, a stimulus to reflect on the conditions imposed by what Foucault called the *order of discourses*. Revisiting these pages in our present time, we are struck by an indefinable but persistent sense of foreignness: everything is familiar, but we are separated from this very familiarity by an irrevocable sense of distance; we directly perceive the rigorous conditions by which discourses, simply in their continuous flux, become heterogeneous to the very people – including ourselves – whom they traverse and envelop. It is impossible for us, therefore, to step back into the era of this book, even if we see no reason to 'deny' a single line, a single statement. The determining factor is not so much that 'the world has changed' since we wrote it, or that almost all the people whom we interviewed have disappeared; it is rather, in a far more disturbing fashion, that the very conditions of speaking about such subjects have changed and shifted. Even if we had not budged an inch from the positions that defined the arrangement and orientation of the book, we would not be able today to find the 'manner' in which it was written, we would have lost the 'secret' of its way of speaking – a fact that, on rereading, has the effect of arousing violently shared feelings ('God, what energy, what passion!' on the one hand; and 'What certainty, what poetic excesses' on the other).

In other words, what is at issue here is not so much the inevitable growing distance of a 'world of yesterday', but rather a loosening of connection from what appears today as a 'lost world'. And once again, this is not simply due to the fact of Auschwitz and the mass graves of summer 1941, but for another reason as well: since we wrote *Revolutionary Yiddishland*, a change of era has set in, surreptitiously rather than manifestly. A change that leaves completely open and uncertain the question of the conditions of the reception of this book in the world today.

Two points of contention can serve here to shed light on this issue of the difference between one era and another, and the effects of a break in intelligibility that this produces: the question of communism, on the one hand, and that of collective memory, on the other.

'Communism' is a signifier that runs right through this book, in all the 'chapters' of history evoked by the militants to whom it gives voice. In their memories, this word is far more than simply a political label, a programme or a form of organization. It is a kind of constant perspective in which the notion of another possibility is embedded, a field of radical heterotopies in the face of a present condemned to disaster (exploitation, misery, political terror …). In this sense, 'communism' is a reference that mobilizes and inspires our witnesses well beyond the limits of belonging to a particular milieu – the communist movement or communist parties. There is in fact this perspective of communism, both practical and non-practical, in each of the great 'scenes' in which they variously participated: the Russian Civil War, the building of the USSR, resistance in the camps, the war in Spain, the armed struggle against Nazism, the formation of 'socialist' states in Eastern Europe, emigration to Palestine, etc. 'Communism' is, in this general sense, the word used for a politics with the ambition to establish social justice and apply egalitarian principles. The fact that this perspective was most often blocked by defeat, calculations of realpolitik, the strategic blindness of bureaucracies, etc. in no way changes the fact that this article of faith is embedded at the core of the hope of these men and women, in their activity on every front of struggle: *another world is possible*, and the generic name of this other possibility is 'communism'. A distinct philosophy of history gives this term consistency: it is possible to be radically *different* from the present (of oppression, misery, injustice) inasmuch as the mass of humanity *inhabit history*, which presents itself as a field of action in which they possess the capacity to produce decisive shifts, bifurcations. History is open, the future is the surface on which the human possibility of emancipating itself from the present is inscribed. And once again, 'communism' is not simply the name of this unbounded freedom, but its master signifier.

However, what is precisely epoch-making in our present is the horrified rejection of any such presupposition and the historical sensations that accompany it. We have entered the age of the supposed universality and eternity of the democratic paradigm, in such a way that any notion of a sidestep decided outside the conditions of present historicity now appears as a promise of inevitable disaster and unreasonable exposure to multifarious risks. An ideal of 'immunitarian' democracy has replaced the perspective of that social refoundation which, for those who attached themselves to it, implied full exposure to the winds of history. It is not simply because the collapse of the Soviet bloc created a wide gulf between our present and the historical sequence that was the very milieu in which our characters acted, the twentieth century of sound and fury, that their 'world' has become enigmatic in the eyes of the great majority of our contemporaries. It is, more radically, and in a manner less reducible to 'particular circumstances', because the horizon on which their rebellion against the existing order was inscribed has grown misty, with the effect that the signifier 'communism' has lost all its power and shrunk to the dimensions of a pejorative signifier, synonym of everything that, in the past era now rejected, bears the mark of the unreasonable and monstrous.

The same type of observation is needed when the question of collective memory arises. When this book was being written, there was a rage for 'voices from below', as witness the great success of the Maspero collection 'Actes et mémoires du peuple'. René Allio outbid Michel Foucault with his film *I, Pierre Rivière* ... acted by peasants in a Norman village, etc. And so we were hardly original in considering that rescuing the memories of these militants who came for the most part from the poorest sectors of the 'Jewish street' in Eastern Europe was part of a genuine process of regeneration – rediscovered memory supposed to lead, not principally to a better knowledge of the past, but rather to a better capacity to inform the struggles of the present. This was indeed for us the amazing actuality of these diffracted accounts, their intact power to transmit a revolutionary 'legacy' that, preserved against wind and weather by these survivors, came down to us as the most precious of deposits ... But things turned out rather more complicated: the theme of collective memory has effected a complete about-turn, to become, in the hands of 'elites' happy to turn anything to their advantage, a privileged instrument for the government of the living (ritualizing of memory, obsession with commemoration, 'duty of remembrance', victimological cult of the 'terrible' places of the past, religion of 'traumatism', etc.).

The beginnings of this turn can be seen already in the film *Les révolutionnaires du Yiddishland*, made by Nat Lilenstein and partly inspired by our own research. This is a monument, a sumptuous cenotaph erected to the memory of those whom it celebrates, yet it only rekindles the flame of what it celebrates the better to facilitate its transition to the status of cultural object: a page is turned, that of the album of memories, while a supposedly implacable reality principle tends to impose itself. 'Bundism', which was indeed an immense militant epic, attested to in our book by its last survivors washed up in Israel, has meanwhile become a kind of memorial tourist agency (specialized in teaching Yiddish language and culture) – but solidly

moored to the communitarian establishment and the fate of the
Hebrew state.

In this twilight hour when the French president seeks to promote
the 'adoption' of a child of the Shoah by primary schools today, as one
plebiscitary ruse among others, it seems hard to understand the 'uto-
pianizing' of the memory of the defeated that was our main impulse
in embarking on the quest for these survivors, inspired by a strong
enthusiasm, even the sense of fulfilling a mission. We could even recall
here that our sense of having collected a folder of almost sacred words
was so strong that we delivered to our editor, Françoise Adelstein, an
initial version of the book consisting of a pure and simple montage,
without commentary, of 'words' gathered – so convinced were we
both of the intrinsic power of these testimonies, and of the incon-
gruity of any irruption into this untouchable text. Collective memory
was then our fetish, and self-effacement before its speech our credo.
We were at first quite stunned by the refusal of our editor to endorse
this cult – and we had to go back and play the tapes again in order to
start actually writing this book.

In our day, in 'our' part of the globe, it is almost impossible to
understand these revolutionaries of yesteryear, ready to put their
lives in peril for a 'cause' – the most eloquent example of this being
the Spanish Civil War – or to penetrate what inspires those men and
women who, in other parts of this same globe today, are ready to die
to promote their 'cause'. Let us say with Zygmunt Bauman that our
liquid society, which promotes the interests of consumers and man-
ufactures celebrities, is at the opposite extreme from the hero who
sacrifices a personal present in the name of a collective future.

Most of the individuals who found their way into this book were
unknown to us before our field study in Israel, in the early 1980s, led
us to meet them and conduct the interviews that form the basis of
this book. And we lost sight of most of them after completing this
work, sometimes learning of the death of one or the other. However,
a few exceptions to this general 'ingratitude' (familiar enough to
researchers practising oral history) must be mentioned: Yankel Taut,
a Trotskyist militant since the earliest time and a political friend of
Sylvia Klingberg, active together with her in the 1960s in the Israeli

organization Matzpen, and Hanna Lévy-Hass who settled in Paris in the 1980s, and whose *Journal de Bergen-Belsen* Alain Brossat published in French.

But to end this preface, we would like to mention the case of a 'hidden' witness, who appears in this book under the pseudonym of Isaac Safrin (the only person, in fact, whose name had to be changed).

We interviewed Marcus Klingberg in Tel Aviv in 1981 and, at his request, referred to him by the name of his great-great-grandfather, Isaac Safrin. In the same interest of concealing his identity, we changed his profession of epidemiologist to that of surgeon. Some two years later, on 24 June 1983, his daughter Sylvia handed him a copy of our book, in the presence of his wife and grandson, under the strict surveillance of a colonel of the Shabak, the Israeli counterespionage agency, and a flanking acolyte. This scene took place in the prison at Ashkelon, a seaside town some sixty kilometres from Tel Aviv. The prisoner was then registered under the name of Abraham Grinberg, and described as a publisher.

At the time when we interviewed him, we thought that this imposture indicated a certain cowardice unworthy of this man, who concealed himself and kept silent about a past that was precious to him – as we could hear from his voice, which trembled with emotion. Regretting the lost Jewish world of Central Europe, remaining nostalgic for the 'exile' condition, and above all glorying in having fought in the Red Army, albeit in the Second World War – all that was viewed poorly in Israel. The combination of fidelity to Yiddishland and attachment to the Soviet Union was seen as improper, even suspect, all the more so on the part of a man who managed to carve out a position in the high realms of the state.

Marcus Klingberg, alias Isaac Safrin, alias Abraham Grinberg, was arrested on 19 January 1983, and condemned to twenty years' imprisonment for spying for the USSR. For more than a quarter of a century, from 1950 to 1977, he regularly transmitted information on the highly confidential work that was conducted first of all in the army, then in the context of the Israel Institute for Biological Research at Ness Ziona, where he had long occupied the post of deputy scientific director. He was tried and imprisoned in secret, and for the first ten years of his detention kept away from almost all contact both within and outside the gaol. When the news got out, there was a shock wave across the country, and the press, with rare exceptions, mobilized its whole palette of invectives against this 'traitor to his country'. The divulging of this case of espionage cast a ray of light on the work conducted at the Ness Ziona institute. Though the list of the 'ten plagues of Egypt' (or maybe twenty or thirty …) manufactured in its laboratories remains undisclosed, the business it conducts is today an open secret: chemical and biological weapons.

There are still some major areas of uncertainty around this story that its protagonist is forbidden to disclose. In his biography published in 2007 (co-authored by M. Sfard), Marcus Klingberg reveals that he did not act alone. He recruited his wife, a biologist employed at the same time, as well as a close friend who would later become both an eminent scientist at one of the country's leading universities and a discrete protagonist in strategic research for the Israeli state. Verbal reports, photographed documents and even a test tube containing a sample of microbial culture were handed to agents of the Soviet Union. Until 1967, these exchanges took place at the Russian church of Abu Kamir, in a district of Tel Aviv; after Moscow broke diplomatic relations with Israel, the rendezvous were abroad, generally in Geneva.

Like many of his kind, Marcus Klingberg never found it hard to let go of the moorings holding him to a particular place and letting himself be carried by the current, ready always to reach a new country (today, Paris). Yet he spent fifty-five years of his life in Israel, including twenty behind bars. He extracted himself from the contradictions in which he found himself by conveying to the Soviet Union, the state that had enabled him to accomplish the actions he was most proud of, the panoply of formulae for weapons of mass destruction invented (or copied) by Israel, the state conceived from the start as a counter to his submerged Yiddishland.

Alain Brossat, Sylvia Klingberg
December 2008

Introduction

Out of the eleven million Jews in the world as a whole, Russia held more than five million; scarcely a tenth of these in the countryside or outside the 'Pale of Settlement', and around four and a half million pressed into the cities and towns of this 'territory'.[1]

Behind the double wall of this territorial and urban ghetto the mass of Jews lived, thought, suffered and acted, a whole world, a complete society, with the requisite variety of elements – workers and intellectuals, scholars and financiers, managers and labourers, etc. At the top of the pyramid, a financial bourgeoisie as in the West, but without any influence; below them a middling bourgeoisie, intellectual and commercial; and finally an immense Jewish proletariat. An unknown proletariat, if ever there was one! For this largest and most homogeneous class, the mass that was truly characteristic of the nation, the Jewish proletariat, has always been ignored. Bernard Lazare was quite correct in writing that only the Jewish bourgeoisie had been studied, and that Jewish historians had only written the history of the Jewish bourgeoisie for a readership of the bourgeois Jews of their day.

---

1 The Pale of Settlement comprised twenty-six governorships where Jews were allowed to live, but only in cities and towns. Élie Eberlin and Georges Delahache, 'Juifs russes', Les cahiers de la quinzaine, December 1904. [For several sources cited in this book the French edition does not give page references, and thirty-three years later it has not been possible to retrieve these. – Translator.]

'The Jew as trafficker, dealer in money, merchant, occupied the whole of the historical stage. Anti-Semites attacked him, Jewish historians pleaded attenuating circumstances. But no one wanted to see the proletariat, the Jewish mass, and this is still misunderstood.' These lines were written by Élie Eberlin, and published by Charles Péguy in his *Cahiers de la quinzaine*. In the text from which they are taken, Eberlin emphasizes the powerful organization of this unknown proletariat, stressing that this is where 'the best fighters in the struggle waged in Russia for a better future' come from; he describes the organization and activities of the 'Jewish General Workers' Union', the Bund, and concludes, 'Governmental and public anti-Semitism systematically seek to reduce the Jews, and especially the Jewish proletariat, to the level of pariahs. Despite this, it is the Jewish proletarian organization that the Russian authorities view as most dangerous.'

A few months later, the decisive part played by this Jewish proletariat and its organizations in the strikes and insurrections that broke out right across the Pale of Settlement in the course of the 1905 revolution would confirm Eberlin's observations. The Bund then reached its zenith, and Lenin himself paid homage to the combativeness of the Jewish workers, whose struggle entered history. But what is the position today as regards the paradox mentioned by Eberlin, that of the unknown Jewish proletariat and its struggle? Has history rendered it its due?

Quite the contrary. This paradox is today immeasurably greater, reflected by the tragic dimension of the history of the last century. The Jewish working class of Eastern Europe has disappeared, swallowed up by this history, and this disappearance is now duplicated in historical consciousness, leaving a blank page. It is not the stuff from which official histories and history lessons are made, apologetic myths and images for popular consumption.

This working class, this wretched, over-exploited populace several million strong, concentrated and very homogeneous in terms of its conditions of existence, its traditions and cultural references, its language, no longer exists except through its survivors and scattered traces. This is a unique paradox in contemporary history. The twentieth century is sadly rich in historical defeats, bloodbaths of the working class: from Germany in 1933 to Chile in 1973, not forgetting Spain in 1938 and Poland in 1981. But there is no other example of a proletariat that, after defeat, does not raise its head again one day and rebuild the network of its organizations, its historical consciousness and its combativeness. Just this one: the working class of Yiddishland, erased from the map, disappeared at the same time as the human continent in which it was the most numerous and most dynamic element, set on a different future.

It is not our intent here to undertake yet again, in a proletarian version, the work of mourning (not always disinterested) for the 'holocaust'. As we shall see, the problem is infinitely more complex. Before being the conscious, stubborn and systematic work of the Nazis, this world was already brought into crisis by the effect of two major factors: the growth of large-scale capitalist industry in Central and Eastern Europe, with the social, ideological and cultural upheavals that it inevitably brought in its wake, and the October Revolution – with the economic, social, political and cultural earthquakes that arose from it.

There is no longer a Yiddishland, there is no longer a Yiddishland working class, a point that it has long been unnecessary to emphasize. Between the many and sometimes vivid traces of this vanished Atlantis and the present is a blank, a void, an abyss created by the earthquake of history, which no work of memory, no testimony, no scholarship, is able to fill. And so the imaginary, the emotional and the symbolic necessarily enter into the composition of our attitude towards this vanished world. An attitude that focuses a sum of historical passions and emotions, obstinately held positions, sometimes still vivid, which very often stand in the way of a work of truth.

In this way the paradox continues. The time is not so very long ago, in fact, when this world was still alive. Despite Hitler, despite Stalin and, on a different level, despite the stubbornness with which Zionism rewrites the history of the social and political struggles of the Jewish workers of Eastern Europe, many of the witnesses and actors are still here, albeit as survivors. Yet their very status as survivors of this disarticulated universe, reduced to tatters, pervades and determines their memory of this world in a highly singular fashion. Whatever the precision and quality of this memory, they speak today beyond the caesura that we mentioned, and this pervades their discourse; as escapees, they are as if born a second time, beyond the historical trauma that dynamited their existence. And in a new paradox, this remark seems particularly applicable to the witnesses and actors who speak in this book – because they live in Israel. In the historical geography of this century, ironic and tragic, Israel stands in many ways as the polar opposite of Yiddishland, especially for a revolutionary Jew from Eastern Europe.

In the course of 1981 and 1982 we interviewed in Israel former revolutionary Jewish militants from Eastern, Central and Southern Europe. Some of them had been active in specifically Jewish workers' organizations such as the Bund or Poale Zion. Others were communists, socialists, Trotskyists, etc. Some had joined the revolutionary movement already before the First World War, others in the 1920s, others later still. For the most part, their testimonies related to the interwar period. They had been in all the revolutionary struggles of this time, from the October Revolution to the anti-fascist resistance, from Spain to Poland. The courage and obstinacy to commit themselves to militant activity they had drawn from the credo of revolutionary action of our age: 'The earth shall rise on new foundations / We have been naught, we shall be all!'

They were active when everything still seemed possible, but especially when the shadow descended, when it was midnight in the century. They paid more than their due tribute to this dark course of our history, spared by none of the tyrannies that crushed Europe under their iron heel. As Pierre Vidal-Naquet wrote, 'The Judaism of Eastern Europe really did serve as the blood bank of the proletarian revolutionary movements.'[2] Behind the testimonies that we collected stand the immense cohort of those whose existence came to an end, for most of them at an early age, on the battlefields of the Russian Civil War; in the Belgian, French or Yugoslav Resistance;

---

2   Pierre Vidal-Naquet, *The Jews: History, Memory, and the Present* (New York: Columbia University Press, 1996), p. 204.

in the International Brigades before Madrid; in the ranks of Soviet partisans; etc. It is to their memory that this work is dedicated.

For the most part, the individuals we interviewed were rank-and-file militants or medium-rank cadres in the movements and organizations in which they participated. They had not shaken hands with Stalin, received the confidences of André Marty at Albacete, or dined at Borochov's table.[3] But they were at the point of struggle; they were the movement. Their point of view was hardly embarrassed by the diplomatic concerns and apologetic preoccupations that retrospectively mark the memoirs and testimonies of leaders. In actual fact, however, is the anonymous fighter a subaltern actor in the revolution – the fighter who holds the rifle and writes the leaflet, who knows prisons and camps, who has no time to pose for history, and has also to worry about feeding his children? At all events, the density and strength of the testimonies of these men and women give the lie to the doubtful aphorism attributed to Mao Zedong, that the rank and file are 'a blank page on which you can write whatever you want'.

These militants were carried along by a history that submerged and suffocated them like a tidal wave. They did not surface from this

---

3   Ber Borochov (1881–1917), a socialist Zionist born in Ukraine, attempted to achieve a synthesis between scientific socialism and the national dimension of the Jewish people, between the class struggle and Jewish nationalism. His fundamental idea was that the 'social physiology of the Jewish people is organically diseased', that the Jews of the diaspora were condemned to an abnormal situation. They lived in an economy dominated by backward petty production and lacked access to modern heavy industry; in sum, the social structure of the Jewish people in the diaspora formed an upside-down pyramid. There was thus no chance of emancipation for it in the diaspora; assimilation was an illusion. The central task of the Jewish people was to gain access to genuine national sovereignty by emigrating to Eretz Israel. As a militant of the Russian Social Democrat Party, Borochov founded the Union of Socialist Zionist Workers of Yekaterinoslav in 1901. He played a determining role in the foundation of the Poale Zion movement, leaving the eighth Zionist congress in The Hague in 1907 to take part in the founding of a world union of Poale Zion – thereby asserting the necessity of the independence of working-class Zionism. He left Russia in 1907, living in Western and Central Europe until 1914, then emigrated to America. On return to Russia in 1917, he took part in the Poale Zion conference in Russia in August of that year, arguing for the establishment of 'socialist colonization' in Palestine.

whirlpool intact, and they still question themselves today about the certainties and commitments of that time. But they have not for all that renounced the attempt to understand; they still have the passion of their history. They committed themselves as actors; they carried the burden of what they saw as their historic responsibility. Today they stand on the margins of history. They are witnesses. They have not renounced their lucidity.

The effort we made was to reconstitute, by way of their accounts, the broader spectrum of movements, commitments and ideologies. It is essentially what we call Yiddishland, the Jewish communities of Eastern Europe, that constitutes the backcloth of these testimonies. As will readily be seen, this Yiddishland was the cultural, linguistic, social and political soil of the majority of our informants. From Yiddishland to the revolution: that is the guiding thread of the great majority of experiences recounted in this book. We sought, accordingly, to give voice in an equitable manner to representatives of the three major currents of red Yiddishland: the communists, the Bund and Poale Zion. Reading their stories certainly makes it easy to measure the complex reality that these three labels cover: communist may mean Stalinist, but also Trotskyist or Brandlerite.[4] In the period between the world wars, the Bund swung between communism and social democracy, while the trajectories of Poale Zion allegiance were also multiple, from Moscow to Tel Aviv. Where these narratives seem to leave too much implicit, we have supplemented them with historical notes.

In a general way, these stories seem to bring out a number of salient elements: the commitment of Jewish revolutionaries from Eastern, Central and Southern Europe that finds expression here is a nomadic one. From Poland to France, from France to Spain, from Spain to the USSR … an atlas is needed to follow their wanderings and the

---

4   Heinrich Brandler (1881–1967) was a member of the Spartacus League, then a co-founder and leader of the German Communist Party (KPD). Opposed to Stalin, he was detained against his will in the Soviet Union for four years. Expelled from the KPD on his return to Germany, he co-founded the KPD-Opposition along with Paul Frölich and August Thalheimer. From 1930 he opposed the Comintern and became a member of the bureau of the International Communist Opposition, before being forced into exile when the Nazis seized power.

succession of their struggles. This is because the world from which they came, the European 'East', was in the early twentieth century a turbulent volcano, a social and political powder keg, a world that was constantly rumbling and moving. On top of this, in this zone of insta-bility, the situation of the Jewish communities and populations from which they came was in most cases particularly unstable – from the pogrom at Kishinev in 1903 to the state anti-Semitism of interwar Poland. This double instability, the danger in simply being Jewish in Eastern Europe, this misery that was the everyday experience of the great majority of these communities, clearly formed the roots of the availability for revolutionary commitment of a large fraction of Jewish youth in the early decades of the century. The enforced nomadism of their commitments expressed its lack of roots in this unstable world, but also all the vacillations of the century's history. The trajectory of the Yiddishland revolutionaries was a long one, erratic because it followed the broken and sinuous course of a history that was itself erratic. They were in the vanguard of this.

Besides, these intersecting testimonies, sometimes converging and often contradictory, even implicitly critical of one another, these stories in which the dimension of history, of the universal, is mingled with that of the private, the intimate and the infinitely particular – these retraced experiences amount to a manifesto against schematic discourses. They bring out the infinite complexity of the situations within which these militants had to find their way; they emphasize the insurmountable contradictions that they came up against in their commitments; they show how derisory are all clichés, self-interested legends, 'official versions' and half-truths in relation to the jungle of this history. They convince us that the time has not yet come for objec-tivity on this page of our history. One writer, for example, devoted an impassioned book to the participation of Jews in the International Brigades in Spain, but he was too orthodox a communist to mention there the Jewish fighters who joined the supposedly Trotskyist POUM, or the liquidation of Jewish – among other – oppositionists by Jewish executioners.[5] Another put his pen and his patience in the service of

---

5   Cf. David Diamant, *Les juifs dans la Résistance française* (Paris: Le Pavillon, 1971).

rehabilitating the Bund, but, carried away by enthusiasm, stigmatized the 'Bolshevik victors who physically liquidated the Bund in Russia',[6] failing to remember that in the wake of the October Revolution there existed a Kombund which owed very little to terror or the Gulag, but much to the tremendous attraction exerted by communism on all the Yiddishland revolutionaries. For the Jews of Eastern Europe born in the first decades of the century, the name of Simon Petliura would be forever synonymous with pogrom. There are excellent reasons for this, and it was not by chance that this Ukrainian nationalist should have fallen to the bullet of a young Jew in 1926. But what is forgotten, which is unfortunate as this also belongs to the same history, is that in 1917 and 1918 this Petliura sat in the Ukrainian parliament, or Rada, and in the government of the ephemeral Ukrainian republic alongside deputies and ministers who represented Jewish socialist parties, and that Jabotinski, the mentor of the present Israeli prime minister,[7] maintained excellent relations with him between 1919 and 1921 … Others have made their task easier by writing, for example, that 'during the first eleven years of the Soviet regime, they [Jews] were treated, if not as enemies, then at least as second-class citizens'[8] – which is particularly laughable in view of the exceptionally high proportion of Jews in the party and state apparatus of the 1920s, not to mention the struggle against anti-Semitism that the Soviet leaders (starting with Lenin) waged at this time, the rights newly granted to the Jewish population, the real flourishing of Yiddish culture, the efforts made to develop agricultural colonies in southern Russia, etc. There were mistakes, failures, inadequacies, and undoubtedly an underestimation of the national dimension of the Jewish problem; there was the weight of the past, and later the crimes of Stalin; in short, in this field as elsewhere there were the formidable contradictions that beset the 'new world', the 'homeland of socialism'.

---

6   Editorial, 'Le Bund en Pologne', *Combat pour la diaspora*, 1980.

7   A reference to Menachem Begin, who was Israeli prime minister when these lines were written in 1983.

8   Chimen Abramsky, 'Le projet de colonisation du Birobidjan (1927–1959)', in Lionel Kochan, ed., *Les juifs en Union soviétique depuis 1917* (Paris: Calmann-Lévy, 1971).

But it is precisely this jungle of contradictions that one has to plunge into, with rose-coloured versions on the one hand and black ones on the other, each a peremptory short cut that makes the advance of knowledge impossible.

From this point of view, the mosaic of testimonies that we present in this book (with the contradictions, enigmas, paradoxes and zones of shadow that emerge) often goes against the grain of these short cuts and other 'official' versions. We learn, for example, in a mortal sin against the mystical version of Jewish history in which the Jew is the eternal innocent victim – that in the dark twists and turns that the Yiddishland revolutionaries experienced, they were sometimes on the side of the tyrant and executioner.

In more than one respect, the fate of the Yiddishland working class concentrates the fate of the revolutionary workers' movement of the twentieth century, in both its brightest and its darkest colours. Is it accidental that we discover these Yiddishland fighters everywhere that the revolution brilliantly flared, from the barricades of Łódź to the St Petersburg soviet of 1905; in Berlin in November 1918, Munich and Budapest in 1919, Poland between the two wars, Extremadura against the fascist generals in 1937, in the Resistance in France and Belgium and Yugoslavia, and again in the struggle within the concentration camps, from Auschwitz to Vorkuta?

We will not make a fetish of the particularity of this red Yiddishland whose archaeology (however partial and limited) we undertake here; we follow this thread less because it supposedly leads to a specific irreducibility of Jewish 'being-in-the-world',[9] than because it leads to the tragic universal of our history, its breakthroughs and blind alleys, and to the only great positive utopia of this century – that of the 'emancipation of the human race' under the red flag. Nor is it by chance, yet again, that this 'Jewish and red' illumination of the history of the century should emphasize its contrasts and enable us to approach in striking fashion those moments when everything was in the balance – Petrograd 1917, Madrid 1938, Warsaw 1939 … – as a springboard for

---

9   Even if the characteristics of Jewish society and culture must naturally be taken into account here.

historical reflection on the century, an encouragement to go beyond fables and lessons learned by heart.

Of course, if this 'Jewish thread', this 'Jewish history', teaches us much about the enigmas of our era – fascism, Stalinism – it does not give a miraculous key. Contrary to what is often imagined (a form of reassurance like any other), we are not today so removed from these phenomena that our historical reflection can grasp them, if not as 'things', then at least as historical objects comparable to others. On the contrary, we are still 'within', immersed in the history that these monstrosities wove, in the same way that, psychoanalytically speaking, each of us is 'in' their family, and anthropologically 'in' their society – precisely unable to grasp them as objects. This situation shows itself in a particularly spectacular fashion when we tackle our history from this 'red and Jewish' angle: why, in fact, are the most obvious and best-established facts about the Jewish workers' movement in Eastern Europe, its struggles and traditions, its organizations, its relationship with other populations and the powers of this region, so easily dissolved into the passion and emotion of discourse, prejudged positions and ideological blindness? Why is there no consensus among researchers and witnesses about the analysis of the most basic facts regarding these questions?

It is precisely because this 'Jewish and red' thread, traversing the seven circles of hell of our history, leads us right into the dark places of our era, to the absurd, the illogical, the unreasonable and irrational of this time; this juddering of history that no reason, no balance-sheet, no a posteriori discourse, no dissection of the past, can manage to exhaust, tame, reduce to the state of an objective past. The tragedy of this story remains the motor of our own existences.

It could indeed be a cruel and cynical game to bring one witness into 'dialogue' with another as we do in this book: the former militant of the Bund, the former communist, the former activist in Poale Zion. Each stresses the historical bankruptcy of the other, and each in their way is right. None of them, though, will admit that on this or that question they were blind. Beyond self-interested pleading and self-criticism, this situation reflects the density and irregularity of our history: its twists and turns disjointed and shredded the revolutionary discourse of these militants; their principles for understanding the world around them, their reason and concepts (historical, political, etc.) were cast on the sand like so many wrecks. Nothing is easier, for the Zionist, than to 'prove' the bankruptcy of the Bundist concept of 'national and cultural autonomy' for the Jews of Eastern Europe; they need only ask what remains of this fine dream? Nothing easier than for the Bundist to denounce the fate of the Poale Zion dream of the 1920s – a red and socialist Eretz Israel – in the face of the obscurantist and rapacious state of today, the scion of American imperialism. Nothing easier for both of these, the militant of Poale Zion and his enemy brother of the Bund, than to denounce in a single voice the collapse of their communist comrade's utopia (the USSR, Poland, etc.), where anti-Semitism reared its head (again) under cover of the 'new world'. Nothing easier for the communist …

These aporiai of historical and political reason on every side, these balance sheets with no bottom line, refer us again to the stifling unreason of a figure of history that has not faded into the past, with which we still have to deal, if not blind then at least blinkered. In fact, if none of the witnesses and actors we questioned can boast that they were not at some moment or other caught short by the course of history, belied by the sudden and disconcerting turns of the situation, it is also true that their efforts to anticipate the future, understand the laws of social and historical development and act on them, were not entirely vain or derisory. With their programme of cultural and national autonomy, the Bundists sought to offer a response to the exceptional situation of the Jews of Eastern Europe: that of a community extremely concentrated in certain urban zones but without a tie to a homogeneous territory. In large part, the politics of the young Soviet power towards the Jewish population, in the wake of the Revolution, linked up with this thread, in line with the proposals developed by Lenin and Trotsky in the first years of the century.

The militants of the left Poale Zion, for their part, stressed that the Jewish national problem – just like any other national question – could not be genuinely resolved without the Jewish communities being given the possibility of gathering in a territory, in Palestine, and devoting themselves to productive work. After the October

Revolution, and reflecting on the difficult problem posed by the existence of territories on which several nationalities or dispersed national communities coexisted, Lenin reached the conclusion that certain forms of national concentration were the necessary guarantee of national equality:

> In order to suppress any national oppression, it is urgently necessary to create autonomous districts, even very small ones, having a homogeneous national composition, around which the members of the nationality in question, dispersed at different points of the country or even the globe, can 'gravitate', entering into relationships and free associations of all kinds

– a conviction that is in the end quite 'territorialist'. Another Bolshevik leader, Kalinin, propagated the idea that, in order to preserve its nationality, the Jewish people in the USSR should turn to the land and create agricultural communities. The realization of the 'autonomous Jewish territory' of Birobidzhan – in a bureaucratic form, and beset by considerations that had nothing to do with the Jewish national problem – fitted naturally into this line of thought.

The element of unreason that took hold of history in the 1930s dismissed these concrete solutions, prospects and visions to the lumber room of accessories of utopia. Yet they were not lost for all that: there still exist, in countries such as France and the United States, a Jewish culture and problems of the diaspora that continue, for example, the inspiration of a cultural 'Bundism'. Nor should we forget that the militants who speak here embodied in their action values that were eminently positive, indeed the most elevated that the century saw. Their discourse certainly illustrates very often what we have known since the 1930s, the Moscow trials, the first revelations on the horrors of the Stalin system: that the seed of irrationality finds its way into the very heart of revolutionary practice and commitment for a 'new world'; that the weight of history, its ruses and Moloch-like cruelty, can come into collision with the revolutionary intention, this enthusiasm for the good, to divert or crush it. This disassociation between revolutionary enthusiasm and the objective consequence of action often raises agonizing questions, particularly for former communists, and this is a thread running through the whole book.

These texts are also a spur for us to challenge the premature 'verdicts of history', supposed 'good sense' and short-term 'realism'. Our perception of the history of the century is encumbered by arguments, paralogisms and a posteriori rationalizations that serve only to obscure this perception. And this is particularly clear, for obvious reasons, when Jewish history is in question. As Pierre Vidal-Naquet put it, 'to illuminate the Dreyfus affair by way of Auschwitz and Treblinka means having a tragic and unhistorical view of history'.[10] A view that is mystical and most often mystifying, we can readily add. And mythology is the opposite of history.

It is precisely because the history that injured the witnesses and actors presented in this book still sticks to our heels, that we have to guard against hasty 'judgements', overly smooth accounts, balance sheets on the backs of others. It should be emphasized that Zionist historiography, whether of right or left, has made a speciality of this kind of writing history backwards, a posteriori. It is common, for example, to hear in Israel that the Bund or the Jewish communists of Eastern Europe bear a heavy responsibility for not having spurred their fellows to emigrate to Palestine when there was still time, before 1939. This type of argument has the appearances of good sense and realism – today. But it does not need very much 'scratching' to find that it rests on a combination of sophisms or, at best, omissions. Is it not notorious, for example, that in their great majority the Jewish bourgeoisie of France still viewed Zionism before the war as an unrealistic utopia? The least that can be said is that the leaders of the Jewish communities of our country (and of Germany) tended in the 1930s to view the 'Bolshevik' danger as far more serious than the Nazi peril. It was only after the genocide, after 1945, that Jewish leaders in Western Europe and America invented the subtle dialectic of 'diaspora Zionism' and were converted to the reality of the state of Israel. And still more striking that in its majority the Zionist 'establishment' of interwar Poland was far from devoting the

---

10   Vidal-Naquet, *The Jews: History, Memory and Present*, p. 88.

greater part of its efforts to practical organization for emigration to Palestine.

It is true that in any case the policy of the British authorities of the time made it impossible to envisage the emigration at an early date of several million Jews. Even if some tens or hundreds of thousands of additional emigrants had managed to reach Palestine before 1939, the 'historical' question was not yet settled: Palestine might well have become a bloody trap for the Jews there if the clash of arms had had a different outcome; it was not the hand of God but the success of the British Eighth Army that fortunately tipped the scales in the right direction.

In the same way, it is wrong to evoke the action of Yiddishland militants in the 1920s and 1930s as if the concept of the unity and universality of the Jewish people, a religious concept that only the victory of Zionism made a political reality, was 'self-evident' at that time. This is again an anachronism: in their immense majority, the Jews of Eastern Europe did not attach any historical or social content to this religious notion. Even a militant so deeply pervaded by the sense of his Jewish identity (which he had deliberately chosen) as Vladimir Medem explicitly rejected this abstract and often mystic notion of a universal Jewish community. And then, in the 1920s, how did the leaders of the Zionist establishment, the heirs of Herzl who propagated the 'return' of the universal Jewish people to Eretz, conceive the 'fusion' of its different components?[11]

---

11   Adolf Böhm, historian of the Zionist movement from its origins to the 1930s, gives an insight into this in his work *Die zionistische Bewegung*, 2 vols. (Berlin: Jüdischer Verlag, 1935). He discusses the serious problem of conscience raised for progressive Zionist ideologists and the early Jewish colonists in Palestine (originally from Eastern Europe) by the presence on Palestinian soil of an Arab 'labour force'. There was a great risk, in fact, that an unequal relationship, even one of exploiters and exploited, would be formed between this frustrated labour force and the new immigrants. Better therefore to 'dispense' with these Arab workers. From this point of view, the influx of Yemeni Jews to Palestine from 1909 onwards, fleeing persecution in their countries, was manna from heaven. In Böhm's words, 'The Yemenite Jews were accustomed to the torrid climate, and also in many cases to arduous work, they were akin to the Arab workers in terms of their absence of needs, they spoke Hebrew and Arab, and besides were subjects

We can thus see that the 'verdicts' of history are not as clear as people are often tempted to imagine, and the mystical conception (Maxime Rodinson, after Salo W. Baron,[12] calls it 'lachrymose') which 'raises Auschwitz to the rank of a metaphysical phenomenon' only erects obstacles to examining the enigmas, contradictions and paradoxes of our century. That men have not been able, in this century, to become masters of their history, is a self-evident fact that the fate of the European Jews illustrates in all its tragic dimension. But how and why did history get out of control in this way? How can we understand today that the great majority of leaders and theorists of the European proletariat at the start of the century, such people as Lenin, Trotsky, Bauer, Jaurès, Kautsky, Martov, Plekhanov, Rosa Luxemburg and many more, viewed assimilation as the path of emancipation for the Jews, and the Jewish proletariat in particular? Did this prognosis reveal, as some people are unafraid to say, a scarcely concealed hostility towards the Jewish people – even (for the large number who were Jews themselves) a reflex of self-negation? Yet none of these failed to speak and militate against the oppression and persecution to which the Jews of Eastern Europe were particularly subject. In other fields, their anticipatory sense proved itself. What, then, is proved by the refutation that the course of history brought, at least in part, to their prognosis as to the 'historical' solution of the Jewish problem? Their absolute blindness, or rather the regression of history in the 1930s? After all, the years up to the Second World War saw the integration of

---

of the Ottoman Empire. It seemed appropriate to replace Arabs for unskilled work – work for which the Jew from Eastern Europe, an intellectual with a high level of needs, would be quite unfitted' (Böhm, *Die zionistische Bewegung*, vol. 2, pp. 425–6). Prophetic anticipation of a certain reality of contemporary Israel.

12   Rodinson cites one of the best and greatest historians of the Jews, Salo W. Baron: 'It is not without hesitation that the present author undertook some years ago, and has continued ever since, to reveal the historical foundations of the "lachrymose conception of Jewish history" along with its insufficiencies ... Very clearly, this lachrymose conception served as a basic mechanism of social control ever since the age of the ancient rabbis, and its rejection today could contribute to weakening still more the authority of Jewish community leaders.' These prophetic words were pronounced in 1938. Maxime Rodinson, *Peuple juif ou problème juif?* (Paris: La Découverte, 1997), pp. 278–9.

the Jews of the USSR into the general Soviet population, the destruction of the ghetto, the opening up to the wide spread of human culture and world revolution. In the same way, the rise of the Jewish workers' movement at the end of the nineteenth century in Eastern Europe, then the massive involvement of the working-class and intellectual youth of Yiddishland in revolutionary struggle during the first few decades of this century, went together with the toppling of a closed and immobile world, weighed down with conservative traditions, into modernity, the eruption of the universal into this world.

Even before setting itself up as the defender and promoter of Jewish culture and national identity, the Bund was a deeply internationalist and universalist current, the bearer of secular, emancipatory, rationalist values that went diametrically against the social and religious traditions of the *shtetl*. In this sense, the voluntarist universalism of Trotsky (who, in the opening years of the century, proclaimed that the only 'people' he felt part of was the proletariat, the 'people' of the Revolution) and the revolutionary spirit of the leaders of the Bund at this time (who laid claim to their Jewishness because their soil was the Jewish working class of Eastern Europe) were simply two branches of the same tree. Two attitudes that had their source in the same utopia that rose with the new century as a red sun in the European east.

The cleavages that marked the Jewish communities of Yiddishland at that time did not run between far-sighted propagandists of Zion and blind assimilationists: they opposed a world that was cracked and overthrown by the rise of modern capitalism to the live forces that arose from the young Jewish proletariat, open to the universal culture of the modern world; they opposed this over-exploited populace to the nascent Jewish bourgeoisie who, in the textile plants of Łódź or the cigarette factories of Vilnius, were no more generous than their Polish, German or Russian counterparts.

This aspiration and opening to the world of the new forces of Yiddishland, underpinned by powerful economic and social factors, explains the prognosis of the European socialist leaders that we mentioned. And besides, did not the growing assimilation of Jews in the countries of Western Europe show the way?

The articulation of universalism with the sense of Jewish identity took varying forms depending on the different revolutionary cur-rents: for internationalists such as Trotsky, Zinoviev, Radek and Rosa Luxemburg, the assimilation of a Jewish revolutionary into the con-crete universal party, the dissolution of the 'little difference' into the status of equality of the militant, anticipated the society for which they fought; they did not consider the 'little difference' as called on to crystallize one day in terms of national identity. Were they blind? Blinkered, certainly, in the sense that they underestimated the national dimension of the Jewish problem in Eastern Europe.

As we saw, Lenin admitted, after the creation of the Soviet state, that the rights of all oppressed nations had to be defended without restriction; but in the course of that crucial period, this powerful idea was not applied in any consistent way to the Jewish population of the USSR. In 1937, Trotsky had to admit that 'the Jewish nation will maintain itself for a whole era to come'. But even after the concentra-tion camps, even after the establishment of the state of Israel, has the problem been settled? Elie Wiesel, in his novel *The Testament*, wrote,

> Between a Jewish businessman from Morocco and a Jewish chemist from Chicago, a Jewish rag picker from Lodz and a Jewish industrialist from Lyon, a Jewish mystic from Safed and a Jewish intellectual from Minsk, there is a deeper and more substantive kinship, because it is far older, than between two gentile citizens of the same country, the same city and the same profession. A Jew may be alone but never solitary ...[13]

To which Hélène Elek, a revolutionary Hungarian Jew, replied,

> I do not feel Jewish when I meet an orthodox Jew from Poland, for example. I tell myself that I have nothing in common with him. In Hungary, the Jews were assimilated, which I was very happy with. But I was never ashamed of being Jewish ... You are a Communist first, and being a Jew comes second. You can be a very good Jew without Judaism.[14]

---

13   Elie Wiesel, *The Testament* (New York: Schocken, 1999), p. 68.
14   Hélène Elek, *La mémoire d'Hélène* (Paris: Maspero, 1977), pp. 188, 223.

The Bundists, for their part, linked the universal dimension of their struggle indissolubly to the emancipation of the community from which they came, to the promotion of the positive values and culture of this community, to the promotion and flourishing of the specific identity of this community within the universalism of the 'new world'. We can understand how Henri Minczelès wrote, 'The Bund was more than a party; it was a set of moral principles, an ethic bound up with the Yiddish-speaking people of Poland.'[15] Poale Zion, for its part, connected the universalism of its struggle with the rather mystical vision of an Eretz Israel that would be red and socialist … which did not prevent it from fighting under the tsarist empire, then in Poland and the USSR, etc., for a 'new order communism', from activism in the trade unions, and the promotion of a secular and progressive Yiddish culture.

It is, of course, possible, like Elie Wiesel, to see the commitment of all these Yiddishland revolutionaries as simply a transfer, or more precisely a diversion, of Jewish faith and identity ('You are a Jew first and foremost; it is as a Jew that you aid humanity'), which when push comes to shove will rediscover its *tefelin*. It is likewise possible to trace back to Abraham the territorial claims to 'Judea and Samaria', on condition of renouncing any principle of rational intelligibility in history, or surprise when the dark forces of history are unleashed on Sabra and Shatila.

If we resist this dangerous mysticism, we can only be struck by the strength of the universalist current that bore the positive forces of Yiddishland in the early part of the twentieth century. How else to understand the way in which the militants of the Bund and Poale Zion were swept up in the great current of the Russian Revolution, set off by the events of October 1917 (a fact that the heirs of Medem and Borochov are reluctant to admit today)?[16] How to understand the enthusiasm that impelled many hundred workers from Yiddishland to join the International Brigades in Spain? Did these commitments

---

15   Henri Minczelès, *Le mouvement ouvrier juif* (Paris: Syllepse, 2010).

16   This paradox was given spectacular expression by the rallying to communism of a number of leading figures from the Bund, including Gina Medem, the partner of Vladimir Medem, who fought in the Spanish war.

mean abandoning or rejecting Jewish identity, as maintained today by those who champion a return to real or imaginary ghettos, those who, playing dangerously with words, dare to write, 'Assimilation = new genocide'. In no way. If there is a chapter of the contemporary history of revolution in which the dialectic of opening to universalism and the sense of Jewish identity is strikingly apparent, it is that of Spain. It was, of course, for the cause of humanity, in the name of its positive values, that these militants went to fight in a distant land. But as we shall see from their interviews, there was also for them in this war, as another invisible and subjective front, a separate challenge: to show that the Jewish worker could fight, that he was no less courageous than the German or Polish brigader – in short, that the atavistic prejudices were a lie. There is also from this time the famous episode of the Botwin company.[17]

Our history's share of shadow has stretched over their struggle, muddied the tracks, diverted its ends; it has turned their hopes to derision and dismantled their convictions. Those who survive often share the sentiment of having been cheated. More numerous still are those who were cheated in death. Yet their struggle was not a blind one. It was nourished by light; it sought to repel the shadow. Nor were they victims in the sense that a certain conception of history appoints the Jew as 'eternal Victim'.[18] It is only certain martyrologists who seek to dissolve the meaning of their combat. Even after the camps, the struggle of the 'Botwinists' still had nothing in common with the action of the leaders of the Union Générale des Israélites de France (UGIF). Even after the camps, Rabbi Jacob Kaplan's friendship with colonel de La Roque and his Croix-de-feu remained different in kind from that between the Jewish communists in 1930s Warsaw and their Polish comrades.[19]

---

17   See below, Chapter 3.
18   Maxime Rodinson, *Cult, Ghetto, State* (London: Al Saqi Books, 1983).
19   On the good relations between the future chief rabbi Kaplan and the Croix-de-feu, cf. David Weinberg, *Les juifs à Paris de 1933 à 1939* (Paris: Calmann-Lévy, 1974); and Maurice Rajsfus, *Sois juif et tais-toi!* (Paris: EDI, 1990). The Union générale des Israélites de France was a body set up by the Vichy government's law of 29 November 1941, in response to a German demand. It played an ambiguous

The discourse of the state of Israel has sought at all costs to erase this boundary. It has largely succeeded, and the *union sacrée* around a general, a 'leader' and certain symbols, is the most valued fuel of Israeli politics. In the official history of Israel, and its prehistory, the fighters of Yiddishland have no place, the red shadow of Yiddishland is a stain of infamy that has at any price to be eradicated, rather in the way that photos were retouched in the Stalin era. In the eyes of the young *sabras*, the survivors of this time seem figures led astray into derisory adventures. It was against the traditions of this revolutionary movement, against its utopia, its history and its memory, that the Hebrew state was established, along with its own founding myths. As we have said, the movement was internationalist, universalist, secular and progressive; whereas Israel is separatist, chauvinist, clerical and conservative. The movement headed for a future of a better world, a more just and humane society; Israel has reinvented the ghetto, and embedded itself in the irrational exaltation of a mythical past. It perceives its future only in the intoxication of its strength, its proud isolation defended by tanks and fighter planes. Yes, it has indeed reinvented Masada.[20]

It is only too understandable that institutional Zionism has stubbornly stifled the memory of this movement; that the schoolbooks of Israeli children are silent about the Bund and the commitment of Jewish fighters on the side of the Spanish republic; that in Israel, Yiddishland is buried in museums, and the Yiddish language in libraries; that the witnesses and actors who live in Israel are never called on to recount their struggles, but are even blamed for their history. In actual fact, the traces of this movement indicate sufficiently that the triumph of Zionism did not flow from the implacable 'logic' of history, some kind of ontological necessity, but was rather

---

role in the Nazi deportations, misguidedly trusting to Marshal Pétain to protect Jews of French origin at the expense of immigrants and refugees. See Rajsfus, *Sois juif et tais-toi!*.

20   A fortress to the north of Sodom, close to the Dead Sea, the last stronghold of Jewish resistance after the conquest of Jerusalem by the Romans in 70 CE. The Zealots who took refuge there are said to have committed collective suicide rather than surrender.

the product and avatar of the most irrational phase of our time. Today, however, this 'self-evidence' is heading towards a reversal in the blind alleys of Israeli policy, to the point where this 'triumph' of Zionism is heavily burdened by the debts of the illogical moment of history from which it arose. Today, the figure of 'Israelocentric' universal Judaism that emerged in the wake of the Second World War is in crisis. This crisis has a multitude of facets: emigration from Israel, the development of tensions between Sephardic and Ashkenazi communities, the incapacity of the Israeli state to tackle the Palestinian problem in a rational manner, the growing dependence of the country on America, and the development in Europe and America of a new diaspora culture that rejects Israelocentrism. By the same token, it reactivates the questionings and problematics that, beyond the conquering myths of Zionism, rehabilitate the positive values of Yiddishland, bring out from the shadows the pages of history that had been cast aside, retying threats and reweaving traditions. Is it accidental that we see today, for example, a major revival of interest among certain researchers and activists in the Bund and the 'territorialists'?

The common point of the testimonies collected here is that at the end of their tormented trajectories they all live today in Israel. It would be quite wrong to believe that, by confining our study to Israel, we sought to demonstrate the 'necessity' of this end of the journey. Quite the contrary. We might well have questioned other protagonists of this history, in France, America, Poland, Belgium, Germany, etc. Their memories would have been no less passionate than those that we collected; above all, the framework and guiding thread of their stories, the 'moral' of this history and these histories, would have been the same. By questioning witnesses who today live in Israel, most of whom, for the greater part of their lives, did not give a fig for a Jewish state, and always considered Herzl, at best, a harmless illuminatus, and today view Begin as a dangerous adventurer, we focus yet again on the illogicality of history. We emphasize its bitter irony, its juddering, seeing these internationalists caught up by their Jewishness, these utopians converted to realism by the tragedies of our time ('All things considered, after everything that happened, why shouldn't we also have a right to our country?'), these Bundist veterans trapped in the contradiction of embodying the Bund in Israel, these Poale Zionists who abandoned the red flag on the banks of the Vistula or the Volga, keeping only their other blue and white one, these former communists who tell themselves that, after all, Israel is no worse than the United States ... But who would dare set themselves up as judge of their trajectories and their present convictions? In the worst of historical earthquakes, they took the risk of commitment. They had, as it was then said, chains to lose and a world to win. It is for them and them alone to draw up their balance sheets.

We did not conduct our interviews as journalists, as curious bystanders, but above all as militants of the same utopia as that which took them so high and so low. The codes of their stories are mostly familiar; we know from our own itineraries what is a factional struggle within a revolutionary party; a security service for a public meeting; who Thälmann, Manuilski and Erlich were. We know very well that our history, just like theirs, continues to swing between socialism and barbarism. And yet, throughout this work, we were able to measure what was incommensurable between our experience as militants and theirs. The tragedy of history has shifted (for how long?) to other skies, and, from the depth of the soft somnolence of our own 'crisis', our utopia turns towards theirs by way of procuration.

One final word. These stories, these testimonies, are not a scholarly communication. At twenty, thirty, forty or even fifty years' remove, the memory of dates and facts may be uncertain, certain memories that are painful to recall are bowdlerized. Some of them are unduly modest; others tend to strike a pose. Sometimes, also, the witnesses reinterpret their memories and past acts in the light of their later convictions. These are the risks of oral history. But one thing is certain: the motif, the insistent melody that steadily emerges from the mosaic of these testimonies, speaks the integral truth of this history.[21]

We have chosen to interview people who were active in three currents: the Bund, Poale Zion and the communist movement. This decision does not seem arbitrary to us: first and foremost, our study

---

21   Need we spell it out? The ideas that we develop in this book are our own, and in no way commit those people who have agreed to give the testimonies that are gathered in the following pages.

is not one of ideological currents, but of a social and political movement, the Jewish workers' movement. From their origins through to
the eve of the Second World War, these currents explicitly appealed
to the working class – whose emancipation they worked for – and
the movement that embodied this emancipation at the international
level, i.e. the workers' movement born in the mid-nineteenth century.
The centre of gravity of their implantation, likewise, was the working
class – whatever the particularities of the social formation of the
Jewish population in Eastern Europe. From this point of view, they
are clearly distinct from such currents as Hachomer Hatzaïr,[22] which
certainly made reference to socialism, but whose implantation in the
factories and workshops was negligible, and whose activity took place
on the margins of the Jewish workers' movement of Eastern Europe.
A fortiori, they are distinct from organizations such as Poalei Agudat
Israel, which had a genuine hold on Jewish workers, but whose programme espoused the principles of religious conservatism. The Bund
(Algemeyner Yidisher Arbeter Bund in Lite, Poyln un Rusland) was
founded in Vilnius in 1897. A diffuse agitation had developed since
the 1870s among workers in the small workshops and early factories,
essentially in Lithuania and Byelorussia. New forms of organization
then made their appearance; radical intellectuals organized circles
designed to promote socialist ideas among these workers. By the early
1890s, while anti-Semitism was steadily growing, and combining
with the ambient misery to trigger an ever more massive emigration, the inspirers of these 'circles' active in the Jewish working-class
milieu considered that conditions were ripe to pass to 'mass agitation'.
The Yiddish language was adopted in this spirit as a privileged means
of communication and propaganda. At the same time, the radical
intellectuals who laid the foundations of this movement considered
that the struggle of the Jewish proletariat had to be linked by 'indis-
soluble bonds' to that of the Russian workers' movement in general.
The movement spread in the main industrial centres of the Pale of

---

22   The Young Guard: a movement of Zionist pioneers founded at the end of
the First World War in Poland, which gave its name to a party of the same orientation. It claimed to be both Marxist and Zionist, and was always attached to the
World Zionist Organization.

Settlement, notably marked by the rise of hundreds of *kassy* (mutual aid funds).

Ever since its foundation, the Bund viewed itself as an integral part of the Russian Social Democratic movement. Three of its delegates were present at the foundation of the Russian Social Democratic Labour Party (RSDLP) in 1898, and it was represented on the party's central committee. Endowed with a solid organizational structure, and with thousands of members (between 25,000 and 35,000 in the years from 1903 to 1905), it rapidly became the motor of political activity for the Jewish working class. It was the promoter of powerful and effective self-defence groups in response to the pogroms of the first years of the century. It possessed a very popular press and conducted tireless agitation: from mid-1903 to mid-1904 it held 429 political meetings, organized forty-five demonstrations and forty-one political strikes, and distributed 305 leaflets. In 1904, some 4,500 Bund militants were in prison. It created a youth organization and published a daily paper. Its influence reached a peak at the time of the 1905 revolution, in which it played an essential role in the Pale of Settlement.

Over the years, the Bund's programme evolved and deepened. In 1901, it raised the slogan of political and civic equality for Jews. Bit by bit it oriented itself towards the slogan of national and cultural autonomy for the Jews of the tsarist empire. In the context of the RSDLP, it stood for the establishment of a federal structure, and claimed the prerogative of sole representative of the Jewish proletariat. These views clashed with those of the party leaders, Plekhanov and Martov as well as Lenin, and in 1903, at the second congress of the RSDLP, the Bund broke away. Rejecting any collaboration with the other Jewish parties, the Bund particularly denounced all the Zionist groupings as bourgeois and reactionary. It was disturbed by the competition within the Jewish working class of different socialist Zionist currents that emerged in the early years of the century.

Between the 1905 and 1917 revolutions, the Bund experienced a definite development; in 1906 it rejoined the RSDLP. But the period of terror and counterrevolution that then opened was particularly unfavourable to it. Its numbers fell, its political activities were banned, and in response it moved more towards semi-legal activities, essentially cultural, particularly championing Yiddish language and culture. This perspective led it to participate in various Jewish community institutions. It turned increasingly sharply to asserting the national dimension of the Jewish problem in Eastern Europe, more clearly emphasizing the programme of national and cultural autonomy. From 1912 it made common cause with the Mensheviks, whose break with the Bolsheviks was then definitive. At the start of the war it adopted a pacifist position.

The revolution of February 1917 gave a new fillip to the Bund, and by the end of the year it grew to some 40,000 members. It acted as advocate for the civil and political rights of Jews, and divided between right and left Mensheviks; its leaders denounced the October Revolution as an illegitimate *coup d'état*. In Ukraine, the Bund leadership pronounced in favour of an autonomous nation in the context of a federal Russian state. In the elections to the Jewish National Assembly of Ukraine in November 1918, it won 18 per cent of the votes. But the outbreak of the Civil War, accompanied by numerous pogroms, then impelled many of its militants towards communism. In March 1919 a Kombund appeared, which soon merged with the Communist Party of Ukraine.

In April 1920, the Russian Bund split. The majority joined the Communist Party, with the minority forming a Social Democratic Bund that was soon after outlawed.

In Poland occupied by the Germans after 1915, the Bund formed into an independent entity, its activities favoured by the relatively liberal regime imposed by the occupiers. When the new Polish state was founded, it fused with the Jewish Social Democratic Party of Galicia. From 1921 to 1939, it published a daily, *Folkstsaytung*. As a legal party, it generated a dense network of youth organizations, sports associations, cultural and educational bodies, etc. Divided in its attitude towards the Russian Revolution and the Soviet state, it adopted the principles for membership of the Comintern in 1921, but this decision was not put into effect. A minority of its militants left it to form a Kombund, which soon merged with the Polish Communist Party. In 1930, the Bund decided by a small majority to rejoin the Socialist

International. As a declared opponent of both Zionism and religious orthodoxy, the Bund registered substantial successes in the local elections and inspired the Jewish trade union movement in Poland, which had 99,000 members in 1939. It also played an important role in the Central Yiddish School Organization (CYSHO), a secular and progressive Jewish educational movement, where teaching was conducted in Yiddish. It pursued a stubborn battle against anti-Semitism, organizing self-defence and protest movements against the exactions of the Polish far right. Under the Nazi occupation, the Bund took part in the Jewish Resistance, particularly in the Warsaw ghetto. Many of its militants found refuge in the Soviet Union, where two of its leaders, Viktor Adler and Henryk Erlich, were murdered on Stalin's orders in 1941. After the war, those of its militants in Poland who survived tried to recommence their activities, but these were banned by the new regime in 1948.

Poale Zion ('workers of Zion') was a proletarian movement that sought to combine Zionism and socialism. From the origins of Zionism in the last decade of the nineteenth century, intellectuals such as Jitlovki and Syrkin attempted in Russia to develop this combination. At the turn of the century, several organizations under the name of Poale Zion were formed independently of one another in the Pale of Settlement. Some of their members were Jewish workers who belonged to the general Zionist movement, others came from the Bund or the Social Democratic Party. They rapidly created their own trade unions. In the early years of the century, Poale Zion groups developed particularly in Lithuania, southern Russia and Warsaw. The basic idea of their founders was that the solution of the economic problem of Jewish workers was their establishment in Eretz Israel. But some believed that in the immediate future it was better to confine themselves to the domain of economic struggle, while others leaned in favour of a revolutionary political activity alongside non-Jewish socialist organizations. It was this current that formed self-defence groups in 1903, after the Kishinev pogroms. Another current oriented to 'territorialism' appeared at the same time. In 1905 it established itself as a separate fraction and adopted the name of Zionist Socialist Workers' Party, taking its distance from the essentially 'Palestinian' perspective.

The Jewish Social Democratic Workers' Party was founded in 1906, under the leadership of Ber Borochov, who systematized the idea of a territorial concentration of Jews in Eretz Israel, with the perspective of transforming the social structure of the Jewish population and reconstructing Jewish existence around productive labour. Like the Bund, Poale Zion was outlawed after the 1905 revolution, and its influence considerably declined. In 1905 it had some 20,000 members, but this fell to a few hundred in the years that followed. Before the First World War, groups attached to Poale Zion also developed in Austria–Hungary, the United States and Palestine. In 1907 a Poale Zion world union was founded, which gradually distanced itself from the World Zionist Congress.

In the course of the First World War, the Poale Zion world union drew close to the Socialist International. While reaffirming the objective of a socialist Eretz Israel, it increasingly emphasized the necessary recognition of the civic and national rights of Jews in the diaspora. During the 1917 revolution, one section of Poale Zion in Russia joined the Bolsheviks and abandoned Zionism; the other section, while supporting the objectives of the October Revolution, continued to maintain the validity of 'class Zionism'.

In 1920, the movement divided. At the fifth congress in Vienna, 178 delegates voted in favour of joining the Communist International, while 179 abstained. The right, essentially representing the parties of the United States, Argentina, Great Britain and Eretz Israel, joined the 'Two-and-a-half', then the Second International in 1923. Though the left demanded membership of the Third International, the Comintern executive refused dual membership of both organizations (the Poale Zion world union and the Third International), rejected the notion of a national concentration of the Jewish people in Palestine, and demanded that Poale Zion militants join their respective national communist parties.

The sixth conference of the world union, in June 1922, rejected these demands and proclaimed itself an integral part of the world communist movement. A new split followed in Russia, expressed in the formation of the Jewish Communist Party (Poale Zion) and the Social Democratic Poale Zion. The latter was soon transformed into the Jewish Workers' Party Poale Zion, and existed in the Soviet Union as a legal organization until 1928.

In Austria, the USSR and Czechoslovakia, Poale Zion dissolved itself into the respective communist parties. In Poland, on the other hand, it remained independent between the two wars; this was then the largest party in the Poale Zion world union, which in 1926 transformed itself into the Communist Union of Jewish Workers Poale Zion.[23]

The history of the social democratic and communist parties in which many of the individuals we have interviewed here participated can hardly be summed up in a few pages. But it is also far better known. We have indicated works of reference whenever this seemed necessary.

---

23   This information is basically drawn from the entries for 'Bund' and 'Poale Zion' in the *Encyclopedia Judaica*.

1.

The Immense Pool of Human Tears

A terrifying abyss opens
in the immense pool of human tears
marked by a flow of blood.
It cannot grow more deep or dark.

'Song of the Bund'

A former communist cadre trained in the schools of the Comintern, who held important positions in Poland after 1945; a Bund militant who found refuge in the Soviet Union in 1939 but spent long years on the banks of the Kolyma in Siberia; a member of the left Poale Zion who sought to realize the impossible synthesis between the Zionist aspiration and the communist programme in 1930s Poland – these men were opposites in so many ways: the political battles they waged, their itineraries, their versions of history, their summing up of the century. But behind their political commitment in each case, they evoke their childhood years in Poland, Lithuania or Romania; their family; and the social and cultural environment in which they grew up. The picture then changes and the originality and unity of the world in which their consciousness was formed reveals itself: Yiddishland.

A social and cultural space, a linguistic and religious world, rather than a territory in the strict sense. Yiddishland had no frontiers, and at the time our witnesses were born it had long overspilled the limits of the Pale of Settlement invented by the tsars. A space interwoven with other cultural and national worlds, intersecting them, supervening on them, yet remaining so readily identifiable when these men and women speak:

> My father was a practising *Hassid* who prayed three times a day and wanted above all else that his children should continue his path. My parents never had a stable source of income. Most often they went from one market to another, cobbling bits and pieces together to sell – they were what we called *Luftmenschen.*

Or again:

> My father worked for a bank. He was a believer, but not fanatical. He kept the traditions, wore a beard but not side-locks. He wore the *Hassid* dress on Saturdays, prayed every day, but didn't wear the skullcap at work. He insisted that the festivals were properly kept up, that we ate kosher at home, and that the Shabbat should be respected, but despite this he was very open to the world; he was very cultivated and read a lot, particularly in German. He'd started work very young, after studying in a *heder.*

When our witnesses came into the world, at the turn of the century, this universe was rapidly changing. From the mid-nineteenth century the advance signals of the irruption of modernity into Yiddishland made themselves visible. The Pale of Settlement in which the majority of Eastern European Jews were concentrated, on the western borders of the tsarist empire, was not a backward and unchanging Orient, untouched by the great economic currents that were sweeping Europe. It was, on the contrary, a crossroads of exchange and influence where capitalism sprang up in the 1860s, basically in the form of petty industry, but soon also larger enterprises such as the match and cigarette factories in Byelorussia where the first concentrations of a modern Jewish proletariat appeared.

This rise of capitalism overturned the structures of traditional Jewish life in Eastern and Central Europe. A process of social differentiation rapidly developed within the Jewish population, coinciding with a process of concentration in urban agglomerations, from the

shtetl to the big city. The first systematic census of the Jewish population in the tsarist empire was conducted in 1897. It showed that
Jews made up more than 50 per cent of the urban population of
Byelorussia and Lithuania; that in Minsk 52 per cent of the population were Jews, 64 per cent in Białystok, 41 per cent in Vilnius and
48 per cent in Grodno. If we take into account the transition from a
type of activity that was principally intermediary (in 1818, 86.5 per
cent of the Jews in Ukraine, Lithuania and Byelorussia were traders)
to the new functions promoted by the rise of capitalism, far more dif-
ferentiated and dominated by manual labour, this completely upset
the social and cultural universe of Yiddishland. The second half of
the nineteenth century, in fact, saw the rise of a new Jewish culture
in Eastern Europe, a culture that broke with traditional Jewish life
in the sense that it was open to the influences of the modern world,
seeking to realize a synthesis between modern culture and Jewish
values, attacking the 'formalism' of religion and the forms of existence it imposed, and drawing its inspiration from the rationalism of
the Enlightenment.

In the 1850s, under Alexander II, who relaxed somewhat the discrimination against Jews, a stratum of enlightened intellectuals and
traders developed. As increasing numbers of Jews began to attend
high schools and universities, in the last decades of the nineteenth
century, this Jewish intelligentsia who had mastered Russian (while
Yiddish remained the mother tongue of 96.6 per cent of the Jewish
population of the Pale of Settlement in 1898) would play an essential role of intermediary between the Jewish population and modern
ideas, between the nascent Jewish workers' movement and that of
both Russia and Western Europe.

The abolition of serfdom in the tsarist empire quickened the decom-
position of the feudal world, clearing the ground for the development
of capitalism. The 1880s saw an influx of landless peasants into the
towns, seeking work in the factories, where they formed the nucleus
of the Russian and Polish proletariat; for them the Jewish worker was
a competitor. In 1881, in the wake of the assassination of Alexander
II by the Narodniks, pogroms broke out in many towns of the tsarist
empire – anti-Semitism would be a major element of modernity in

this part of Europe. The early 1880s were a turning point in Jewish history, seeing the first waves of massive emigration and the appearance of the first embryos of a Jewish workers' movement, forerunners of the Bund, as well as the first Zionist circles.

If a large fraction of the Jewish population in this watershed period turned to productive work in urban centres, they remained largely concentrated in the handicraft sector, a type of production with a low technological level at the end of the production chain: tailors, shoemakers, weavers, carpenters, locksmiths, etc. This specific character of Jewish labour was defined as follows by Borochov, the theorist of Poale Zion: 'The more a trade is removed from nature, the more Jewish labour is concentrated in it'.

It was this wretched complex of workshops and petty industry that would essentially form the base of the Jewish workers' movement at the end of the nineteenth century. Misery and isolation from the other national proletariats that were forming at the same time (Russian, Polish, etc.), were two fundamental characteristics of the Jewish populace of the towns. This explains the radicalism of the first manifestations of the Jewish workers' movement, as well as the emergence of forms of organization that were exclusively Jewish.

Until the revolution of 1905, the lead taken by the Jewish workers' movement over that of its Russian, Polish, Baltic, Ukrainian and Caucasian counterparts was an evident and remarkable feature of the situation in the tsarist empire. In the 1880s, the first *kassy* developed in Lithuania and Byelorussia, mutual aid funds designed to support the needs of workers on strike. Radical intellectuals organized the first study circles specifically for Jewish workers. The organic connection that was then established between revolutionary intellectuals and workers would make for the great strength of this movement at the turn of the century, a time when the theorists of Russian Social Democracy were still very weakly linked to the proletariat. In the 1880s, the first groups of Jewish Social Democrats in Lithuania undertook a systematic agitation among Jewish workers and artisans, inspiring strikes and publishing the first socialist newspaper in Yiddish, *Der yiddisher arbeyter* (The Yiddish Worker). When the Bund was formed in 1897, the movement already had solid roots in the Jewish proletariat, particularly in Lithuania and Byelorussia. At this time, 1,500 workers paid contributions to the *kassy* in Vilnius and 1,000 in Minsk.

Soon after the foundation of the Bund, the first congress of the RSDLP was held; it was the Bund that took charge of the congress arrangements, possessing as it did material resources and an organization that were far superior to those of the Russian and Polish Social Democrats. It was also the Bund, in the western part of the empire, that helped the Russian Social Democrats to print their first publications and secretly distribute them to the industrial centres. And on 1 May 1899, the Bund organized the first big public demonstration of the Jewish proletariat in Russia. After the Kishinev pogrom of 1903, it organized Jewish self-defence. And when the 1905 revolution broke out, while the Russian party had 8,500 members, the Bund had close to 30,000.

This lack of synchrony between the growth of the Jewish workers' movement and the other national movements it was in contact with would have significant consequences. The intellectuals who gathered the first circles of Jewish workers, and inspired the first strikes of the Jewish proletariat, originally conceived this activity as a work of socialist propaganda and agitation among Jewish workers, not as the construction of a specific Jewish workers' movement distinct from the organization of workers in Russia in general. It was naturally necessary to address Jewish workers in their own language, in order to be effective, and likewise appropriate to take into account their particular conditions of work and existence, but this was no more than one moment in the development of the awareness of the Russian proletariat in general; the development of capitalism in Russia, it was then generally believed, would soon lead to the disappearance of what distinguished the Jewish proletariat from the Russian, Polish or Ukrainian.

At the turn of the century, however, the growth of the workers' movement in the Russian Empire gave the lie to this prognosis. It became apparent in particular that the development and class consciousness of the proletariat and its organizations that were forming at this time responded not just to the development of capitalism, but also to the perpetuation of national oppression; organizations such as the Polish Socialist Party (PPS) and the Bund developed along the dual track of struggle against capitalist exploitation and the fight for national identity. The great strength of the Bund in its hour of glory – around the revolution of 1905 – was precisely to have been far more than simply a vanguard organization of the Jewish proletariat, but rather what Vladimir Medem, one of its most prestigious leaders, called 'a living creature', whose many-sided action, on the terrain of class struggle but also that of the promotion of Jewish culture and the 'new Jewish man', crystallized the aspirations of all the popular classes of Eastern European Jewry; it embodied, at a moment when the world of this population was being ruptured, all the positive values of a new way of life, the outlines of a new culture, the promotion of a modern and progressive figure of Jewishness. But this was not the orientation of all the radical Jewish intellectuals of the tsarist empire, and above all it was not that of the Russian Social Democrats represented by Plekhanov and Lenin, nor even Jews such as Martov, Trotsky and Rosa Luxemburg. The 'nationalism' of the Bund led to a 'federalist' view of the revolutionary party in Russia; when the Bund demanded, at the second congress of the RSDLP in 1903, that it should be recognized as representing the entire Jewish proletariat, including that in the southern provinces of Russia where Jewish workers were far more integrated into the general working class, the split was consummated with those who, like Lenin, dreamed of organizing the whole of the Russian proletariat in a centralized and disciplined party, as the unequal battle against the tsarist autocracy required.

After the 1905 revolution, the Bund drew closer again to the Bolsheviks; then, from 1912, it made common cause with the Mensheviks. But this was not the main thing: it was the split of the Bund in 1903 that really inaugurated a break in the Jewish workers' movement that would continue until the destruction of the Jewish working class during the Second World War. On the one hand, there was the Jewish radicalism that developed on the terrain of Jewish identity, the cohesion of the Jewish working class – but this could not spread beyond the limits of this world, and was vulnerable to everything that might shake or unbalance it. The Bund in interwar

Poland was the embodiment of this current. It was no accident that it dominated the Jewish trade union movement, that it appeared the embodiment of the new Jewish culture against a Jewish bourgeoisie that sought in vain to coexist with the Polish ruling class; but it was also no accident that the most radical fraction of the Jewish proletariat and youth escaped its hold and experienced the force of attraction of the Russian Revolution, or that it failed to survive the Second World War as an active political current. On the other hand, in the diatribes of Trotsky and Martov against the Bund at the second congress of the RSDLP, and the sarcasm of Rosa Luxemburg against the 'Jewish shop-keeper' of the Bund, we see the other current of Jewish radicalism, a universalist current that wagered on the extinction of the Jewish question, the discrimination that Jews were victims of, as a result of assimilation – a trend that seemed to them inscribed in the iron laws of capitalist development. And so thousands of Jewish communists in interwar Poland assimilated, or believed they assimilated, into the great current of the revolution.

Yiddishland in the early years of the century remained a relatively homogeneous and coherent ensemble, but powerful factors were working towards its destabilization. Even if held back by a multitude of social and political factors, the integration of Jewish workers into large-scale industry (textile, engineering, chemicals) was advancing, creating among the Jewish proletariat an opening towards wider groupings – Russian and Polish. On the other hand, the irruption of modernity into Yiddishland precipitated a crisis of the religious conservatism that had until then been dominant. The intellectual and everyday life of the Jewish population of Eastern Europe was now increasingly marked by a tension and antagonism between these traditional forms and the 'new culture', particularly the emergence of a new secular identity of the young Jews who broke with tradition. The rapid rise in the cultural level of the Jewish population in the early twentieth century, and the growing attendance of Jewish youth in secondary and higher education, brought about a growing opening towards the non-Jewish world and a secularization of Jewish life.[1]

---

1   Cf. Rachel Ertel, *Le Shtetl*, Paris: Payot, 1982.

The multiple effects of the Russian Revolution would amplify this destabilization of the Yiddish universe. The geographic, social and cultural unity of Yiddishland, however relative, was broken. The Russian Civil War, particularly in Ukraine, destroyed all the traditional structures of Jewish life, drawing the Jewish population into a formidable whirlpool. The establishment of a collectivized economy, the destruction of the social fabric of old Russia, the 'reconstruction of lifestyle' in the USSR in the 1920s, overturned the social existence and consciousness of the Jewish population from top to bottom: many people were proletarianized, assimilated to the Russian working class; others became more than ever *Luftmenschen*, suspended in the air; others again 'assimilated' into the new society by finding a place in the Party or the new state's body of functionaries. In the newly independent Poland, Jewish workers and their movement were confronted immediately after the First World War with a double adversary: a chauvinist Polish bourgeoisie incapable of giving any consistency to the 'miracle' of renewed independence, and the Jewish capitalist bourgeoisie.

These upheavals brought about a complete recomposition of the political forces of Yiddishland. Many militants from the Bund joined the communist movement, not only in Russia and Ukraine, but also in Poland. The Polish Bund experienced the attraction of the Russian Revolution in the early 1920s; the socialist Zionists were torn between sympathy for Soviet power and their 'Palestinian' utopia. A new generation of communist Jewish militants appeared in Eastern Europe, providing many cadres for the international communist movement, from the Spanish war through to the 'building of socialism' in Poland after the Second World War. It was into this unstable and rapidly changing world that our witnesses were born. The lines of fracture that pervaded it are clearly drawn as soon as they describe their milieu and their youth.

Léo Lev was born in 1905 in the small town of Ostrowiecz, near Radom. 'Until the beginning of the century', he says,

> The rabbis were the masters of our community, all social life was dominated by religion, the Jewish community was under the thumb

of the rich. But the First World War overthrew the traditional state of affairs. The workers' organizations began to exert their influence, and Poale Zion developed in our region. A broad debate took place in the [Polish] workers' movement of the 1920s: what perspective was most favourable for Jews? To settle in Palestine, or to integrate ourselves into the struggle of each country? The petty bourgeois leaned in the direction of Poale Zion; but among the youth, communism was dominant, so great was the prestige of the USSR.

Elija Rosijanski was born in Kovno (Lithuania) in 1902. He passed the matriculation exam and began studying medicine, but was bored to death in the 'big village' that Lithuania was at the time. He dreamed of a wider world. Besides, he didn't always have enough to eat. At the age of twenty he abandoned his studies and left for Palestine. It wasn't that he was a Zionist, but he was stifled in the garrison town of Kovno, 'where nothing had happened since the day that Napoleon established his bivouac there while his troops were crossing the Niemen'.

The family was a microcosm in which the tensions and conflicts that beset the world of Yiddishland were focused. The theme of generational conflict, the clash between old and new within the family structure, returns like a leitmotiv in the statements of many of our witnesses. A conflict whose protagonists seem fixed in their roles, so similar are the situations described by various individuals.

Yaakov Greenstein:

My father was a learned *Hassid*, a rabbi who did not practise as such. He lived with his books – four walls covered with religious and classical literature in Hebrew, Yiddish and German. He wasn't at all concerned with material contingencies: my mother's parents were very well off and they met the needs of the family so that my father could study the Torah. As a child, however, we often went hungry. When the situation became too precarious, my father did a bit of peddling or gave lectures in biblical history at a religious school. All his children naturally received a deep religious education and we assiduously attended the synagogue. When I was twelve or thirteen, I began to be troubled by doubts, and to question the religious metaphysic. I had long discussions with my father, who put great store by philosophical debates on the existence of God. He was very learned, but could not find a convincing response to my questions. He told me: 'Perhaps you'll understand later.' Then I began to read all the progressive literature that could be found in Yiddish, and grew interested in Marxist ideas.

Bronia Zelmanowicz:

We were poor and very religious. Despite our wretched condition, my father spent much time studying the Torah. My childhood was very pious: I was taught to read Hebrew, to pray in Hebrew, but I didn't understand the words and phrases that I pronounced in this unknown language. I read the Yiddish translation at the bottom of the page. Because of our poverty, all us children began work very early. I would have liked very much to continue my studies after elementary school, but that wasn't possible: I worked in a shop, then as a clerk in an office.

Yankel Taut:

There were seven of us children at home. My father was very pious, a kind of *Luftmensch* who practised all kinds of little trades before he found regular work as a butcher's assistant. Our situation then improved a bit. We lived in the Scheunenviertel, a popular district in Berlin where *Ostjuden*, Jews from the East, flocked together. The extreme poverty of our family, and the revolutionary climate in working-class Berlin at that time, certainly determined my later commitments. What is sure is that right from childhood my brothers and sisters, like me, turned away from religion. On that question, we were always in conflict with my parents, my father in particular.

The rupture made here was again a multiple one. It was first, as we see, a break with the rigidity of the traditional Jewish life that invaded every sphere of existence. Just to take one example, the religious teaching that was dispensed to children from the youngest age was, in the words of the Jewish historian Simon Dubnow, a genuine torture: 'Children were criminally tortured, in both their minds and their bodies.[2] They were told nothing about the real world, nature and life, they were only told about death and the beyond.' Hersh Mendel, the very archetype of the Yiddishland revolutionary, gives in his memoirs an image of the *heder* that confirms Dubnow's cry of alarm:

> I cannot remember one single joyful hour. Obviously, my teacher did not know very much about education. He loved to hit the bottle and had a red nose … His lessons were given to several of us at once; he would recite something and we would have to babble it back. Since we were all supposed to hear him, he screamed at the top of his lungs and we screamed in return.[3]

From the earliest years, therefore, existence was invaded by this hollow formalism, this absurd rote learning, these rituals and obligations. Tamara Deutscher relates how at the age of thirteen her future husband was deemed worthy of becoming a rabbi:

> [He] started on a two-hour discourse on the theme of Kikiyon: once in seventy years a bird appears over the world. The bird is big and beautiful and unlike all other birds. Its name is Kikiyon … When the bird makes its flight … it spits on the earth, and it spits only once. This saliva is extremely precious; it has miraculous qualities, for it can cure any illness or deformity. What Isaac had to debate and give his most considered opinion on was this: is the bird's saliva kosher or *treyfe*? In other words, does it fulfil the requirements of the Jewish ritual with regard to food or not? Isaac quoted at length all that had been written on the subject before – all the commentaries, all the learned discussions that had been going on for millennia among the wisest of the wise … All this

---

2   Simon Dubnow (1860–1941), historian, born in Byelorussia, was the author of a *World History of the Jewish People* (in ten volumes). In 1906 he founded a 'folkist' party. He saw the diaspora as 'not only a possibility, but a necessity, from a historical and non-dogmatic point of view', and considered the Jewish people one 'whose country is the whole world'. He campaigned in favour of autonomy for the Jews and saw Zionism as a pseudo-messianic adventure.

3   Hersh Mendel, *Memoirs of a Jewish Revolutionary* (London: Pluto Press, 1988), p. 30.

pseudo-knowledge cluttered and strained my memory, took me away from real life, from real learning, from real knowledge of the world around me. It stunted my physical and mental development.[4]

It was hardly surprising, in such conditions, that rejection of this way of life sunk in rituals and dogma should be organized around symbols and symbolic actions.

When he was fourteen, Deutscher made the acquaintance of a young Jewish worker, an atheist and communist. Under his influence he vacillated in his faith. His friend then decided to put him to a test. On the day of Yom Kippur, he took Deutscher to the Jewish cemetery, sat him down on the tomb of a rabbi, and took two ham sandwiches out of his pocket. The blasphemy was enormous: 'I was petrified by the iniquity of my behaviour. I munched the sandwich and swallowed each mouthful with difficulty. I half-hoped and half-feared that something terrible would happen; I waited for a thunder that would strike me down. But nothing happened. All was quiet.'[5]

Another highly symbolic break was that of Yankel Taut:

One day, one of my mates from the *heder* – we were not yet ten years old – asked, 'Don't you want to come to the Red Pioneers with me?' He said so many good things about all the activities of this organization that I decided to go along with him. 'But there's a little problem,' he said. 'You can't go with your *peyes* [side-locks], they'll make fun of you.' In order to avoid this, I decided to have them cut. The barber was shocked: 'Have you asked your father's permission?' – 'No.' – 'You know that you'll get the biggest thrashing of your life', he continued. I insisted, and he cut them off.

But he wasn't mistaken. When I came home, my father literally knocked me down. I had committed one of the most serious crimes he could imagine. All the same, I continued to go secretly to the Red Pioneers.

---

4   Isaac Deutscher, *The Non-Jewish Jew*, London: Merlin Press, 1968, pp. 6–7.

5   Deutscher, *The Non-Jewish Jew*, p. 21.

Breaking with the old, for our witnesses, meant a break with the traditions of the *Luftgeschäft*; an escape from misery; a break with the
condition of the *Luftmensch* living on air, on expedients, on tricks,
on little jobs; breaking with a form of existence perceived as para-
sitic. It meant leaving this Chagallian world (and it is no accident that
Chagall's characters so often seem suspended in air) for a different
and more solid one, broader and with positive values: the world of
the workers.

In this 'choice' there was, of course, a share of necessity, as Yaakov
Greenstein notes:

> In our home, all the children began work very young, so that the family
> could live. I became a weaver in the factory. You have to understand that
> in Poland at that time [the 1930s], a boy of twelve was seen as almost
> an adult.

This does not mean that the choice was not often conscious and active,
as Haïm Babic explains:

> We had a different relationship with work from my parents' generation;
> we started work very young, at thirteen or fourteen, as we wanted to
> learn a trade, get a qualification. I myself became a carpenter.
> This different relationship with work determined the ideological rup-
> tures and tensions that arose within the family. When I joined the Bund,
> my elder brother was already a member. This commitment broke my
> parents' heart. Everyone in our little town knew that I was a Bund activ-
> ist, and my parents were ashamed of it. On 1 May 1925, I remember, the
> workers' organizations organized a meeting; I spoke in the name of the
> Zukunft, the Bund youth. Immediately, a neighbour rushed into our
> house and said to my mother: 'Your son Haïm is up on a table making a
> speech, in the middle of the square.' Red with shame, my mother locked
> herself in the house.

This relationship between a productive trade and political commitment recurs in many of our witnesses. Moshe Green, the son of a
well-to-do trader, chose to become a locksmith, just before the First

World War. David Sztokfisz, whose father was also a trader and religious, became a typographer in the late 1920s and a militant in the left Poale Zion, as did three of his sisters and brothers. But they went rapidly on to communism:

> We never stopped quarrelling at home, as I was the only one to remain loyal to Poale Zion. Our father was in despair: 'What's going on?' he asked. 'Before, at least you were all in agreement, and now there's all these different schools. It's stopping me sleeping!'

In the same way, Yankel Taut, son of a *Luftmensch*, became an engineering worker, a communist, and a trade union activist. 'My father wanted me to become a salesperson', he said, 'but nonetheless he signed the contract permitting me to become an apprentice in a large engineering company. That was how I got into the workers' movement, which I never left'.

It may seem rather strange that these young Jews from religious families had scarcely emerged from childhood when they were captivated by revolutionary ideas, took part in strikes and became militants. But this precocious commitment often followed from a precocious entry into the world of work.

Yehoshua Rojanski, for example, began working in a tannery in Slonim at the age of seventeen. He was a militant in Poale Zion. The party then asked him to form a section in the factory, to compete with the influence of the Bund that was dominant at that time, 1913. A few months later, when the Poale Zion section was established, Rojanski called a strike:

> It lasted a month, and the boss had to give in. The working day was cut from ten hours to nine, and our wages were raised. After this struggle, we held a secret meeting in a forest. I spoke to try and convince the workers that it was time to move from economic to political struggle. 'Comrades', I said, 'aren't we all Jews? Why do you follow the Bund, which isn't a genuine national organization of Jews, but first and foremost a Social Democrat organization? It's true that the Bund champions the Yiddish language, but it refuses to see the Jews of the whole world as

a single people, a nation. We, Poale Zion, defend the idea of the Jewish nation; we are the genuine national organization of Jewish workers!

Rojanski, a former *yeshiva* pupil, transferred the skill in argument and casuistry he had acquired there to political discussion. But the break with the old world was sharp: he did not become a rabbi, but a virtually professional agitator, travelling throughout Byelorussia on behalf of his party and running one strike after another. He has not forgotten his first arrest, on 9 January 1914. The Okhrana, the tsarist police, suspected him of having posted on the walls of the town a leaflet commemorating the anniversary of 'Bloody Sunday' in 1905.

As explained, acquiring a trade, a qualification, was also an attempt to escape from poverty. It is hard today to conceive the distress in which a substantial part of the Jewish population lived, not just at the beginning of the century, but also in Poland in the 1920s and 1930s. Hersh Mendel traces a sensitive portrait of his childhood in a Warsaw alley: 'My first childhood years completely lose themselves in the abyss of darkness' – the gloomy building where his family lived and his father worked, a pious and taciturn man who 'never conversed with us kids', and a leatherworker whose work never ceased. 'No matter how late I came home and every morning when I woke up, he was always in his small work room.' On Saturday, the father went to the synagogue in his grubby work clothes – that was all he had. The mother, who suffered from a chronic disease, was 'covered completely' by the wig she wore.[6] Despite the father's incessant work, the children did not have enough to eat.

Mendel joined the Bund and became a militant, and escaped to Paris and then Russia, where he took part in the October Revolution. When he returned to Warsaw, the neighbours told him that his father had died of hunger in 1915, followed by his mother and sister in the famine two years later.

Reading the memoirs of this militant gives the impression of a nineteenth-century naturalist novel. But this was no fiction, as other testimonies confirm. Bronia Zelmanowicz:

---

6   Mendel, *Memoirs of a Jewish Revolutionary*, pp. 27–9.

We were poor, but there were people poorer than us. My mother was known for her goodness, and a constant procession of hungry, sick and wretched people descended on us. When mother was unable to help them, she sent us children to the better-off households to beg for food and money. I saw then what real poverty was. These children of six or seven who sold doughnuts illicitly in the street, who were caught and beaten by the police. And so I very soon began to ask myself: how can God permit such injustice? I started going to public libraries and reading socialist literature – Marx, Plekhanov, etc. – and I came to the conclusion that the only way to achieve justice in this world was to struggle.

Yaakov Greenstein:

I remember a neighbour's family where there were eight children at home. The father went from village to village with a colleague, collecting scrap metal. They had a cart but no horse to pull it; one of them took the front, the other pushed, and they went along the roads in this way, among the *goyim*, from dawn to night. For the evening meal, my mother bought a loaf of bread. But she waited to cut it until father came home, afraid that the children would swallow it all; they couldn't wait. 'When will father come home?' they kept asking.

These were everyday scenes of Jewish life in Eastern Europe, and make a striking contrast with the stereotypes of Russian or Polish anti-Semitism: the Jew as well-to-do trader or prosperous industrialist. We should note, however, that despite the cleavages that ran through Yiddishland, despite the instability of this world, community spirit and family ties remained strong: a continuation of traditional values that is explained by the persistent mechanisms of rejection by the surrounding society.

Bella Greenstein describes this community spirit, this solidarity of the disinherited:

There was often unemployment in our little town of Krinki. But mutual support was a regular feature. My mother and some of her friends did their shopping before Shabbat, buying challah – the Saturday bread –

fish and a bit of meat, and gave what they could to people who had nothing. No one went completely without food. A few years ago I visited Argentina. In Buenos Aires I met a woman from Krinki, and she slipped around my neck a thin chain supporting a little gold heart. 'It's the heart of your mother,' she said. Why? One day, in the 1920s, this woman's husband left for Argentina, abandoning her and her five children – and a sixth that she was pregnant with. He had had an affair with a *goya* and in any case felt unable to support his family. The poor woman lived on what my mother and some others gave her. Sometimes her children ate with us. One day my mother wrote to the association of people from Krinki in Argentina, asking a favour. A few months later, visas for the woman and children arrived. My mother and her friends made up a trousseau for her, then accompanied her to Danzig where they took the boat. In Argentina, the Krinki association met them and took them to the husband, who was obliged to take care of them.

In families, the solidity and intensity of relations between parents and children most frequently trumped the conflicts triggered by the children's commitment to revolution. Moshe Green, a Bund militant, quarrelled with his father, who was religious and annoyed that the Bund published its newspaper even on Saturday. Moshe argued; his father got angry and slapped him. 'But that didn't stop us from still living together on good terms', he immediately added.

Did the children reject their values, their way of life, their faith? The first reaction of traditionalist parents was to ignore them, sometimes to disown them. But when repression struck, when they were thrown into prison or threatened with a trial, the reflexes of family and community solidarity took the upper hand; parents did everything possible to ensure the services of a good lawyer, and sent regular parcels to the prison, even if the conflict persisted despite this.

Janine Sochaczewska relates a visit that her mother made to her in prison:[7]

---

7   Janine Sochaczewska was the mother of Pierre Goldman, the author of *Souvenirs obscurs d'un juif polonnais né en France* (Paris: Éditions du Seuil, 1975).

One day in April, my father sent my mother to ask me to eat unleavened bread during the Pesach festival. Well, in the [prisoners'] commune we had decided that as soon as our parents began talking religion, we would get up, turn around and end the visit. My mother arrived in tears, broken to see me in prison, and said to me: 'Pesach is coming, we'd like you to accept a packet of unleavened bread.' I got up, left her in the meeting room, and very quietly went back upstairs. I was a good communist.[8]

A less dramatic example is the example of the solidity of family ties given by Rachel Schatz. Her father, a Polish Jew who had emigrated to Dresden, was the only Poale Zion militant there; he conducted active proselytism in favour of emigration to Palestine. One day, however, when his daughter showed a desire to make her *aliyah*, he cried from the heart: 'Oh no, not you!' He was what she called a 'Zionist for others'.

We have emphasized so far the conflict between old and new that crystallized in the opposition between the pious, traditionalist parents and the children who abandoned religion and traditions to join the revolution. But other accounts present a more complex image of the irruption of modernity, the new culture and values, into early twentieth-century Yiddishland. In the tales of our informants, this image emerges from the distinction that they make between what they called the 'fanatical' and the 'religious'. Many times we heard the phrase 'my parents were religious, but not fanatical'. What becomes clear in this distinction is the plasticity, capacity for evolution and basic internal dynamism of the Jewish world of Eastern Europe. How did the new superimpose itself on the old and link up with it? It is again at the level of family life that our witnesses explain this phenomenon.

Max Technitchek:

My mother came from a family of eminent rabbis who, like her own brother, had written works of interpretation of the Scriptures. But her culture was German and quite indifferent to religion. She had read

---

8   *Le Monde dimanche*, 26 April 1981.

Spinoza and Marx, and had an unquenchable thirst for knowledge. When my brothers and I went to the Ukrainian school, she learned Ukrainian with us, and Polish as well. By conviction, she oriented herself towards socialism and influenced my father, guiding his reading so well that he certainly ended up thinking that socialism was a good thing, that a day would come when everyone would be happy. Of course, the good Lord still had a hand in it – the Messiah, socialism, the vision of future happiness for the Jews and all humanity – all this tended to melt together in his convictions. No doubt his faith weakened somewhat as his reading extended, but he remained attached to the traditions.

David Szarfharc:

My father was a knitter, working at home on a small machine. He was a profound believer and read the sacred texts every day. But he was also open to the world, progressive; he read the Bund daily paper, the *Folkstsaytung*, and was quite familiar with Yiddish literature. He had sympathy for the communists. For him, the prophets were precursors of Marx. I even remember that in 1923 he openly conducted propaganda among his *Hassid* co-religionists in favour of the communist candidates for the Diet elections.

Here, the transition from the closed world of tradition to the open world of modernity is not expressed in terms of violent rupture, rather of evolution, reconciliation between what embodies the deep identity of Judaism and the rationalist, enlightened aspiration for the promotion of a more just and human world. As Isaac Deutscher notes, it was another tradition of Judaism that continued here, renewed in both culture and historical practice, ideas and action: that of rationalists such as Marx, Heine, Rosa Luxemburg, Trotsky, etc.

These parents who, without abandoning their faith, were unrestrictedly open to the world outside, read newspapers, visited theatres and did not make too much fuss about their children not eating kosher when they were away from home, clearly in their own way beat the path to radicalism and revolutionary commitment for their children.

'In our family the intellectual atmosphere steered us to the left', Max Technitchek notes. 'My father knew that my brother and I were politically involved and he did not see any objection. The only thing for him was that he didn't want to see us go to prison.'

David Szarfharc also explains his joining the Communist Youth at the age of fifteen in terms of the 'atmosphere' in his family home. In this sense, the revolutionary commitment of so many young Jews was an expression of the 'new culture' that developed in Yiddishland in the first decades of the twentieth century. This world shaken by modernity was not in fact condemned. It transformed itself, but its internal dynamic was not broken: the vitality of Yiddish culture at the beginning of the century is evidence of this, even in Piłsudski's Poland and Stalin's Soviet Union before it was rooted out.

This is what Rachel Ertel writes on the subject:

> Once again, we are led to observe that Jewish society in Eastern Europe of this time did not correspond to the ideas usually accepted. Its traditionalist character that is often evoked did exist and pervade the atmosphere of the *shtetl*. But the relationship between tradition and modernity was dialectical ... The dynamic element of Jewish society was its secularist sector and more especially the youth ... This youth developed a genuine way of life, a genuine counterculture in which it flourished ... Young people and adolescents, bound up with the social body of the group by all the fibres of their being, could challenge this without disavowing it, combatting those aspects of it that they saw as outmoded and seeking to appropriate what the outside world was in a position to offer them ... They injected [the new culture] into their original inheritance, carrying out a mutation of the entire Jewish society ... Contrary, therefore, to what one might believe, imagination and youth were dominant and reinvented life in the *shtetl*.[9]

We should also note that there was permanent contact and a direct connection (if not always harmonious) between the artists and particularly writers who embodied this new culture, and the Jewish

---

9   Ertel, *Le Shtetl*, pp. 292 ff.

workers' movement. Isaac Leib Peretz, for example, was in permanent dialogue with the socialist movement. Bronia Zelmanowicz relates on this subject a story that struck her from her youth:

> One day, during the 1905 revolution, workers came to seek out Peretz and asked him why he wasn't coming to fight on the barricades. He replied to them with a parable: 'Two cities in ancient Greece were at war. The battle was exhausting and deadly, and the survivors few in number. One of the cities then called on its oracles, the priestesses who tended the sacred fire, and their participation in the battle actually led to its victorious outcome. But when the people returned to the city to celebrate, they noticed that the sacred fire had gone out. And they killed the priestesses. With us, too,' Peretz concluded, 'someone has to tend the sacred fire; if I went to die on the barricades, what would happen to your soul?'

Hersh Mendel, likewise, remembers how before the First World War it was his custom each Saturday to place himself, along with some revolutionary workers among his friends, in the Saxon Garden at Warsaw, where Peretz would always come to promenade. They accosted him and listened to him passionately … except when the writer attacked Marxism or maintained that it was right for Jewish workers to attend the synagogue. Then there was a lively argument, though without affecting the respect and affection that existed on both sides between the artist and the revolutionary workers.

Moshe Zalcman, in his memoirs, mentions a meeting between the great popular Yiddish writer Shalom Asch and a group of young communists who revered him. Unfortunately, the discussion took a bad turn, and when Moshe asked the writer why he supported the Piłsudski government instead of exalting the heroes of proletarian struggle, Asch became annoyed and put an early end to the exchange: 'I don't know you and don't want to know you; I don't see you and don't want to see you!'[10]

---

10   Moshe Zalcmann, *Histoire véridique de Moshe, ouvrier juif et communiste au temps de Staline* (Paris: Édition Recherches, 1977).

These exchanges in no way detract from the resonance that writers such as Shalom Asch, Sholem Aleichem and Isaac Leib Peretz met with among the progressive and even revolutionary Jewish youth. Very often, moreover, their work bore witness to both the upheavals in the Jewish world and the deep originality of the constitutive features of *Yiddishkeit* that persisted despite this. Thus the misadventures of his character Tevye the dairyman, whom Sholem Aleichem portrays so robustly, show a permanent contrast between the procession of miseries that beset the ordinary citizen of Yiddishland and his incorrigible optimism. 'And what about hope and trust?' Tevye cries out. 'Well, that's just how it is, not otherwise; the more misery there is, the more we need trust; and the more poverty, the more we need hope' – a profession of faith that is often echoed in the utterances of the Yiddishland revolutionaries.

The tribulations of Tevye are also an occasion to illuminate the key role of the family in this world, since, as he recalls, 'the grandson of the cousin of a grandmother's cousin is still something for a Jew. If you're family, then you're family, as the saying goes'. But at the same time, and again echoed in the stories of our witnesses, this traditional family shows cracks on all sides, and it is in vain that Tevye arranges an advantageous marriage between his daughter and a prosperous widowed butcher; in secret, and without asking her father or mother's opinion, the girl was already engaged to a young – and poor – tailor.

Basically, this modern Yiddish literature detected and depicted a paradox that casts a sharp light on the situation of *Yiddishkeit* at the start of the new century: it was a literature of rupture that the rabbis rejected as impious, a literature turned towards the realities of life, towards the world of the underdog, but if it testifies in this way to the earthquakes that were shaking Yiddishland, it did not take flight beyond the linguistic and cultural frontiers of this world and set foot in universal culture. Though very many Jews in Poland were moved by reading Mickiewicz, how many Polish intellectuals between the two wars were aware of Peretz? This literature remained entirely focused on the Yiddish world, its fund of religious mythology, its customs and traditions, a literature that prospered at the heart of the crisis this world was undergoing, for the exclusive use of those who were its direct witnesses or its agents. Curiously, it is only posthumously, one could say, decades after the disappearance in fire and blood of the world from which it arose, that this literature has begun to enter the pantheon of human culture in general, and, paradox of paradoxes, the broad non-Yiddish-speaking public has begun to discover Sholem Aleichem and Shalom Asch by way of Isaac Bashevis Singer.

The massive revolutionary commitment of a fraction of Jewish youth in the early twentieth century cannot be equated with a flight from the Jewish world, an unqualified rejection of this world. This is clear enough as far as the Bundists and Poale Zion militants are concerned. But it is also true to a great degree of the communists – their commitment to the movement was not a sign of forgetting or denying their identity; they participated in it as Jews, drawing Jewish workers into the great movement of universal emancipation. The Polish Communist Party of the 1920s and 1930s was a party in which Jews were sufficiently numerous for the specific dimension of their struggle, their traditions and culture, to be taken into account. It was only later, after 1945, that Jewish communists in Poland began to 'Polonize' their names, could not hope to hold important positions if they did not have a Polish 'profile', and were driven to disguise their Jewish origins from their children. Even if the Polish Jewish communists of the 1930s believed in theory in assimilation, as they wrongly imagined that the USSR showed the way to a harmonious and peaceful assimilation of Jews with respect to their culture, the reality of the country in which they struggled rooted and consolidated them in their Jewish identity. Their battle, like that of the Bundists and the militants of Poale Zion, was both an indication and a factor of the dynamism of the world that had produced them.

Of course, there was still resistance to this dynamism: the social and political conservatism of the majority of the Jewish community of a country like Poland, the blindness of its leaders in the face of rising perils, their loyalty to existing institutions and the state, even when this stubbornly treated Jews as second-class citizens. But the conflicts of perspectives and interests, the confrontation between classes and world views within the Jewish communities of Eastern Europe, precisely attest that this world was not fixed and frozen. On the eve of the

Second World War, the national dimension of the Jewish problem in the European East was fully apparent, especially in Poland but also in the USSR – as against the prognoses that Lenin, Trotsky and Rosa Luxemburg had made at the start of the century. Paradoxically, it was then the Jewish working class and the Jewish revolutionary intelligentsia who appeared as the real supports of national identity, and it was they who held the key to the resolution of the Jewish problem as a social and national question.

In the wake of the revolution of 1905, the Bund turned towards a 'nationalist' approach to the Jewish question in Eastern Europe, and was increasingly perceived as promoting Yiddish culture and national sentiment, particularly under the slogan of cultural and national autonomy for the Jewish population. This, for example, is what *Di hofnung* (Hope), the Bund's daily paper, wrote in October 1907:

> [The Bund] has created a Yiddish culture ... The first step of the Jewish workers' movement, the transition from propaganda circles to mass agitation, begins by putting the Yiddish language first. Jews have to speak Yiddish! And everyone is certainly obliged to accept that the Bund has greatly developed the Yiddish language, enriching it and making it more flexible. It has transformed the jargon of the marketplace into a language in which the most serious scientific questions can be discussed. Speak with an average Jewish worker and you will see how greatly the publications of the Bund have influenced his manner of expressing himself ... And then, the Bund has taught the Jewish masses to read ... It has created a broad public of readers who demand good books and newspapers, it has created a new literature for this public ... The Jewish masses have not received any cultural legacy from the upper classes [of the Jewish community], neither literature nor art. They have to create this legacy entirely on their own account.[11]

Beyond the *pro domo* argument here, the text illustrates a basic idea: that of an intimate connection between the development of a new

---

11   Cited in Vladimir Medem, *The Memoirs of Vladimir Medem* (New York: KTAV, 1979), p. 475.

Jewish culture in Eastern Europe and the rise of the Jewish workers' movement. In this sense, the slogan of national and cultural autonomy for the Jewish population of the geographical Yiddishland, which the Bund was alone in defending from the first years of the twentieth century, appears as the concentration of a historical perspective that remained genuinely realistic for the Jewish masses of Eastern Europe until the eve of the Second World War. This slogan corresponded to the deep 'diasporic consciousness' of the great majority of Jewish workers, who wished to continue to live in the cultural, linguistic and geographical space in which they were born; and despite the fact that the discrimination and hostility displayed towards them by the nationalities among which they lived or came into contact scarcely declined, the slogan matched very well what made for the specificity of their 'nationality' condition: unity and identity in dispersion, and the intertwining and certain forms of osmosis between their culture and those contiguous to it. It corresponded to the development and dynamism of the new Jewish culture that emerged from the ghetto and the marketplace and breathed the free air of the modern world, without denying its ancient roots. It took account of the situation of the Jews of Yiddishland as an oppressed national minority, whose basic national rights were not recognized in a country such as interwar Poland.

It is true that in the 1930s the evolution of the Bund towards social democracy and reformism attenuated the radical and revolutionary import of this slogan, or tended to fix it in certain partial conquests such as the CYSHO, the secular Yiddish-language schools that the Bund sponsored together with other socialist currents. Today, it is less frequently this loss of radicalism on the part of the Bund that is criticized as much as the unreal character of the historical perspective that it continued to defend on the eve of the Second World War: against assimilationist illusions on the one hand, and the Zionists on the other. But this amounts to reproaching it for not having foreseen the full consequences of the Second World War, the invasion of Eastern Europe and the Soviet Union, the application of the final solution by the Hitlerite bureaucracy, an escalation of horror with consequences that no head of state anticipated; for not having foreseen either the singular new beginning of Jewish history after the war, in the wake of the genocide. It is not true, however, that the solutions proposed by the Zionists, of whatever shade, represented historical realism as against the inconsistent utopianism of the Bund. Certainly the prophets were not numerous, but they have to be given their due: Kurt Tucholsky, for example,[12] who already in the mid-1920s sounded the alarm, in a Weimar Republic prey to the demons of order, nationalism, xenophobia and dreams of revanchism; Leon Trotsky, who in the late 1920s warned that the fate of Europe was being played out in Germany, and understood that the bankruptcy of German communism in the face of Hitler bore within it the inexorable unfurling of horror. At this time they were preaching in the desert, including the desert of Judaea. The rabbis who called for obedience to the temporal power in all circumstances, and the inspirers of Begin and Sharon who at the time paraded in black shirts, are not best placed to cast the first stone at these Jewish visionaries and militants who were struggling at this time for a better world.

---

12   Kurt Tucholsky, *Bonsoir révolution allemande!* (Grenoble: PUG, 1982); and *Chroniques allemandes* (Paris: Balland, 1982).

2.

Rally Round Our Flag!

In serried ranks, the enemy attack.
Come rally round our flag!
No matter that death may threaten,
We'll suffer gladly for the cause.
'The Warsawian'

B etween the two world wars, an interval of twenty years when the history of the century was in the balance, militancy was the key word in the existence of our witnesses, the centre of gravity of their lives. Some of them had already begun their activity before 1914, with others this reached a high point after the Second World War, but all were fully engaged in the interwar years.

Militancy did not just mean joining a party, a particular political activity. It meant, far more broadly, making a moral choice; adopting a cause; a creed, a set of values; rooting one's individual practice in the world view of a collective action. It meant accepting both what was explicit in this view of the world and what was implicit, its commandments, its codes and its references. For those who made this commitment, whether as communists, Bundists, or Zionist workers (left Poale Zion), the foundation of their belief was the concept of the historic mission of the proletariat, the actuality of proletarian revolution and the promotion of a new world, the optimistic vision of a future in which man would be reconciled with man, and men with their history, a faith in the speedy advent of a world from which all injustice, discrimination and exploitation of man by man would be banished. Each party's 'utopia' certainly had its particular coloration. But these different branches all sprang from the same root: the great utopia of a new world, the New Covenant that was prefigured by the writings of the socialist thinkers of the second half of the nineteenth century, that was consolidated with the growth of the workers' movement in the early 1900s, and that stormed the heavens with the Russian Revolution.

For all its great diversity of places, times and ideologies, this militancy was always messianic, optimistic, oriented to the Good – a fundamental and irreducible difference from that of the fascists with which some people have been tempted to compare it, on the pretext that one 'militant ideal' is equivalent to any other. It was young people who were caught up by it, a youth whose social and political consciousness was born at a moment when history was in flux and seemed to promise still more colossal transformations. They lived in what Wolf Biermann called the 'waiting room of the revolution'.

Irène Gefon, born in Łódź into an intellectual family, finished her studies in Paris, writing a thesis on Balzac at the Sorbonne. On return to her own country, far from the libraries of the Latin Quarter, she became active in the working-class districts:

> I covered my head with a scarf, and went into the workers' quarters. I made propaganda in support of political prisoners, collected money … It was an emotional commitment above all; these workers often opened their doors to me, offered me a soup that I would never have eaten at home (times were hard); but I had to swallow it if I didn't want to be seen as a bourgeois intellectual preaching to the workers!

Haïm Babic, a young carpenter, became active in Warsaw in the Bund's youth organization, set up circles of young Jewish workers, saw to their political education, ran from one district to another, argued with the communists in his trade union, and still found the time to read the writings of Marx, Plekhanov and the Austro-Marxist Otto Bauer on the national question. 'It wasn't just a matter of action, militant activity,' he says; 'the young workers also had to be educated'.

Hanna Lévy-Haas, the daughter of an unsuccessful shopkeeper in Sarajevo, managed to get into Belgrade University thanks to great sacrifice on the part of her mother. She was successful in her studies, but caught up in the agitation that was rife among the students:

> We were always demonstrating, whether on educational issues, or economic and political questions. One day, we skipped a maths lecture to go to a demonstration. When the exam came round, the professor, a real reactionary, took his revenge with a vengeance and failed us all. Another time, the police entered the university precincts despite the supposed autonomy and gave us a thrashing. By way of protest, we spent the night in the lecture theatre.

Hanna soon found herself marked out as a communist, even before joining the party.

Yaakov Greenstein, from a very poor family, started work in a textile plant in Łódź at the age of fourteen. A few months after he was taken on, the workers went on strike, and sent him – a Jew, into the bargain – to make their demands to the boss. 'I'm not going to discuss with a *smarkatch* [wretch] like you', were the boss's disdainful words. 'On the contrary, it's precisely this "*smarkatch*" you're going to discuss with', responded the workers who accompanied Yaakov. As a militant in the Young Communists, Greenstein became one of the main 'agitators' in the factory, until the day that the Defensiva, the Polish political police, arrived to arrest him: he had still not turned fifteen.

David Sztokfisz, a typographer in Lublin, joined the left Poale Zion at the age of sixteen. He didn't have an easy time of it. In his union, the Bundists were the dominant party and tirelessly denounced the Zionist utopia as reactionary; the communists infiltrated and undermined the ranks of the socialist Zionists; and in the Zionist camp, Poale Zion were shunned as crypto-communists, mocked with the rhyme '*Fun Zion a leck, fun Marx a schmeck*' ('a lick of Zion but a taste of Marx'). 'Basically', says Sztokfisz, 'there was some truth in this joke: we were caught between the hammer and the anvil'.

Elija Rosijanski, born in Lithuania, also rowed against the current in Paris. A Trotskyist, he published along with a few other comrades a little newspaper in Yiddish which he secretly distributed among the Jewish workers who frequented the offices of the Kulturliga, the Jewish cultural association controlled by the French Communist Party (PCF). His bundle of copies often ended up in the gutter, thanks to Stalin's acolytes, while Rosijanski was also shunned by the orthodox Trotskyists for his unorthodox position on the Soviet Union. Isolated and out of funds, he soon had to close operations. So much for the dissident Yiddish revolutionary paper *Klorkheit*.

There were tens of thousands of Yiddishland revolutionaries who followed the different paths of their utopia to the four corners of Europe in the interwar years. From the aftermath of the Russian Revolution to the Nazi invasion of Poland was a long and bumpy journey. But the constancy of these militants' commitment was remarkable, as was the firmness of the ideas and aspirations that underlay it. No matter how the scales of history came down, the 'great socialist dream' remained basically the same: how otherwise to explain the fervour that took thousands to Spain at a time when the German workers' movement was being massacred under Nazi jackboots, or the enthusiasm that brought them into the ranks of the Resistance when the rule of Nazi barbarism stretched across all of Europe? How to explain even the return of tens of thousands of them to the ruins of their culture in Eastern Europe after 1945, to homes where their nearest and dearest had suffered a horrible death – if not by the hope that utopia would finally become reality despite everything?

A strange paradox is apparent here: the maintenance of this flux of revolutionary heroism, militant readiness, élan for a new world among these fighters despite the trajectory of their parties and organizations, which increasingly turned their backs on the 'great dream' to accommodate to the realism of the established order, or even scuttle themselves in a horrific waste of human life and hope.

There is no mystery about the commitment of Yehoshua Rojanski in the maelstrom of the Russian Revolution. A militant since 1913 in Poale Zion, an agitator pursued by the Okhrana who opposed the 'imperialist' war right from the start and organized Poale Zion in Tsaritsyn when the February Revolution broke out, it was the most natural thing in the world to join in with those who undertook to build the 'new world' without reneging on his socialist Zionist commitment. At this point utopia was clearly marked out and unstained, the dividing line clear between the camp of revolution and that of counterrevolution:

> Our movement was riven by factional struggles; some leaned towards the Bolsheviks, others towards the Mensheviks. I aligned myself with the Bolsheviks, convinced that the defeat of the Russian army could only lead us towards our goal, a socialist revolution. I was under the strong impression made on me by the Bolshevik leader in Tsaritsyn. The son of a priest, he returned from Siberia in May 1917. He arrived in the town brandishing a flag on which he had written: 'Down with the war!' I was twenty years old then, and that kind of militant made a greater impression on me than the Mensheviks with their moderation.

No more mystery either in the way that Solomon Fishkowski, likewise a militant with Poale Zion in Poland, crossed the Rubicon of commitment on the side of the Russian Revolution. Arrested as a leftist in 1920, he was sent to a punishment battalion on the front at the height of the Russo-Polish war. There was a prevailing climate of anti-Semitism, and one insult and humiliation followed another. On 2 January 1920 he decided to cross the Bug and join the Red Army. When they saw him coming, with his sparkling Polish uniform, the Red soldiers in their rags ironically shouted, 'Look at the *pan* [Polish 'gentleman'] we have here!' And Fishkowski replied, 'From now on I'm a *pan* like you; I'm on your side!'

No mystery, finally, in the commitment of Hersh Smolar, who, scarcely fifteen and already a socialist activist, watched in amazement the entry of the Red Army into his little Polish town. 'That's when I saw the men from the Red east for the first time: dressed in strange costumes, half military and half civilian, with pistols on their belts and their eyes on fire – men who were hollow and sleepless, with rather hoarse voices.' One of the officers met with the local socialist militants at the town hall, talked to them and shook their hands. Taking Smolar aside, he asked him not to shirk his responsibilities but play a part in the revolutionary administration that was being set up.

'What can I do, then, a simple Jewish boy like me?' Smolar asked. The Red soldier stared at him:

You're still an element without political consciousness. If the Revolution sent me and the others here, it's to put an end to all inequalities – Jew, non-Jew, who cares? What counts is to drive out our enemies, all of them without exception. But among friends, in our camp, what does it matter what language someone speaks or where they come from?

Smolar became a member of the town's revolutionary committee. When the Red Army fell back and the Poles recaptured the town, all members of the revolutionary committee they could lay hands on were tortured and massacred; Smolar spent long weeks hiding on a farm. He finally managed to escape and reach the Soviet Union.

The 'great dream' was still intact like a cloudless sky. Even the Polish Bund, traditionally linked to the Mensheviks, was a hair's breadth from joining the Communist International. Moshe Green, a Bundist since 1915, remembers the great stream of the revolution that carried away everything on its course:

The day after the Russian Revolution we organized a meeting in our Warsaw premises. Vladimir Medem took the floor, the Bund's historic leader who was traditionally hostile to Bolshevism. His whole speech was directed against the revolution, but the audience were against him and milled out into the street shouting: 'Long live the revolution!' Medem remained inside by himself, but eventually he came out and joined the crowd. At that time, the climate in the Bund was favourable to the Bolsheviks. Medem predicted that things would take a bad turn. But the majority of militants were further left than he was, myself especially. It wasn't an accident that Medem left for the United States shortly after.

By the mid-1930s, however, the political landscape had changed considerably. In the USSR and the communist movement internationally, there was no question any more of the burning actuality of the world revolution, the struggle of the German proletarians joining with that

of the young Russian revolution, but rather the building of socialism in one country and unconditional support for Stalin's domestic
and foreign policy. In Germany, the most powerful workers' movement in Europe, the most powerful national Communist and Social
Democratic Parties, had just experienced a historic defeat; the war
in Spain would soon show the irresistible rise of fascism in Europe; in
France, the promising experience of the Popular Front collapsed after
only a year; while in Poland, the anti-Semitic nationalist currents
were in the ascendant and Stalin would soon administer a kick in the
teeth to the clandestine Polish communists by dissolving their party.

Despite these reverses, despite the fossilizing of the big workers'
organizations, despite the collapse of all the driving ideas of a socialist
utopia into their opposite, the militants were still there and the idealism and messianism of their action still just as great. How was this?

First of all, Shlomo Szlein replies, because misery and anti-Semitism
were still the same:

> The situation of Jewish workers was generally wretched, and even that
> of the small Jewish employers. In Galicia where I lived, the workshops
> were full of children who worked from dawn to dusk. The eight-hour
> day was hardly enforced. Except for a small stratum of big entrepre-
> neurs or businessmen, the Jews lived in indescribable poverty. Besides,
> our region was attached to Poland even though not basically peopled by
> Poles. The Ukrainians suffered discrimination along with the Jews. We
> were on the border with the USSR, and the way in which the national
> question had been solved in Soviet Ukraine or Byelorussia, especially
> the Jewish question, struck us as extraordinarily positive.
>
> Younger Jews, in the late 1920s, had joined the communist move-
> ment in eastern Galicia on a massive scale. The movement's power of
> attraction was that it seemed to promise to resolve both the social ques-
> tion and the national question in a short space of time. There was such
> a high proportion of Jewish youth in the communist movement here
> that you could almost say it was a Jewish national movement. In any
> case, the question of any stifling or denial of Jewish identity absolutely
> didn't arise. The majority of Jewish young people joined it with a Jewish
> national consciousness.

Léa Stein, a student in Zagreb, was active in Hachomer Hatzaïr before joining the Young Communists. This had given her an education in Zionism, but also something of the Marxism that was *de rigueur* in that group; she had stayed on a *hakhchara*, a kind of kibbutz where young Zionist activists prepared for their emigration to Palestine. One thing, however, failed to satisfy her: in 1930s Yugoslavia, under the heel of a police regime, these young socialist Zionists were completely absent from the sites of class struggle; their combat for the 'new world' was confined to Palestine. She accordingly moved towards the Young Communists, who not only studied Marx and Engels but also acted: 'They struck me as representing a broader perspective, with very positive values. I was about eighteen years old. In 1934 and 1935, most of the young people from Hachomer in Zagreb joined the Young Communists.'

Shlomo Shamli, a communist of Bulgarian origin, relates an experience that is completely comparable. A Hachomer Hatzaïr activist in Sofia, he failed to understand why this organization supported the Spanish Republican side in 1936 but refused to recruit fighters for the struggle in Spain; for this reason, many Hachomer militants joined the Communist Party. Almost half the members of Hachomer in Sofia had done so by the start of the Second World War, the Communists being, as Shamli said, the only group to organize armed struggle against the Nazis.

'Becoming a communist', added Yaakov Greenstein,

for me meant taking the shortest and most natural way to put an end to my miseries. It meant marching in the footsteps of the Soviet communists, of the USSR, of what I believed this then was. In my home we generally had bread, because several of us children worked, but that was far from being the case everywhere. The worse misery, anti-Semitism and political repression grew, in the 1930s, the more convinced I was that socialism was the only possible solution for us. The communist movement was like a fountain at that time for the Jewish youth in Poland.

For Hanna Lévy-Haas, communism at that time was more a moral and philosophical ideal than a political practice. It was the very meaning of humanity, she said, and the incident that convinced her of this was totally everyday:

> In Yugoslavia in the 1930s, under King Alexander I, it was dangerous even to utter the word 'communist'; the Communist Party was illegal. But that was when I had my first contact with communism. I was about fifteen, and someone gave me a leaflet at school. I hid it, went home, and waited until I was alone in the children's bedroom before reading it. I learned that a sixth of the world had already been freed by socialism, that in the USSR there was no more exploitation or oppression – simplistic propaganda, rudimentary explanations, but for me it was an intellectual discovery, an intellectual opening. I felt that the message contained here resonated with my own sadness, and that I could draw a great strength from it to overcome that sensation.

Around that time, one Friday, Hanna was carrying on the way to school a big dish that her mother had entrusted to her: a Shabbat bread prepared in the Sephardic style, which she was supposed to take to the baker's for cooking. She saw her maths teacher coming towards her, a Jewish man whom she knew to be a communist, good-looking, well-dressed, whom all the *lycée* girls were a bit in love with, and she herself liked a lot. It was raining, and the teacher wore a trenchcoat and carried an umbrella. As a shy and awkward adolescent, Hanna felt terribly embarrassed and stupid coming down the road with her baking dish towards the young and handsome maths teacher. 'He felt this,' she says,

> and made an unforgettable gesture, taking his umbrella in the other hand and raising his hat to greet me. Without the least irony. Just to show me that he respected me as a person. A pedagogic gesture, if you like. But only a communist could have done this. At that time, things were simpler than they are today; that kind of simple humanity was more or less synonymous with communism.

The young teacher joined the Resistance and was killed by the Nazis; his portrait is in Sarajevo's Jewish museum, and he is remembered there as a hero.

Perhaps, though, things were no longer quite as simple as Hanna Lévy-Haas recalled. Certainly, objective conditions fed the revolutionary idealism of the militants, their courage and their devotion, but this enthusiasm constantly broke against the policy of their organizations. It was what Isaac Deutscher called in relation to the Polish Communist Party the time of 'bureaucratized revolutionary heroism':

> The movement had reached the stage of bureaucratic uniformity. The Polish party was affected by this even more painfully than were other European parties because its revolutionary tradition had been deeper and stronger, and it operated in conditions of complete illegality; appealing continuously to the spirit of revolutionary self-sacrifice and to the heroism of its members, which never failed. Bureaucratic uniformity and revolutionary enthusiasm are a contradiction in terms.[1]

In the everyday practice of militants, this bureaucratic degeneration signalled the promotion of new behaviours and values in place of the old: loyalty and obedience to leaders and hierarchical superiors rather than aptitude for critical reflection; likewise sectarianism, triumphalism, unbridled dogmatism. Bronia Zelmanovicz describes very well the 'contradiction' in this militancy:

> We were working under very difficult conditions. For us Polish communists, five-year prison terms were quite commonplace. Yet our optimism was unshakeable, we were convinced that our children would know true freedom and happiness, the emancipation of the human race. I remember having read in the party paper, while I was in prison, that in the USSR prisoners were able to continue their education, and I said to myself, 'How lucky they are! And I'm rotting in here!'

That was in 1937, at the height of the terror and the colossal purges in the USSR ...

---

1   Isaac Deutscher, 'The Tragedy of Polish Communism between the Two Wars', in *Marxism in Our Time* (London: Jonathan Cape, 1971), p. 126.

The other side of our radicalism was our sectarianism. As a general rule, in Łódź where I was active, our relations with the Bund and the PPS were very bad. It was exceptional for us to march together. We had our own fraction in the unions, kept strictly separate from the others. One of my friends was a Bundist, another was Poale Zion. I liked to discuss things with them, but my aim was always to indoctrinate; I explained to them that there was no more anti-Semitism in the Soviet Union, that the most complete equality prevailed, that all medical care was free, that everyone was well housed … I believed it.

When our party was dissolved by Stalin in 1938, I was certainly shocked. But I told myself that our own leadership was undoubtedly to blame. I continued to believe religiously that the USSR and Stalin were infallible. I remember a terrible quarrel with friends of mine who practically threw me out of the door because I argued that Stalin had been right to dissolve the party and conclude a pact with Hitler. I was a true believer, a mystic, if you like.

Less spectacularly, this involution of revolutionary spirit also affected an organization as powerful as the Bund, even though it did not have to face such ferocious repression as did the communists. In the late 1930s, it dominated the Jewish trade union movement in Poland, and often did very well in municipal elections and those for the *kehilot*, the representative assemblies of the Jewish community, but it was no longer the revolutionary party that in 1905 had led the Jewish workers of Poland and Lithuania to attack the tsarist monarchy – it had lost the flame.

'The Bund,' notes David Sztokfisz, a militant in the left Poale Zion at that time,

> bureaucratically led the unions, with its full-time officials whom we called by the Jewish nickname of *Bund-zen*, trade-union 'bonzes', as they still say in German. From this point of view, you could say that the trade-union apparatus was a kind of anticipation of the Histadrut.[2]

---

2   The Israeli trade union federation, but in that period also a state-building institution and the largest employer of Jewish workers in Palestine. [Translator's note.]

These Bund bureaucrats were far removed from the workers, and rather corrupt.

Basically, you shouldn't forget that at this time the Bund had become social democratic. It was struggling to improve working conditions and increase wages; it mobilized against anti-Semitic campaigns when need arose – but there was no question of its calling on workers to mount the barricades! The left Poale Zion was more radical, more combative, and the communists still more so.

Although a faithful activist in the Bund, Haïm Babic moved in the same direction:

I took part in the Bund congress of 1930 at which it was decided to join the Second International. I was against that orientation, part of the strong minority that opposed it; we then saw the European social democrats, especially German socialists of the kind of Noske and Scheidemann, as rightists, incurable reformists. We didn't feel any affinity towards them. As a general rule there was a gulf between them and the socialist youth: one side had voted for war credits, the other had the broken rifle as its emblem. For ourselves, as Jewish youth, we suffered so many inequalities in Polish society that we demanded immediate and radical solutions, which pressed us to turn towards the east, the USSR. Without being communist, we were influenced by writers such as Barbusse, Rolland, Alexis Tolstoy, Mayakovsky. You could say we were rather leftist.

As we shall see, militancy inspired by this kind of ethic, and in these conditions, was very far from being a picnic. It involved every kind of risk and sacrifice. In exchange, however, embarking on this path meant joining a social and intellectual collective and receiving from this all its values and codes of behaviour, being initiated into the view of the world that held the collective together, and inheriting the sense of a new strength, feeling strong and almost indestructible within this new family – even if one's own situation was that of a besieged fortress.

Our witnesses describe very well the experience of joining this world against the other world, the intellectual pathway that led to it, the way in which political commitment involved a quest for cultural identity, and the structures and organizations that served as links in this chain.

Reading and discussion first of all. As a 'Young Pioneer' (the youth organization of the KPD) in Berlin, Yankel Taut discovered Marx and Rosa Luxemburg in the pamphlets his comrades passed on to him. At night, together with one of his sisters – a future officer in the Haganah – he deciphered *Wages, Price and Profit* in the family kitchen, by the light of a candle. 'I'm sure that we didn't understand very much', he recalls, 'but was that the important thing?'

At seventeen years old, Haïm Babic was president of the Bund organization Zukunft in Nowy Dwor, near Warsaw. He was a tireless militant but also a passionate reader. He devoured Barbusse's *Under Fire* standing up in the rain. After hurrying back from work, he swallowed *Crime and Punishment* in a night. Educating oneself and militancy was all one and the same thing for him. It was by reading along with action that he became convinced that the Polish Jews would never escape from their misery without a worldwide overthrow. For a young Jewish worker, that was a route from way back, simply bringing up to date in a revolutionary sense the 'Jewish' idea that knowledge is man's most valuable capital and highest value.

'Even the poorest Polish Jews', notes Yaakov Greenstein,

dreamed of their children gaining an education, becoming 'scholars' – no matter in the end whether this was in religion or science, or even politics. The essential thing, so typical of the Jews, was the inspiration to see their children escape from poverty. There were several million illiterates in Poland at that time, but this was rare among Jews.

Nor was it just by chance that the radical movements which a large proportion of young Jews joined were so concerned not only for the political education of their militants, but for their social and cultural education as well: libraries, cultural circles, history lectures, meetings with committed writers, language courses, political presentations, schools, seminars and theatres, as well as institutions such as the Bund's famous Medem sanatorium, and sports clubs inspired by the different workers' parties whose practice and results signalled the path to the new world that everyone aspired to build. In this sense, knowing history and culture, hearing a brilliant intellectual or an experienced militant explain that Yiddish was not a vulgar 'jargon' but a language no less respectable than any other, meant becoming more sure of the cause one was fighting for, more aware of one's own identity. Moshe Green recalls how, as an apprentice locksmith, he joined the Zukunft, the Bundist youth movement, in 1915:

> At the invitation of a Bundist militant, a group of apprentices from my trade school met up in an apartment on Mila street [in Warsaw]. I knew nothing about the Bund, and was very intrigued. The comrade arrived – known as Mordechaï 'Schneider', Mordechai the tailor – and he explained to us the dignity and importance of the Yiddish language, the need for teaching in Yiddish. At the end of this meeting, a Bund circle was started at the school, and I was a member.

Bella Greenstein, likewise a Bund member, stressed that this organization 'was a big family' in her little town of Krinki, in Byelorussia: 'We received from it a socialist political organization, but it also gave classes for those who had not finished their studies, courses in Polish and in French for those wanting to emigrate.'

Whatever the circumstances, educating oneself and learning meant continuing the struggle. Militants who were thrown into prison found themselves in a kind of red university. And if the party was banned, its activity was reborn in a number of forms, on the border between the political and the cultural. Shlomo Szlein recalls,

> As the [Communist] Party had to combine legal and illegal activity, when it was banned it set up in my town [Stanislawów, in eastern Galicia] broad legal organizations with a cultural aim – at least officially. We had our choirs, our dramatic clubs, our orchestras, our libraries, our Yiddish classes, etc. We invited writers such as Peretz Markish, who came and lectured to us, and in his honour we gave a big banquet.

The high point of all this cultural activity linked with political struggle, at least in Poland, was certainly the Centrale Yiddishe Schule Organisatsia. Founded in 1921, the CYSHO was a network of secular schools in which teaching was given in Yiddish, inspired by the Bund, the left Poale Zion, and progressive Jewish intellectuals. Despite the hostility and sporadic repression of the Polish government, this network continued to grow between the two wars, with a total of nearly a hundred schools and several thousand students. Kindergartens and evening classes were also attached to it, as well as a teachers' training college in Vilnius and the Vladimir Medem sanatorium for children.

As Haïm Babic explains,

The CYSHO was the first secular school for the Jewish people. Up till then, Jews could not imagine a Yiddish-language school in which religious teaching would not be the essential component. The CYSHO was a genuine popular school, open to workers and promoting a modern, socialist world view. Then there was a passionate debate. Some people maintained that the fact that teaching was in Yiddish was a heavy handicap for children educated in these schools; they would not have sufficient mastery of the Polish language. But it was quite the contrary, former CYSHO students generally went on to do very well in *lycée* and university, because they had acquired the basic education in their mother tongue and had therefore assimilated it perfectly. The Polish state never gave the CYSHO a penny's subsidy. It was the ordinary Jewish people who kept it going. A long battle was needed for the validity of the diploma it awarded to be recognized.

In 1930s France, where at one point there were three Yiddish daily papers, one Zionist, one Bundist and one communist, it was the Kulturliga dominated by the communists that formed the pole of attraction for everything radical in the Jewish emigration from Eastern Europe. It had choirs, a Jewish theatre, Yiddish-language schools and a popular university; it organized lectures, ran the Yiddisher Arbeter Sport Klub (YASK) sports club and the AIK club for young people. It served as a rallying point for new immigrants, and its offices served as a 'labour exchange', housing office and information bureau for Yiddish-speaking workers in Paris. Its press reported events in the 'home country' and worldwide, as well as new works of Yiddish culture. Its activists worked closely together with the leadership of the MOE (Main-d'œuvre étrangère), which later became the MOI (Main-d'œuvre immigrée), likewise attached to the PCF's central committee.

Bureaucratically led, sectarian and broadly aligned with the orientation of the PCF and the Communist International it might have been, but this welter of activities in which culture was intermeshed with politics expressed nonetheless the vitality of Yiddish radicalism in the very difficult conditions of emigration. In September 1937, on communist initiative, a World Congress of Jewish Culture was held in Paris, with the participation of a hundred or more delegates, including many intellectuals and celebrated artists. This congress was presented as a response to the rise of fascism and anti-Semitism in Europe. But the chairs of the Soviet guests remained empty. The year 1937 was when the first major pogrom against Jewish culture and institutions was unleashed in the USSR, and those who had been involved in promoting this culture and leading these institutions disappeared by the hundred.

In the course of our research, we were able, as it were, to feel this very particular relationship that the revolutionary radicalism of Yiddishland had with culture. The great majority of our informants were not intellectuals in the classic sense of the term; most often they had not attended university or even secondary school; most of them had practised a manual trade for a more or less lengthy period of their existence. But despite this, almost all of them seemed 'intellectuals' of a particular type, intellectual proletarians, autodidacts who, through the many wanderings and experiences of their tumultuous existence, had acquired a form of culture that was highly original, both universalist and typically Jewish, if not indeed 'Yiddish'. A polyglot culture, made up of the taste for historical and theoretical reflection (they all had their own ideas on the roots of Stalinism, the nature of the Piłsudski regime, the underlying reasons for the victory of Hitler), but also of good sense, an ironic realism drawn from the legacy of Yiddish-language culture: Peretz, Sholem Aleichem and so on. A culture nourished by remarkable libraries that even the most modest of their number had steadily and stubbornly expanded and carried within them, as shown by their habit – a virtual mania – of constantly leaving the recording machine to go and check a date or find a quotation or reference.

There is no exaggeration in the expression 'revolutionary heroism' that Isaac Deutscher uses to describe the militant courage of the Polish communists. From the proclamation of Polish independence in 1919 to the dissolution of the party in 1938, it was constantly tossed between legality and illegality, almost every few weeks. It was perceived as the 'Moscow party', the party of the foreigner, of Poland's hereditary enemy, the 'fifth column' that had supported the Red Army's advance on Warsaw in 1920. That is the time when the concept of 'Judaeo-Bolshevism' (*zydeokommuna*) was forged by the nationalist right, to combine the Jewish 'plot' and the communist 'plot' in a single word. After the *coup d'état* that brought him to power in 1926, Piłsudski thanked the communists for having supported his putsch by increasing the repression against them. During the decade in which he presided over the destiny of Poland, thousands of communists were imprisoned and dragged before the courts. At the end of his reign, the concentration camp of Bereza Kartuzka was established – after the model of Dachau, it was openly said at the time – designed, officially, for all extremists, but after the death of Piłsudski reserved exclusively for revolutionary militants, particularly communists. In 1934 (still under Piłsudski), Poland signed a non-aggression pact with Hitler's Germany, and from then on the nationalist right and extreme right, fiercely anti-communist and anti-Semitic, held the high ground both in the institutions, from the government down, and in the street. From 1935, pogroms again began. It was in this context that the majority of our informants, Jews born in Poland, were radicalized and became militants. Not all were communists. But the repression spared neither Bundists nor Zionist workers, even if the communists were the main target.

Poland after 1918 was a multi-ethnic state that included ten million people other than Poles – though the great majority of the Polish population refused to accept this reality. Jews made up around 10 per cent of the country's total population. Contrary to other nationalities (Germans, Ukrainians, Byelorussians, etc.), they did not challenge their attachment to the Polish state, in which the great majority of them wished to carry on living. Jewish emigration (to America and Western Europe) in the interwar years was basically an emigration forced by misery and social and political discrimination. As we have seen, these conditions were the key to the radicalism of a large fraction of the Jewish youth in Poland, even if, as Pavel Korzec emphasizes, 'the dominant feature of the Jewish community was its religious conservatism, which went together with a loyalty towards the government in place',[3] and even if the conservative religious parties accordingly continued to influence the majority of the Jewish population in the interwar years.

As indicated above by Shlomo Szlein, the young Jews who turned towards the Communist Party in his region of Galicia did not feel they were abandoning or betraying their Jewish identity, precisely because so many of them met up in the communist movement. This is an essential factor that many other witnesses confirm.

Bronia Zelmanowicz, in the mid-1930s a militant in the MOPR,[4] rapidly came to the attention of the police and was thrown into prison. 'I found myself together with thirteen other young women – militants or communist sympathizers – twelve of whom were Jewish.' Later, as a militant in the Communist Party, she was attached to a cell that was completely made up of Jews (in fact clothing workers), who had mostly begun to work in the industry when they were only ten years old. She says something very interesting about them:

> Their mother tongue was naturally Yiddish, but in the context of the party they wanted to speak only Polish. They certainly spoke it very poorly, but it was very important for them. Polish was the language of social advance. If you wanted to change your condition, become a

---

3   Pawel Korzec, *Juifs en Pologne* (Paris: Presse de la Fondation nationale des sciences politique, 1980), p. 112.

4   Międzynarodowa Organizacaja Pomocy Rewolucjonistom (International Red Aid), an organization set up to support militants who were victims of repression.

white-collar worker, for example, you had to master Polish. For myself, before being a militant I read only in Yiddish, the great classics, Sholem Aleichem, Asch, etc. After I joined the party, I only read Polish. Everyone who could do so spoke Polish in the party and the trade unions.

Here we touch on an important difference from the Bund, which valorized and championed Yiddish while the communists merely accepted it. 'Jewish youth', Yaakov Greenstein emphasized,

were attracted by communism because it proposed global solutions. The Bund certainly maintained that we had to struggle to improve the condition of the Jews, but the emancipation of the Jewish people that it proposed was not bound up with that of other peoples. That did not satisfy me.

This is undoubtedly only one aspect of matters, and in the 1930s a large portion of radical Jewish youth continued to be oriented either to the Bund (whose great asset was to crystallize the strength of a purely Jewish identity, progressive and socialist, as an alternative to the conservatism of the religious parties and institutions), or to working-class Zionism. For David Grynberg, socialist Zionism was certainly the most radical solution, the only alternative to the prevailing misery:

We saw ourselves as Jewish communists. We could see on the one hand that conditions for Jewish workers in Poland were deteriorating, and on the other hand that something was amiss in the USSR, where our movement had just been made illegal. We thought, therefore, that our best chance was to make Eretz Israel a communist country. Left Poale Zion was present in every field: in the trade unions, in elections. It gave its militants a Marxist political and economic education, it had its sports clubs, and ran Yiddish-language schools along with the Bund.

Indeed, in more than one respect the balance that the left Poale Zion militants tried to maintain between what they called *da* and *dort* ('here' and 'there') – activity in Poland and propaganda for a socialist

Palestine – was a dangerous one. Despite being traditionally favourable to the Soviet regime, they were rejected by this as Zionists, while in the Zionist camp they remained isolated, as they were alone in organizing the greater part of their activity around Polish realities with a socialist perspective. For the communists, who sought to attract their militants and shared the greater part of their ideological references, they were dangerous rivals among the Jewish youth, while for the Bundists they were propagators of the petty-bourgeois and reactionary utopia of Zionism. In the 1930s, however, taking advantage of the setbacks of the Polish Communist Party and the reformist turn of the Bund, they managed to capture a significant share of the radicalized Jewish youth.

To militate under the constant threat of repression, trial and prison; to accept a provisional life under the eye of the Defensiva, abandoning any 'normal' existence; to have from one day to the next to leave your town, perhaps emigrate, deal with spies, move around secretly, not sleep at home the night before a demonstration, not fall into the hands of anti-Semites, wage constant rhetorical jousts with militants of rival organizations, adapt to sudden changes in the situation or the 'line': that was the stuff that the everyday 'revolutionary heroism' of the militant was made of, many episodes of this being fixed in memory. As Yaakov Greenstein recalls,

We put up red flags and banners, and we held ourselves ready. When a shift came out, a thousand workers, the Young Communists placed themselves across the road and a speaker gave an illegal speech, agitating against the regime and for socialism. We threw leaflets to the wind and rapidly scattered before the police arrived.

In 1935, at the age of fourteen and a half, I was arrested for the first time at one of these demonstrations. We were going to hold a meeting in front of a factory where a few years earlier some workers had been killed by the police during a strike. It was a commemoration. But one of our people, who turned out to be a Defensiva agent, had denounced us, and while I was speaking the police surrounded us. I finished my speech and they took me away. Despite my age, I was thrown into prison awaiting trial.

In April 1936, Shlomo Szlein was in Lviv, taking part in a big demonstration against unemployment. The police fired, and a demonstrator was killed. A general strike was called for the day of his funeral. The police tried to smuggle away the coffin so that the burial would not give rise to a popular demonstration, but the opposite happened; a demonstration of tens of thousands of people turned into a riot. The fighting lasted for several hours and there were dozens of dead, perhaps a hundred. On 1 May, the agitation had not subsided. All the shops were closed; there was not a single policeman in the streets. The crowd paraded, intoning the Song of the Martyrs. The local authorities called on the army, but it refused to intervene; and except for a few broken windows in the facade of a factory on strike, the great demonstration finished without incident:

> That was an extraordinary experience for me. It was the time when the pogrom instigators of the far right were raising their heads. Instructed by the [Communist] Party, I made contact in my town with the secretary of the PPS. In many towns, self-defence against the Endecy was organized jointly,[5] by Jews and non-Jews. I remember that in Stanislawów, my home town, it took the heavies of the building union only a few minutes to deal with the fascists, to 'bend them in four', as we said.

Szlein's activities were noted by the police, and he found himself in prison. He was released, then imprisoned again. Unable to carry on being active, his only choice was to leave for Spain.

Trials, prisons, camps … In 1938, David Sztokfisz, a left Poale Zion militant, was brought before the court. There was nothing particular against him, except that his brothers and brother-in-law were all communists. He was accused with them in a 'family trial', of belonging to an illegal party. This was a critical affair for left Poale Zion. If it was decided that Sztokfisz was a 'communist', then their whole organization

---

5   The Stronnictwo Narodowo-Demokratyczne (National Democratic Party) or 'Endecy' was an ultra-nationalist Polish party founded in 1897. It was very influential and led by Roman Dmowski. It not only preached hatred of Germans and Russians, but also the rejection of all national minorities in Poland, particularly the Jews. The Endecy organized several pogroms between the wars.

would be treated as a branch of the underground Communist Party, with all the dangers this entailed. They therefore called on one of the leading Polish lawyers for his defence, Henryk Erlich, who was also the leader of the Bund. In the trial, Sztokfisz openly proclaimed his membership of left Poale Zion. 'And how many members are there in this organization in Lublin?' the judge insidiously asked him. 'That is not the kind of information that a militant gives, your honour.' Erlich relished this dignified response, but the court would not put up with such insolence. Sztokfisz was given two years.

There were thousands of left-wing political prisoners in Poland at this time. By their struggles, they succeeded in being granted special status, and were very well organized.

Yaakov Greenstein:

In prison we had what we called the 'commune'. All the food we received from outside, whether from our families or the MOPR, we held in common. In my cell there was a communist doctor who received every day a meal cooked in one of the best restaurants in the city; this was divided up like everything else. In each cell there was a 'president', and a 'foreign minister' responsible for relations with the administration – that was my role, even though I was the youngest.

We waged struggles in the prison. For example, we were separated from visitors by a grille, and we demanded its removal. We refused visits until the regulations were changed. We gained a certain number of advantages: we no longer had to wear prison clothes, we didn't work, and we even managed to have the cell doors left open during the day. One day, the authorities decided to tighten up. We went on hunger strike for several weeks. Demonstrations were held for us outside. We were bound together by the commune. Anyone who dissociated from it would have been mercilessly rejected, their life would have become hell.

Each cell was a university for the political prisoners. In Greenstein's cell the inmates got up at 4 a.m. – the prison regulations specified 7 a.m. – and studied Marxist theory, dialectics, historical materialism. 'My teachers weren't Jewish', Greenstein explained, 'but they were very learned all the same'.

Communication between cells was done in code, tapping on the walls. Directives and information were exchanged, even documents. Security problems were not neglected: in the women's prison where Bronia Zelmanovicz was held, there was a 'secret troika' in each cell made up of three trustworthy comrades. It alone was empowered to question militants who had recently arrived on the causes and circumstances of their arrest. In fact, these questionings were so severe that the detainees often cracked and told everything they knew – so the less they knew about other people's activities, the better for everyone.

The communists were the largest contingent of political prisoners in Lublin, but they did not shun the left Poale Zion militant David Sztokfisz:

> The other detainees, who were practically all communists, knew that I belonged to the left Poale Zion; and for my part, I respected the collective discipline. On the anniversary of the death of Borochov, in December 1938, I organized a commemorative ceremony with their agreement. I gave a presentation of the life and work of the founder and theorist of Poale Zion, and they sung with me Borochov's anthem, whose words I had written on the board in Latin letters.

The political prisoners were strongly supported from outside by workers' and humanitarian organizations, in particularly the Red Aid run by the communists. Irène Gefon was very active in this in Łódź:

> I was responsible for bringing the prisoners underground literature. In order to do this I drew on the service of one of my uncles, who was blind and sympathized with the left. He had learned to make brushes, to occupy his time and earn a little money. Between the cover of the brush and the wood he slipped messages that I gave him. In this way a great deal of information reached the prison.
>
> We were also helped by a dentist who treated the prisoners; she fell in love with a Soviet prisoner and conveyed messages so as to be useful to him. One time, I found myself in her waiting room – I was taking her a document – at the same time as the wife of the prison governor. 'You don't know how sensitive my husband is', she blabbered, 'he can't stand

the dentist hurting me'. And all the time in that prison detainees were
mistreated and beaten.

In the late 1930s, in fact, the condition of political prisoners steadily
deteriorated. The administration did not spare any effort to challenge
the special status that they enjoyed. In the sinister camp of Bereza
Kartuzka, their conditions of detention were basically similar to
how communists, social democrats, radical intellectuals and Jews
were treated in the Nazi camps. The government of Leon Kozlowski,
moreover, which took office in May 1934 – under Piłsudski – openly
pinpointed Jews as future detainees in this camp – another singular
similarity with Nazi plans.

In March 1938, David Szarfharc, also a communist militant from
Łódź, was arrested in the middle of the night. He had not been home
for two months, while the Defensiva was awaiting his return. He was
thrown into prison, and on 11 April it was announced that he had
been deported to Bereza Kartuzka.

When he reached the camp, in a group of about eighty prisoners
that day, he was welcomed by what was called 'the music'. He had
to pass between two ranks of guards who shouted 'Up! Down! Run!'
while striking the new detainees with their truncheons. The game
continued while they were searched: 'Dress!' 'Undress!' until the thugs
were tired. Then the new arrivals were taken into a bare hall with
broken windows, where they had to stand the whole day against the
wall with their hands up. It was forbidden to move, even to go to the
toilet. 'Do it in your pants!' the guard replied when a prisoner begged
to be excused. At night they were taken to a cell where they had to
lie on the cement floor in their underclothes, without any cover. The
doors were open. The 'sleepers' had to keep motionless and only turn
round when the guard gave the signal.

This initiation to life in the camp lasted two weeks. Then began
the 'normal' existence at Bereza Kartuzka: the prisoners were
crammed into cells containing thirty-two or even thirty-eight
persons. They were forbidden to speak to one another. The cell doors
remained open and the guards made sure that the rule of silence was
respected. Offenders were severely punished, either being sent to the

dungeon or given thirty blows with the stick, as was the case with Szarfharc.

Each day the detainees had to do several hours of gymnastics, on marshy ground under the thumb of several guards. The guards' favoured exercise was the duck walk or 'frog', interminably to the sound of a whistle. Anyone who fell and did not get up quickly enough received a volley of kicks. They were made to keep running, falling, getting up again, relentlessly. Work in the camp was obligatory. There was so-called 'normal' work, and pointless work. The former consisted of paving roads and digging ditches. It had to be done entirely with bare hands, without the help of any tools. Pointless work consisted of carrying stones from one place to another, then taking them back again.

In the morning, the prisoners received coffee and bread; at midday, soup, a potato and a tiny quantity of meat; in the evening, a liquid soup. There was no canteen. Many of them could not stand the diet and fell ill. Newspapers, books and visits were forbidden. Only parcels of clothes got through. The guards confiscated food. Once a month prisoners were allowed to write to their families – to say that they were all right.

The camp administration used all means to try and get the detainees to sign an undertaking not to resume communist activity when released from the camp. Only very few signed, however. The prisoners' 'commune' was also very active in Bereza; each cell was 'led' by three militants, in contact with the central leadership of the prisoners' organization, the 'central commune', which conveyed information and directives from outside. It was the commune that restored the morale of those whose strength or courage weakened, dissuading them from signing. It defined the code of conduct for prisoners: to do only 'normal' work, but in such a way as not to use up their strength too much; to do the least possible in terms of gymnastics and pointless work; not to call strikes, as the administration would only seize the opportunity to break the prisoners' organization.

David Szarfharc, prisoner number 1063, spent six months in Bereza Kartuzka. 'When I left the camp', he concluded his story,

I naturally resumed political activity. And I was again arrested several times, the last time in March 1939. The attitude of the police towards me was no longer quite the same – everyone felt that war was imminent. But communists were still sent to Bereza until 1 September 1939, the day that the Germans invaded Poland.

During the interwar years, the constant flow of emigration led hundreds of thousands of Jews away from Central and Eastern Europe: a diaspora within the diaspora, from France to Argentina, from North America to South Africa, from Australia to Palestine. An economic or a political emigration? Certainly the majority of these immigrants were workers, artisans or petty traders who left Poland, Hungary, Romania or Lithuania because they hoped to find less wretched conditions of existence elsewhere. But very often politics and economics were intimately connected: in Poland, 1929 and 1935 were years in which the figures for Jewish emigration sharply rose. The first peak in the statistics coincided with the world economic crisis that struck all the capitalist countries, the second peak marked the sharp deterioration in the condition of Polish Jews with the arrival in power of a semi-fascist government. In interwar Poland, however, any social, political or economic difficulty was almost automatically expressed by a discharge of aggression against the Jewish population, as if, says Pavel Korzec, 'solutions' to the Jewish question 'constituted the panacea for the country's main socio-economic and political difficulties'.[6]

In these conditions, was the emigration of Jewish workers economic or political? Workers who could not find employment in large-scale industry because the bosses (quite often including Jews) rightly or wrongly viewed them as agitators and fomenters of strikes, who, on top of everything, refused to work on Saturday? Or the emigration of small shopkeepers whose premises had been sacked by Endecy pogromists? These examples show how the two factors were intimately connected.

It was workers above all who left Poland. In 1939, there were some 150,000 Jews in Paris, of whom 90,000 were immigrants from Central

---

6   Korzec, *Juifs en Pologne*, p. 19.

or Eastern Europe, half of these from Poland. Maurice Rajsfus explains that

> 60 per cent of the immigrants worked in the industrial or handicraft sector, but more than 80 per cent of these, around fifty thousand, worked at home or in small workshops – most often in clothing, fur or leatherwork. Some ten thousand worked for small Jewish middlemen and were ferociously exploited.[7]

The predominance of the working-class element in this immigrant community largely explains its ideological orientations and political reflexes, just as it illuminates the antagonism between it and the French Jewish community, whose traditions and social composition were completely different. In the early 1920s, years of economic reconstruction, immigrant labour was welcomed with open arms in countries such as France. But a few years later, with the advent of the great depression, the picture rapidly changed: borders closed, laws were passed restricting the number of immigrants, a brake was put on naturalization and foreign 'political agitators' were expelled. The immigrant trajectory then became an odyssey, a leap into the unknown.

Elija Rosijanski left his native Lithuania for Palestine as an adolescent, in the early 1920s. He stayed there for a number of years, but was 'restless'. With a friend, he embarked on a boat armed with a visa for Las Palmas. When the ship stopped at Marseille, they met a fellow Lithuanian who said, 'Las Palmas? Are you crazy? You won't find any work there. Go to Paris!' And the two friends took the train for the capital. But where to stay? They remembered having noted the address of a vague acquaintance from Kovno who was living in Paris.

As soon as they got off the train, they hastened to the address in question, a hotel on the place Denfert-Rochereau:

> We presented ourselves at the reception and asked for our friend. 'Thirty-three', the woman said. We didn't understand and wondered:

---

7   Rajsfus, *Sois juif et tais-toi!*, pp. 29–30.

'What does that mean? Is he here or not?' We questioned her with our looks and she repeated again: 'Thirty-three! Thirty-three!' We still didn't understand, and decided to explore the upper floors. She followed us and showed us the number on a locked door. Now we understood: he wasn't there.

As was inevitable, the two companions went walking in the Luxembourg gardens, and naturally came across their friend. He gave them some good advice: it was hard to find work without a resident's card, and in order to get that, the best thing was to enrol at university – in Grenoble. Reluctantly, the two inseparables followed this advice, obtained their student cards and went to the prefecture to ask for resident's cards. But as their French was still very hesitant, the clerk there thought that they wanted a 'certificate of expulsion' to leave French territory. 'Very well. Fill in your request', he said. But they were quite incapable of filling in anything. So the man began dictating to them:

> He spelled out: 'Je, J-E …' But my friend stayed with his pen in the air, quite embarrassed. The clerk got annoyed: 'Write, will you! J …' But in Polish, the letter 'J' is pronounced *iott*. We didn't understand a thing, and I broke out laughing hysterically while the clerk looked at us as if we were mad.

Then a couple of Russians appeared: Rosijanski asked them to act as interpreters, and explain what the clerk meant by his bloody 'J'. The clerk replied, 'I'd like to make out their certificate of expulsion, but they're not even able to write what I tell them.'

When they heard the word 'expulsion' translated into Russian, the two friends picked up their papers and decamped without more ado. They spent a few months working in Grenoble on construction, then returned to Paris. As Rosijanski explained,

> Life wasn't easy there; it was an obstacle course to work legally. You needed a certificate from an employer, but he could only provide this if he had received a favourable report from the authorities. A vicious circle. So we worked on the black, for Jews, of course. I spent some time

as a packager. Then I started attending university. I wanted to study international law – an odd idea: what use would it have been to me?

Along with his friends, he attended the Kulturliga:

> When we joined, in the late 1920s, there was a terrible struggle for influence between left Zionists, Bundists and communists. The last two were on the point of winning. I had two friends, Moulké and Haïmké. Moulké was a communist right down the line; Haïmké and myself were more oriented to Trotskyism. We lived on good terms, shared the same room and went to the Kulturliga activities together.

To manage the difficulties involved in being an immigrant, the Jews of Eastern and Central Europe developed a strong network of organizations that extended the community, political and cultural structures of their own countries, in particular the well-known *Landsmannschaften*, friendly societies for people from the same town. In Paris, the Bundist militant rediscovered the Bund – even if this organization was hard put to survive outside its 'natural milieu' of Eastern Europe; the communist militant was taken care of by the party and its 'language groups' and satellite organizations – even the Confédération Générale du Travail (CGT) had sections for Yiddish-speakers. Thus, despite being subject to often ferocious exploitation, and facing a social and political climate that was hostile to them, the Yiddishland immigrants did not feel isolated, lost or powerless. In certain quarters of Paris, such as Belleville, the *Pletzl* and the Faubourg Poissonière, people spoke openly in Yiddish and you could almost feel at home.[8] The right-minded authorities of assimilated French Judaism, however, were upset by the lack of 'discretion' on the part of these low-class immigrants, to whom the *Univers israélite* of 10 June 1938 gave the following well-meaning advice:

> Do not engage in politics, as the laws of our country prohibit this. Watch your dress. Be polite and discreet. Be modest. Do not boast of the

---

8   The *Pletzl* or 'little place' was the traditional Jewish quarter in the Marais, the fourth arrondissement of Paris. [Translator's note.]

attractions of the countries you have recently come from and that seem to be lacking in France. 'Everything was better at home' is a formula that will shock French people who hear you. Quickly learn to express yourself in French. Do not speak loudly and, if you speak a foreign language, avoid doing so on the street, on public transport or on a café terrace. Respect all our laws and customs.[9]

As for work … in the early 1930s, David Grynberg, a left Poale Zion militant from Radom, left for Paris. Armed with a false passport, he crossed Germany, the Netherlands and Belgium. He found work in his field, the garment trade:

> I worked on the black for a year, as a tailor. It was easier than in Poland, and better paid. But my working days were long: from seven in the morning to eight in the evening. I lived in a maid's room that was also my 'workshop'. I sat on the bed, with the sewing machine in front of me. In order to iron, I had to put boards across the bed. The police very often raided this quarter in central Paris where illegal clothing workers were concentrated.
>
> The working conditions were really wretched, often dangerous. One of my comrades from Radom was killed in horrific circumstances. He stuck garments together with rubber glue, which caught fire, and he was burned alive. He was a leader of the left Poale Zion. As in Poland, our bosses were Jews. Only they would accept us working illegally in such conditions.

And yet, Grynberg notes, despite very hard working and living conditions, these young immigrants 'still found time to do lots to things: study, go to meetings, lectures, the Yiddish theatre (there were two in Paris in the 1930s), etc … It was by attending political meetings, listening to the great speakers of the Popular Front, that I learned French', Grynberg explained, remembering the great hopes this raised for immigrants:

> But the Popular Front government hardly bothered to organize all these immigrants; they certainly had other problems to tackle, starting with

---

9   Cited by Rajsfus, *Sois juif et tais-toi!*, p. 139.

their own survival. We were very sympathetic to them, and for us the arrival of people like Chautemps and Daladier was synonymous with new misfortunes, the return of the truncheon for immigrants. It started with massive expulsions, and the climate became xenophobic.

As we have seen, the horizon darkened as the Second World War approached, and for militants a terrible tension arose between the original movement, the genuine wellspring of their action, and the reality of things. The more historical optimism was belied by events and impending cataclysms, the more they lost the guiding thread of their actions. The final aim was obscured, the profile of the new world lost in the darkness that descended over Europe. Ever more, the militants were forced onto the defensive against the forces of night: anti-Semitism, fascism, Stalinism …

In fact, anti-Semitism was always the sinister background music to the action of the Yiddishland revolutionaries. From this point of view, the end of tsarist rule in Poland did not change things fundamentally. In many Polish towns and villages, particularly in Galicia, the new independence of Poland was celebrated in 1919 and 1920 in the blood of Jews. Piłsudski's advance on Kiev was accompanied by anti-Semitic outrages, which Esther Rosenthal-Schneidermann witnessed in Warsaw:

> Before getting into carriages covered with the slogans 'To Kiev!', 'To Odessa!', 'Death to Bolshevism!', the Polish soldiers had their fun in the Jewish streets of Warsaw. Difficult days began for the Jewish population, days of terror. Shops were closed early, before nightfall; windows looking onto the street were covered up; no lights were lit in the evening. One Saturday, a band of soldiers invaded a *stubbl* [meeting room] where *Hassidim* were singing; they pulled off their *shtreimel* [fur hats], grabbed their caps and left with shouts of joy, breaking the windows of Jewish shopkeepers that they met on the way. We could hear from upstairs their shouts and the clatter of broken glass.[10]

---

10 Esther Rosenthal-Schneidermann, *Naftoulei Derakhim* (Turns and Detours), vol. 1 (Tel Aviv: Hakibbutz Hameukhad, 1970), p. 186.

On the opposite pavement a group of officers arrived in their gaudy uniforms, coming out of the church where the bells were joyfully pealing. They passed in a dignified fashion as if they had not seen anything. 'How I would have liked to have been able at least to drop a chamber pot full of boiling water on them!' Esther Rosenthal-Schneidermann recalls. Later on, uniformed anti-Semites attacked other businesses, promising to send all the Jews 'to Moscow and Palestine'. But the market porters' and butchers' trade union mobilized their members, and the thugs were seen off.

Self-defence of the Jewish population was a tradition that the Bund established at the start of the century. It continued into the 1930s, as we have seen – in the Jewish quarters, but also at times in the university. Isaac Safrin was a student in Warsaw:

The business of benches reserved for Jewish students in the universities exploded in 1936. Already for several years there had been a *numerus clausus* against Jews in certain faculties, in particular: medicine, pharmacy, dentistry, agronomy.

In the university, the reactionary nationalist organizations had the upper hand. Right-wing students were constantly provoking us. In January 1936, Endecy militants started physically expelling us from the lecture halls. Fights broke out. Then the university authorities decided that we, the Jews, should sit separately on the left, in lectures and classes. We refused, and remained standing during the lectures. Some non-Jewish students and even progressive teachers supported us. Often blood flowed, when the fascists tried to start pogroms at the university. We called for support from Jewish porters and carters who came and gave the anti-Semites a lesson.

But this 1930s anti-Semitism was an insidious poison hovering in the air of the time, its expressions being all the more wounding as they sometimes emerged when they were least expected. Yaakof Greenstein had a bitter experience of this in prison:

We communicated between cells by knocking on the walls in the prisoners' code. As I had good hearing, I became the 'knocker' for our cell.

One day, I deciphered for one of the 'teachers' a lecture transmitted from the adjacent cell. A point came when I didn't understand and asked for a phrase to be repeated. The teacher got furious and knocked: *Parszywy zyd*, 'lousy Jew', the ritual insult of anti-Semites in Poland. I was shattered and started crying. That this man was teaching me Marxist theory!

Another time, I was looking through the skylight at a sparrow perched on a bar. A comrade came up and asked me: 'Do you know what that bird is called?' 'Of course,' I replied, 'it's a sparrow.' 'Wrong,' he replied, 'it's a *zydek* [little Yid]; do you know why? Because it doesn't work, but that doesn't stop it eating!'

France under Daladier was not the Poland of the Endecy, yet the propaganda of *Gringoire* and other anti-Semitic rags had its effect. David Grynberg also learned this to his cost:

I was a football enthusiast, and played in a club affiliated to Poale Zion, the *Roïter Shtern* [Red Star]. We played against other working-class teams, made up of CGT activists. One day, it must have been in 1937, we had a match against one of these teams and were well in the lead – we had some excellent players who had come from Poland. Then our opponents got annoyed and started making remarks such as: 'Give them a good kicking, Hitler was quite right.'

Grynberg was scandalized. After the match, the two teams went for a drink together, as was the custom, and a collection was taken for Spain. But he didn't feel like clinking glasses with anti-Semites. He also noted that there was not a great fraternity between French and immigrant workers at this time. Those who worked on the black could not join the CGT. And he still remembers how shocked he was when he heard the communists launch the slogan 'Full up here!' in 1937, which sounded unpleasantly similar to the xenophobic right-wing slogan 'France for the French!', and felt to him like 'an outrage to the immigrants, a refusal to allow us to make a living'.

How to struggle successfully against fascism? That was the question which constantly haunted these militants after Hitler's accession to power, and still more after Franco's putsch in Spain. But in order to struggle, the first priority was to understand: how had the millions of organized workers in Germany been defeated without even a battle? As an orthodox communist, Max Technitchek sought an explanation that would not challenge his political categories; in Prague he met exiled KPD leaders who explained to him that it was all the fault of the Social Democrats, who had rejected any alliance with the communists, that Hitler had no social base, that even a large part of the bourgeoisie and petty bourgeoisie rejected him, that his days were numbered ...

Technitchek was aware that the underground KPD displayed tremendous heroism, as reported in its press. He knew that the German communists had been always the first to campaign against the Nazis' anti-Semitism. He began therefore to attempt an explanation of the German defeat:

> I told myself that it was impossible to blame the policy of the Comintern, the policy of the 'third period', as Germany had been the only developed, industrialized country where fascism had triumphed at the time that this policy was applied. The explanation of the phenomenon had accordingly to be sought in the deep history and mentality of Germany.

For Yankel Taut, the explanation was completely different. From the late 1920s he had experienced how the German Communist Party had embarked on a suicidal policy. In 1930, as a young communist, he was active in a large engineering company in Berlin. In the trade unions, the communists engaged in a relentless war against the Social Democrats, whom they considered 'social fascists', the main enemy. They organized a split, proclaimed a 'red' trade union, and immediately decided to launch an appeal for a general strike. Yankel Taut was responsible for bringing the apprentices in his company out on strike. He objected that the apprentices did not have the right to strike, and that he would get himself fired. The comrades in charge were not interested, and as a disciplined militant Taut carried out orders. He was indeed fired, as he had foreseen. When he asked for an explanation, he was treated as a 'Brandlerite' and expelled from the party. From now on he was simply a renegade.

Another episode indicates very well how far the sectarian folly of Thälmann's party extended. First a follower of Brandler, then a Trotskyist, Taut was sought by the Nazis when they came to power. He hid at his sister's, who had remained a member of the KPD:

> One day, a few months after Hitler came to power, I went home and, as usual, whistled for her to throw me down the key to the outside door. But she came down and said, 'The party has sent a young guy to stay with me. He's wanted by the police; it seems rather important.'

Taut went upstairs and recognized the fugitive: it was Helmut Remmele, the son of one of the party's historic leaders, and himself a leader of the Young Communists. Seated around the table, they began to eat their supper in silence.

'Helmut,' said Taut, 'do you remember who I am?' 'Of course,' Remmele replied. 'All right, I'll tell you, Helmut; I've not changed my ideas since you expelled me; on the contrary, my criticism of the party's orientation is even more radical than it was. You see where your absurd stories of "social fascism" have led us?'

Remmele then got up and replied, 'Listen. I don't discuss with people like you. If I could, I would denounce you and your kind to the police.'

It was, Taut recalls,

> as if I had been hit on the head with a hammer. My sister, although a good Stalinist, leapt up and wanted to throw him out. But I calmed her and said to Remmele, 'You're an idiot. Look at the situation you're in. The Gestapo are looking for you everywhere, and you want to denounce me to the police.'

That was the culmination of a line that also caused damage and disorientation to militants in Poland. In this difficult time, the workers' movement never presented a common front against repression and the blows inflicted by the nationalist right, either in the street or in elections. A few alliances were made, but political enmities could be equally strong and lasting. Haïm Babic gives an example of this:

In my town, Nowy Dwor, the Bund had established a regular alliance with the PPS. In 1927, this made it possible to have a working-class majority in the town hall: the mayor was a PPS militant; the deputy mayor was a Bundist, which was quite exceptional. The Bund had five municipal councillors, including one responsible for finance. That was a minor revolution. Previously, a Jew would hardly have dared to enter the town hall, given the discriminatory attitude of the municipal authorities; and now even a Jew in caftan and beard could come in and speak with a representative in Yiddish.

The picture similarly changed in the carpenters' trade union in Warsaw, where he was now active. The communists dominated this, and, as almost everywhere, they were at loggerheads with the Bund. 'It wasn't just a matter of political struggle', Babic comments; 'often also, unfortunately, there were physical confrontations'.

This reciprocal sectarianism did not benefit either side. Shlomo Szlein sums up the situation as far as the Communist Party was concerned:

In the early 1930s, the Polish Communist Party had adopted an extreme caricature of the Comintern's 'class-against-class' line. What this meant for us was that we formed little groups of agitators convinced of the imminence of proletarian revolution, brought them out into the street, and tried to turn every social movement or strike into a 'class war'. But this orientation in no way corresponded to reality, and was accompanied by a terrible sectarianism towards other organizations. The section of the party that I was active in was shattered. Any discussion was stifled in the ambience of the 'Sovietization' of the party. Only gradually, much later, did I understand what was going on behind the scenes in the Polish party and the international communist movement.

In 1935, when the Polish Communist Party made the turn to the policy of the Popular Front, it was already late in the day, and three years later it would be dissolved by Stalin. As war drew increasingly close, the disorientation of its militants grew. Yaakov Greenstein defines himself as 'completely naïve', his faith in the USSR so great that he accepted without demur the decision to dissolve the Polish party:

> And yet I was rather troubled: I could hardly begin to understand, for example, how a party leader born in Poland, who had been exchanged in prison for a Polish priest detained in the USSR and was shot as soon as he arrived there, could have become such a thing as a 'Japanese spy'. There might possibly have been a couple of spies in the leadership … but all these spies? That Trotsky had become an imperialist agent, then Zinoviev, then Kamenev – then all the old guard. That was hard to swallow, and this phenomenon wasn't just in Poland, but also in Yugoslavia [the exiled party leadership in Moscow was brutally purged in 1938] and Romania. There were a lot of tears, discussions and questions in our ranks.

Despite these worries, the militants accepted the decision. Greenstein, as head of the Young Communists in the Łódź region, went from town to town dissolving local branches. Yet communist activity continued in a doubly clandestine situation (vis-à-vis both the Polish police and Moscow):

> The dissolution came after a period of openness. Having tirelessly denounced the Bund for several years, and the PPS as worse enemies than the bourgeoisie, we had turned to fraternizing with them, even with priests who declared themselves opposed to Hitler. These sudden turns, added to the illegal situation of the party, had developed a great tactical sense among the militants. They penetrated everywhere that was possible: into the PPS, the left Zionists, the Bund. After the dissolution we kept these contacts and established cultural clubs that served as a facade; we continued to organize strikes.

When it was apparent that war was inescapable, Greenstein received an unexpected visit: from the town's police commissioner. 'In all probability,' the commissioner said, 'there will be war between Germany and Poland. What will your attitude be?' Greenstein replied, 'If Poland should be threatened by German fascism, then we'll leave old scores till later, and defend Polish soil against the Nazis along with you.' The policeman shook his hand.

A few months earlier, the Bund and the Zionist movement had adopted the same position. It is rather poignant to see the workers' parties and the Jewish workers' movement adopt this attitude of loyalty towards the Polish 'homeland' and nation, at the very time as the anti-Semitic campaign had reached a zenith; when, rather than preparing for war against Germany, the 'political class' in power was devoting its energies to finding 'solutions' to the Jewish problem – mass emigration of the Jewish population being the favoured option.

This paradoxical patriotism, this 'Polish' loyalty on the part of an organization like the Bund or the 'dissolved' communist militants who did not suspect that behind the scenes Stalin was negotiating with Hitler the partition of the Polish state, contrasts with the attitude adopted at the outbreak of the First World War by the Jewish workers' movement and the left currents of social democracy that would give birth to the communist movement – embodied in Poland by the Social Democratic Party of Poland and Lithuania, the party of Rosa Luxemburg.

One section of the Bund leadership had then adopted a position denouncing the 'imperialist' character of the war, while another rallied to the 'revolutionary defencism' of the Mensheviks. Yehoshua Rojanski, who had joined Poale Zion in his town of Slonim a year earlier, proudly recalls what his reaction had been on 30 July 1914, when the tsarist government decreed general mobilization:

Along with my comrades, we decided to produce a leaflet protesting the war. The leaflet was in two languages, one side in Russian and the other in Yiddish. I carefully wrote out the Yiddish part, then we went and stuck the pages on the town walls. The police chief reacted instantly, calling on the rabbi and ordering him to identify the authors of this appeal. The rabbi knew my handwriting; he had me come to him discreetly and advised me to leave town as soon as possible. I left for the Caucasus.

Of course, in 1939 the situation was made far complex on account of the aggressive policy of Nazi Germany, and the existence of an independent Polish state wedged between two great powers. But that is not the only reason why the militants' compass no longer gave such an infallible reading as when Rojanski had spontaneously written 'Down with war!' in his best handwriting. There was also the growing dizziness of the utopia, as we mentioned above, which would culminate when the proclaimed leader of the world revolution signed a pact with the man who for all revolutionary Jews was the very embodiment of barbarism.

3.

The Spanish Sky

Above our trench the stars of the Spanish sky,
Dawn breaks already on the horizon,
Soon a new battle will begin.

Song of the Thälmann battalion
of the International Brigades

In the revolutionary commitment of the former militants we interviewed in Israel, as for so many thousands of others, the Spanish war was a strong and special moment, both in itself and as a turning point. That was true above all for those who went off to fight on the Republican side, but it was true for the others as well. Here the course of individual existence melds with that of history. Many signs attest to the fact that in the memory of these witnesses the Spanish episode remains marked by a milestone, a memory with a heavy emotional charge and unanswered questions, even half a century after.

One of their number received us in his home, with a road map of Spain spread out on the table. We had scarcely finished introducing ourselves when he started tracing out for us his Spanish odyssey: 'I reached Barcelona on 17 July 1936, the day before the Franco putsch.' His tone was confidential, with a hint of solemnity; he spoke French with a strong Yiddish accent and sometimes Spanish turns of phrase found their way into his speech, particularly when he described the military actions in which he had taken part; his finger followed the map of the marches and battles he described. His story took several hours.

This was not the only occasion when we were able to convince our-selves of the crucial character of this episode for the Jewish militants who experienced it. In the course of our investigation, we learned that there was in Israel an association of ex-combatants from the International Brigades. This group still had several dozen members in Israel, former foreign volunteers who had fought in the Republican forces between 1936 and 1939. These men and women were survivors in the full sense of the word: survivors of the battles of the Spanish Civil War in which thousands of their comrades had died; survivors of the anti-Nazi struggle in which veterans of Spain took such an active part; survivors of the Nazi extermination camps, the Stalinist Gulag and the witch-hunts of the 1950s, as well as the liquidations that accompanied these in the 'people's democracies' (in the Slansky trial in Czechoslovakia,[1] Jews and veterans of Spain served as expia-tory victims – what fortune when they were both at once, such as Artur London!); survivors, finally, of the work of time, which thinned their ranks year by year.

They came from Poland, Hungary, Romania, Yugoslavia, France, Belgium, Palestine, Germany, the United States, Argentina, even from Australia and South Africa, and from July 1936 converged on that Republican Spain which they bore in their heart, for a struggle whose stake seemed to focus the whole of their energy and revolutionary optimism. It is enough today to go through the endless lists of the 'Internationals' who fell in Spain to realize the large proportion of Jews among them, and especially fighters who originally came from Yiddishland – even if they made their way to Barcelona and Albacete starting from Melbourne, Buenos Aires, Chicago, Paris and Liège, and not just from Warsaw or Łódź.

Before the trajectory of their turbulent existence led them to Israel, they had experienced new wanderings after Spain, new defeats and new tragedies. For the most part, these survivors did not know one

---

1   Rudolf Slansky, general secretary of the Czechoslovak Communist Party, was arrested in November 1951 and charged with being the head of a conspiracy in which eleven out of fourteen supposed leaders were of Jewish origin. Eleven of the accused, including Slansky, were condemned to death and executed the following year. [Editor's note.]

another during the Spanish war; they were scattered between the various brigades and military units, and most often the friend, childhood or party comrade, the 'mate' with whom they had decided to leave for Spain, or with whom they had linked up on the front, had fallen in Extremadura or in another later battle. It was always with an emotion hard to repress that they recalled his image in telling us of 'their' Spain. Besides, among the ten or so former Internationals we interviewed, most had been wounded in the course of this deadly war, some of them several times.

The fraternity that bound the former Brigaders in Israel had thus been formed after the event, but it was no less strong for all that. When we started to gather their memories in the summer of 1981, one of the first that we approached – Jonas Brodkin, who lost a leg in the battle of Jarama in February 1937 – replied very simply, 'I'd rather you came to see me a bit later, my wife has just died.' The following week, we felt awkward visiting him in a suburb of Tel Aviv (a social housing block surrounded by sand dunes). We found him surrounded by friends who turned out to be all former Brigaders. We subsequently discovered that they acted as an almost permanent guard of honour and friendship group for him. This kind of unemphasized friendship, indestructible because rooted in a unique common experience, was something we found again a few months later among the survivors of a group of foreign partisans (Jews and Armenians) whose actions had frightened the Nazis in Paris in 1942 and 1943. The photo of the brother of one of them had figured on the famous *affiche rouge* that the Germans posted on the Paris walls in autumn 1943.

Perhaps the *esprit de corps* of the Spanish veterans in Israel was reinforced still more by the fact that in their adopted country their history attracted no particular consideration. Indeed, one could even say that the Israeli state and its institutions scarcely recognized the utopia and values in whose name they had committed themselves to Spain: for the younger generation, these old stories were like 'last year's snow', as the Yiddish expression goes.

Why was the Spanish war the moment of greatest tension, the culminating point perhaps, for the commitment of these Yiddishland revolutionaries? After all, the historical and cultural threads that bound them to the land of Spain and the Spanish people were quite tenuous, and the great majority of them had had no knowledge of Spain before 1936.

It is certainly possible, like one of the former Brigaders we met, to stress the fact that the majority of Jewish militants who fought in Spain were communists; that it was the communist parties that conducted a tremendous propaganda in support of the Spanish republic; and that in this way, by joining the Brigades, these men were only following instructions. Here is how a former communist, Isaac Kotlarz, interprets today his departure for Spain:

> I had left Poland for France in 1932. I was working as a knitter in Paris, and was an active member of the PCF, belonging to a defence committee for *L'Humanité*; foreigners were forbidden to engage in politics, but that didn't stop me from selling *L'Huma* wherever I could. I listened open-mouthed to the party's great orators such as Thorez, Duclos, Cachin and Vaillant-Couturier. The party said that we had to join up for Spain, so I went off.

But that is only one aspect of things, and certainly not the essential one. Many other witnesses told us that it was in an absolutely spontaneous and voluntary movement that thousands of radical Jewish workers and intellectuals from the *shtetls* and industrial centres of Poland, from Belleville or the suburbs of Charleroi, were ready to fly to the defence of Republican Spain.

Pierre Sherf, a communist militant of Romanian origin who had arrived in Paris in 1933, organized aid to Republican Spain among the Romanian community: collecting money, sponsoring volunteers, sending parcels to Brigaders, etc. But this form of solidarity with Spain seemed insufficient. He wanted to go himself, and sought to overcome the reticence of his superiors:

> I went to see a Party official in Paris and told him, 'Listen, it's settled, I'm going off tonight! I've found a mate to take over from me in charge of the Romanian group for [solidarity with] Spain; he's just as competent as I am, if not more!' And I went off with three other comrades, despite

not having any military training – two of them were killed in Spain and the other later on in Palestine.

In Poland, one of our interviewees told us, far more people volunteered than actually went. The Communist Party could not afford to dispense with so many cadres and militants. Those who were wanted by the police were given priority, as was the case, for example, with Shlomo Szlein:

> The police were looking for me in Stanislawów, my home town, and in Lvov where I was a middle-ranking cadre of the Communist Party. There was no longer very much I could do. So I asked the party for permission to leave for Spain, and received this. I crossed the mountains illegally and reached Czechoslovakia. The Czech party took charge of me in Prague. After a few months I reached Paris, along with a comrade who came from the same town as I did, and a Slovak comrade. We enrolled there in the International Brigades.

Léa Stein, a Yugoslav comrade who served as a nurse in Spain, left in similar conditions. A student at the University of Zagreb, she had been arrested for taking part in illegal demonstrations organized by the Young Communists. She was expelled from university and forced to live with her parents in Bosnia, where she was bored to death. When the party asked her to join the ranks of the Spanish Republicans, she accepted without hesitation.

The enthusiasm with which the Jewish revolutionaries of this time committed themselves to Spain was so powerful, however, that it affected more than just organized communists, experienced militants. People who were communist sympathizers, 'non-party' people, anti-fascists, socialists, Bundists or Poale Zionists also mobilized, along with Trotskyists or former Trotskyists who joined the Partido Obrero de Unificación Marxista (POUM), or anarchists who joined the CNT-FAI.[2] On this point the copious official communist historiography

---

2 The Confederación Nacional de Trabajo was a Spanish trade union federation with anarcho-syndicalist sympathies. Very powerful in the 1930s, especially in Catalonia, it was closely linked with the Federación Anarquista Ibérica.

that recalls the activity of the Spanish Internationals is rather discreet. On the subject of anti-Stalinist Jewish militants who joined POUM it is silent. Yet these existed, and we interviewed one of their number, Elija Rosijanski, in January 1981, a few months before his death.

What were the social and political conditions in which these men and women took the decision to abandon everything and continue their struggle in a Spain ravaged by civil war? First of all, for evident reasons bound up with the national, cultural and social position of the Jewish communities in Eastern Europe, internationalism had been a profound and instinctive component of their activity ever since the birth of a Jewish workers' movement in this region. It should not be forgotten that the fighters we interviewed, who had gone to face death in Spain, were not the Jewish industrialists of Łódź or the prominent figures of the French Jewish community. They were the little people, the proletariat of tailors, shoemakers, furriers, carpenters, tinsmiths and other Yiddish craftsmen born to a spirit of revolt and struggle, to trade union and political organization, to the internationalism of the exploited in the wretched workshops of Warsaw, Białystok and Vilnius. A proletariat living in wretched conditions, but rich already in traditions of culture and struggle, ever since the seeds of the Jewish workers' movement in Eastern Europe had first germinated in the late nineteenth century. They were a new generation, most of them extremely young, but who had inherited the experience and traditions of the Bund in the first years of the twentieth century, and of the revolutionary earthquakes that had accompanied the October Revolution and shaken the 1920s.

This was a generation of Jewish proletarians and intellectuals whom the economic crisis and the worsening of political repression throughout Europe – especially in Poland and Germany – increasingly radicalized and made ready for revolutionary action. In France and Belgium, those whom economic crisis and repression had forced to emigrate – from Poland especially – brought new blood to the Jewish workers' organizations. In Poland, the Communist Party – despite its sectarianism and dyed-in-the-wool dogmatism, its suicidal policy that, without going as far as the aberrations of the German Communist Party in the early 1930s, tended to make it what Philippe

Robrieux calls a 'mass sect' – managed to capture a large part of the radicalism and readiness of the Jewish youth. Unemployment, misery, imprisonment and enforced exile, the ever-present threat of expulsion for those who had found work or refuge in France or Belgium, as well as the rise of Hitler, were all factors reinforcing a radicalism that the outbreak of the Spanish Civil War catalysed.

From the 1920s on, and especially in Poland, a new generation of Yiddishland militants emerged, galvanized by the Russian revolution and the utopian aspirations it fed – a new type of militant whose revolutionary optimism, unlimited devotion and unfailing adhesion to the new system of values that this revolution bore with it were reminiscent of the extraordinary qualities of the Bundist generation of the first years of the century. In committing themselves to Spain, however, these militants took a formidable step. In Poland, in Germany before 1933, in Yugoslavia or in France, they knew that their activities exposed them to prison, the hazards of life underground and the rigours of a quasi-professional militancy. But commitment to Spain was of a different order. Leaving the natural ground of their struggle, breaking their links with the Jewish or Yiddish world that was familiar to them, they joined up for a distant battle in which they risked their lives. Yet thousands of them would take this step, most of them lacking any military training, hastily learning to use a rifle or throw a grenade, like the athletes of the YASK who, having left for Barcelona to take part in the counter-Olympics, found themselves on the barricades on 18 July 1936, fighting shoulder to shoulder with Catalan workers against the military insurgents.

It is not enough, then, to say that the commitment of these militants to Spain was natural, basically only an extension of other struggles. On the contrary, we need to highlight what was specific in the enthusiasm that led them to rush to the rescue of a republic to which they owed nothing – except for the few dozen Jewish militants and workers who had already found refuge and work in Barcelona after being forced out of Germany, and who were among the first to take up arms against the putschists.

We need only study the political map of Europe in 1936 to understand this phenomenon. On the one hand, the sinister shadow of fascism that was constantly spreading, the danger of a deadly conflagration that was ever more clear; and on the other, the immense hopes raised by the victory of the Popular Front in Spain (February 1936), and then in France (May 1936). In this parallel rise of antagonistic forces, these militants sensed a polarization taking shape, a tension that heralded historic tests of strength, a confrontation between the forces of darkness and the forces of light. The unleashing of the fascist insurrection in Spain was the trigger that convinced them of the imminence of this confrontation and the necessity of applying all their strength there.

As they emphasize forcefully in their testimonies, it was both as militants for the socialist cause (communists, Trotskyists, Zionist workers, etc.) and as Jews that they joined the Spanish struggle. Shlomo Szlein, for example:

> I've often been asked, here in Israel, what prompted me to volunteer for Spain: did I go there as a Jew or as a communist? That's basically a quite ridiculous question. I was a communist, which obviously determined my view of the world and the commitments I made. But did this mean I had to cast off my Jewishness? After all, recruitment for Spain was on the basis of anti-fascism. The volunteers who turned up at the Brigades' recruitment centre in Paris were simply asked to prove that they were anti-fascists.

Jonas Brodkin would put it similarly:

> My commitment for Spain was above all a commitment against fascism. I had a double motivation, if you like. As a communist and as a Jew, born in Palestine into the bargain. Jewish national feeling was strong in me, and hatred of fascism was natural. It was certainly not by chance that several hundred young people left Palestine to fight in the ranks of the International Brigades – the overwhelming majority of them being Jews. At least forty of them did not return.

It is certainly true that, in the face of Hitler, the Polish far-right groups (Endecy) and the French 'leagues', Jews had no reason to shun

working-class or communist militants. There was complete continuity between the bans on the KPD and the Social Democratic Party,
the destruction of the trade unions, and the Nuremberg laws of 1935
that made anti-Semitic discrimination official, as there was between
the pogrom-style propaganda of the Endecy and the intensification of
repression against the Polish workers' movement in the mid-1930s –
to say nothing of that 'certain France' in which *Je suis partout* regularly sold 100,000 copies.[3]

The particular coloration of the anti-fascism of these militants is
thus clear enough. They understood by instinct, better than others,
that it was the fate of Europe, the fate of the workers' movement and
the European revolution, that was being played out in Spain – and
thus their own destiny as revolutionary Jews. It was from this lucidity
that they drew the energy and courage that led them to converge on
Albacete, the headquarters of the International Brigades. How else to
understand that out of the 35,000 to 50,000 fighters who joined the
International Brigades, several thousand – 6,000 according to some
sources – were Jewish?

Pierre Sherf, who maintains that three-quarters ('no exaggeration')
of the Romanian volunteers who took part in the Spanish war were
Jews, relates a story that indicates very well what this Jewish 'profile'
of the Brigades meant. One day at the front, his senior officer called
on his help: an American delegation from the Lincoln Brigade had
arrived, very discontent, and he didn't understand English. Could
Sherf translate? 'But I can't speak English either,' Sherf replied. – 'You'll
get by,' the commander told him, 'you know so many languages.' Sherf
scratched his head and suddenly had an idea. 'Do any of you speak
Yiddish?' Several hands went up and the litany of complaints began.
'We're not getting mail, the food is lousy ...' Sherf translated, and the
commander summed up laconically, 'You see, you're far too modest!'

In the Spanish proletariat's armed response to the rebel generals' sedition, these men and women saw the opportunity for an

---

3 *Je suis partout*: a French newspaper inspired by the ideas of Maurras, and
edited from 1937 by Robert Brasillach. It became the emblematic press organ of
collaboration politics, fully aligning itself with Nazism and publishing calls for the
murder of Jews. [Editor's note.]

exemplary settling of accounts with fascism, which could show the way to the rest of Europe. Their anti-fascism was radical and revolutionary, since they knew that fascism and anti-Semitism would not be defeated by half-measures, compromise and diplomatic stratagems. They were well aware that the cancer gnawing away at Europe could only be rooted out by attacking the foundations of the system that fed it and that was now in crisis. Besides, until as recently as 1934 the Communist parties and the ideologists of the Comintern had been constantly stressing to these militants that they should beware of the 'democratic' illusions of social democracy, decried as a forerunner of fascism. The fighters who journeyed to Spain with their double account to settle with fascism knew very well that only revolutionary methods (mobilization, arming the workers and peasants) would make it possible to defeat the military insurgents backed by the support of Hitler and Mussolini, and these methods could not be disassociated from the revolutionary objectives that were raised in the first days of confrontation, particularly in the response of the Barcelona workers to the fascist putsch: the formation of militias, the occupation of factories, the establishment of organs of control over the distribution of supplies; and then, for Catalonia as a whole, the occupation of lands, the development of anti-fascist committees and militias in the villages, etc. In short, they could not ignore the fact that behind the confrontation between the military rebels and the Spanish republic a far more radical alternative was being posed for Spain and Europe as a whole: either the victory of the Spanish revolution, whose dynamic was under way from the July days of 1936, or the triumph of counterrevolution as in Germany and Italy. This was the fundamental wellspring of the Yiddishland fighters' revolutionary anti-fascism. An anti-fascism that had little in common with that of Léon Blum, who as early as August 1936 made non-intervention the official doctrine of the French Popular Front government towards the Spanish Civil War.

The tragic paradox of the war in Spain is that this tremendous capital of energy and revolutionary optimism was essentially wasted. Countless testimonies attest that the courage and self-denial that the Jewish fighters displayed throughout the war – they were in every battle, on every front – compelled the admiration of their comrades in the Brigades, of the militias and of the Spanish population. There was certainly for them in this war something like an invisible second front, that of settling accounts with one of the most persistent stereotypes of anti-Semitic propaganda. One of our interviewees, Léo Lev, who had joined the German brigade, relates a telling incident on this subject:

> I felt quite comfortable in the German brigade. I had excellent contacts with young volunteers, but despite that you could feel wafts of anti-Semitism. I was taking a walk one day with a brigade comrade, Max, while we were on leave. We came across a new recruit who had just arrived from Germany, and he started going on about the Jews: 'As far as politics goes, they're ok; but for fighting … that's something else!' I kept quiet, waiting for Max to reply, as he wasn't Jewish. He just pointed at me and said: 'Look at him, then, he's in our brigade and he's Jewish. In fact he's just come from Palestine!' The other bloke was stunned and shut his mouth.

Pierre Sherf also notes that in the Romanian group there was sometimes talk about Jews having too many positions of responsibility. 'But what was surprising about that', he added, 'given that the majority of us Romanian volunteers were Jewish? Was it surprising that the highest-ranking Romanian, commandant Walter Roman, was a Jew?'

As we have seen from the reminiscences of these 'veterans', the motivations of their commitment to Spain remained clear and apparent. But the same was not true when they described their battles and tried to draw a balance sheet of the war – in both its personal and historic aspects. They did this with a mixture of unease, sadness, sometimes anger and rage, which very often prevailed over their pride of having been in this battle, in the vanguard of anti-fascist struggle. Even so much later, they could not think of Spain without a wrench. Not only because they knew very well that the great tragedy of the century was rooted in this defeat, the start of the dark turn for which they paid the heaviest price – as revolutionaries and as Jews. But above all, perhaps, because they also felt that the defeat had been far from inevitable, that the Spanish opportunity had been wasted and they themselves had been swindled, that behind the scenes of the war, crimes had been committed against other revolutionaries, memories of which still haunted them decades later. They felt that the crisis of their utopia began in this Spanish episode, the beginning of a time of doubt, even if, mobilized in other struggles (the Resistance, then the 'construction of socialism' in Poland, Czechoslovakia, etc.), the hour of their verdicts was delayed.

It was in fact at the moment when they threw themselves body and soul into this life-and-death struggle with the forces of darkness, the moment when all their revolutionary energy was directed towards the hope that the defeat of Franco would lead to a reversal of the historic tendency in Europe, which would make everything possible and trace the contours of a new world, that a new communist policy came into force in Europe, laid down by Stalin, which sounded the death knell of these hopes and clipped the wings of the radicalism of these fighters. This new policy was defined by *L'Humanité* at this time in a few lines:

> The central committee of the Spanish Communist Party has asked us, in response to the fantastic and self-interested stories of certain newspapers, to make known to public opinion that the Spanish people, in their struggle against the rebels, in no way aim to establish the dictatorship of the proletariat but have only a single aim: the defence of the republican order with respect for property.[4]

In the same sense, André Marty, the leader of the International Brigades, spelled out,

> The workers' parties of Spain, and more particularly the Communist Party, have clearly indicated the goal to be reached. Our brother party in particular has demonstrated on many occasions that the present struggle in Spain is not one between capitalism and socialism, but between fascism and democracy.[5]

---

4   *L'Humanité*, 3 August 1936.
5   *L'Humanité*, 4 August 1936.

The reasons for this spectacular turn in Stalin's policy are quite clear. Immediately after the defeat of the KPD without a struggle in the face of Nazism, in January 1933, and disturbed by the advance of fascism in Europe, he had embarked on a rapprochement with the Western democracies – confirmed among other things by the signature of a mutual assistance pact with Pierre Laval, the French foreign minister, the consequence of which was that the PCF abandoned all anti-militarist propaganda, and placed the 'Marseillaise' alongside the 'Internationale' and the tricolour alongside the red flag. In Spain, Stalin wanted to show France and England that by aiding the republic, the Soviet Union and the Comintern would steer clear of fomenting a socialist revolution and would guarantee the maintenance of the established order. Until the last days of the Spanish republic, he remained convinced that Blum's France and conservative Britain would intervene to block the way to Franco and fascism.

In practice, Stalin's turn meant that the Spanish Communist Party would ally with the 'moderate' socialists and those bourgeois parties that had not rallied to Franco. It meant a merciless struggle against all the 'excesses' of the mass movement, in both the countryside and the industrial centres: the disarming of the militias, the restoration of a government with a parliamentary façade, the restitution of confiscated firms and lands to their owners. It meant the formation of a 'regular' army, solidly staffed by Soviet military experts and strictly controlled by Communist political commissars; it meant the infiltration of the state apparatus – especially its vital sectors: police, justice, supplies, information (censorship) – by advisers sent from Moscow and by cadres of the Partido Comunista de España. And it inevitably meant a violent confrontation with those political currents that (in however uncertain and hesitant a fashion, as was the case with the POUM and particularly the anarchist CNT-FAI) expressed the radicalization of the Spanish workers and peasants in the course of the struggle against Franco. This confrontation culminated in the insurrectionary days of May 1937, when the champions of the Republican 'order', with Spanish communists and the NKVD agents who 'advised' them in the lead, clashed with the most combative sectors of the working class in the Catalan metropolis, grouped behind the CNT-FAI and the POUM. At the end of this battle, the Stalinists unleashed a witch-hunt against the anarchists, and especially the POUM, that culminated in the murder in a secret NKVD prison of the POUM leader Andrés Nin, and the imprisonment and liquidation of several hundred anti-Stalinist militants by Stalin's henchmen. These events sounded the death knell of the Spanish revolution.

At the time of these events, Elija Rosijanski was in Barcelona, where he had joined the ranks of the POUM. This almost cost him his life, but so many years later he could laugh about it:

After the May days of 1937, the Stalinists decided to liquidate us. The police invaded the Falcón hotel which was our headquarters and arrested everyone. We were taken to an unofficial prison, a kind of cellar. Men on one side, women on the other. We were under the thumb of the NKVD. One of our number, a Frenchman, managed to get hold of a newspaper and read out that we were accused of being spies in the pay of Franco. There were several foreigners among us. A comrade who had escaped arrest ran from one consulate to another, warning the authorities concerned that citizens of their countries had been illegally arrested and were in danger of death.

These initiatives were the saving of us. We were transferred to the big Barcelona prison, the *carcer model*. In an extraordinary paradox, this prison was basically in the hands of the anarchists! In fact, you could say that, while we were suffering this repression, the anarchists were still the real masters in Barcelona. The prison director, in particular, was an anarchist. When we were arrested, we were not allowed to take any of our belongings at all. And so we demanded soap to wash ourselves and our clothes. But there wasn't any. We decided therefore to protest by remaining naked the whole day, including the exercise period: an unaccustomed spectacle of these hundreds of men parading stark naked in the prison yard! The inhabitants of the adjacent buildings began to complain: this spectacle was offensive to their wives and daughters. The director begged us to dress, but we held firm: either soap or we continue … And we did continue.

We then learned that they were planning to transfer us to Valencia, where the Stalinists were in full control. For us that meant certain death.

We made clear to the CNT that they would have to get us out of prison by force if they wanted to take us to Valencia. The CNT was still a power in Catalonia, with over a million members. One fine day, a CNT leader arrived and told us, 'You won't be going to Valencia. You can leave for the French border. Our men will be waiting for you in each village. If they are not there to show that the way is clear, don't go further, it will be dangerous.' The women remained in prison, my partner was one of them. The most extraordinary thing is that the head of the women's section of the prison was herself a POUM member. Everything was possible in Spain. Finally, we managed to reach France.

Elija Rosijanski's story bears the mark of Yiddish humour, in which self-derision plays such a part. But not all the Spanish veterans would react in the same way when they described these events and tried to sum them up. Some stuck to the image of a just and heroic war which they joined in the heat of their enthusiasm, and do not accept any attempt to tarnish the picture by placing too much importance on what they continue to see as regrettable 'mistakes'. Others have tears in their eyes when they speak of a friend or a comrade who, after expressing certain reservations about the orientation adopted in Spain, received a bullet in the back, or was recalled to Moscow to be liquidated. Others again think that it is quite simply time to tell the truth and contribute to this by their testimonies: one of them describes his visit to a secret NKVD prison in Albacete; another the preparations, in a military unit controlled by the communists, for an intervention against a POUM meeting, and how Brigaders were intoxicated by propaganda that presented this party as an ally of Franco.

Today, indeed, everyone assesses differently their relation to this aspect of the war in Spain. Jonas Brodkin emphasizes that he was only a 'simple soldier' who had no 'overall view of things', but he adds,

Now I see certain aspects of the war differently from at that time, more than forty years ago. I didn't know very much of what was happening in the rear, but in the end we were 'orthodox' enough to accept that if necessary, all the POUM militants had to be liquidated. Today, we wouldn't even dare to think such a thing. I know that many oppositionists were liquidated in Albacete, that people were liquidated who didn't want to go to the front, and others who had been sent to spy on the fascists. Later on I learned a lot of things. Particularly in the USSR, where I met some former *revolveros* responsible for this dirty work.

Adam Paszt's comments are in the same vein:

I was aware of the differences between the communists, the anarchists and the POUM. I'd learned Spanish, I read the newspapers. I discussed in my brigade with socialists and anarchists. But I didn't know what was being planned behind the scenes. Later on, after the outbreak of the Second World War, I was imprisoned in the Djelfa camp in Algeria, where I had the opportunity of talking at length with Spanish anarchists, and learned a lot of things about Spain. At the time, however, I still remained a 100 per cent communist. As soon as I heard someone criticize the Communist Party or the USSR, my ears blocked it out.

Max Technitchek, for his part, tried to reconstitute the logic of the positions he held at the time, without justifying the mistakes committed:

In Spain, we were at war. In the anti-Franco camp we were faced with different currents, anarchists and POUM. And then we were shown documents that 'proved' that the POUM were collaborating with our enemies. Were we meant to oppose these documents that presented every appearance of authenticity? And another thing: I was convinced that the turn to the Popular Front was a good thing, that this orientation had to be applied in Spain. I know today that the Popular Front was in reality just a facade, a pure farce. But at the time I saw things differently; I observed that we were trying to give consistency to this front, and against us an organization like POUM was openly acting against this perspective; its militants believed that the present stage was one of social revolution, not just the defence of the republic, and they sabotaged our efforts. By their action, the communists risked finding themselves isolated and deprived of allies. For me, the idea that you could make revolution in Spain, given the objective conditions of the country, was absurd. And from there it was only a step to accepting that it was necessary to 'bring a bit of order' into all that, even brutally, as was the case in May 1937. Who could be against that?

Pierre Sherf mentions that the unity and solidarity of the fighters in the face of danger trumped political differences. 'At the front', he says, 'we hardly discussed politics, even if the fraternity of the fighters allowed great tolerance; even if, in the Romanian group, even the most "fanatical" communists accepted discussions that verged on "Trotskyism".'

These testimonies highlight the most painful aspect of the doubt and confusion that gripped these men and women when they tried to understand why and how their forces were dissipated and their most secure convictions shaken. Basically, these questionings turn around the role of the USSR in Spain, and the reorientation of Stalin's policy as the Second World War approached. Several factors contributed to their growing doubt.

For some of them, it was the conduct of the war, the insufficiency of Soviet aid. Shlomo Szlein recalls a terrible battle in Extremadura:

In February 1938 I took part in the battles that were fought in the Sierra Quemada. We had attempted a breakthrough during the night. This was a major operation in which two International Brigades and two Spanish units were to take part. We were supposed to be covered on our flanks by tanks. But at the decisive moment they failed to arrive. At the price of terrible losses, we clung to the hillside a day and a night. There were three of us from the same region in my brigade: one was killed, myself and the other wounded.

Léa Stein was a nurse in a hospital close to the front. She remembers the state of mind of the wounded:

The hospital was always full to bursting; we had to operate without a break. The wounded were often demoralized and undisciplined. They felt that they had been abandoned, that not enough weapons had been supplied, that the USSR was letting them drop. These reactions were easily understandable: right from the start, our armies were on the retreat, they weren't properly equipped.

Pierre Sherf maintains that the fighters were hardly aware that the Soviet Union, all things considered, was not arming Republican Spain as much as it could have done, since 'we ate Russian grub, tinned food, and our rifles were stamped with the hammer and sickle logo'. On the other hand, his personal experience quite soon led him to question the role of the communist cadres sent to Spain by the Comintern. As a political commissar in Albacete before being sent to the front at his own request, he suffered the bombings of Italian planes along with his comrades:

> That lasted from nine in the evening to six in the morning; we didn't have shelters or anti-aircraft defence. The volunteers took fright and scattered in the fields. Some days later, in my capacity as commissar, I was summoned by Marty, together with other officers, and he said to us, 'If this kind of scene is repeated, that's the end of you, you'll be shot.' I stood there open-mouthed: had I come to Spain to get shot by my own people? Then someone asked, 'What should we have done?' Marty's answer: 'Got out your pistols and fired!' – 'On whom?' – 'On those of your comrades who fled.' Marty was certainly capable of shooting the lads, but most of us certainly weren't.

In his novel *For Whom the Bell Tolls*, Ernest Hemingway gives a transparent portrait of Marty that is hardly flattering: '[Gomez] recognized his bushy eyebrows, his watery gray eyes, his chin and the double chin under it, and he knew him for one of France's great modern revolutionary figures who had led the mutiny of the French Navy in the Black Sea.' Hemingway depicts the leader of the International Brigades showing this 'mania for shooting people', his subordinates and other fighters suspected of being 'spies'.[6]

Despite this incident, however, and despite what he had learned of the events of May 1937 in Barcelona, and the suspect conditions of the death of the anarchist leader Durutti before Madrid, Sherf basically had 'no doubts or unease'. 'I was one of the fanatics', he explains.

---

6   Ernest Hemingway, *For Whom the Bell Tolls* (New York: Arrow, 1994), p. 434.

'The party pointed out the way and we followed. Our motto could be summed up as this: "The party said so, the party is right; Stalin said so, Stalin is right."'

Others were deeply shaken when they heard the news, in 1938, that the Polish Communist Party had been dissolved on Stalin's orders. Max Technitchek was one of these:

I was interim secretary of the Communist Party in the Balkan brigade when I learned that the Polish party had been dissolved; its leadership was said to have been infiltrated by the police. The brigade was made up of Yugoslavs, Bulgarians, Czechs, but also Poles. The secretary of the brigade, a Latin American, was then at the front; he sent me a letter ordering me to suspend all Poles from political or military responsibilities.

I was pretty disheartened. I understood well enough in principle that a party that has been fighting underground for several years could be infiltrated, that certain leaders might have succumbed to the pressure of the class enemy, etc. I told myself that if the Comintern had taken that decision, it was because it had proofs that it would publicize before long. I was a bit disturbed because the leadership that had just been 'unmasked' had come in to replace another one, dismissed only a few years before for right deviation. But then ... Above all, being from Poland myself, I was wounded in my personal dignity, in my dignity as a Jew, so to say.

So I replied right away to the brigade secretary that I saw myself as also suspended, and sent him the name of my replacement, a Serb. As for myself, I added, I would return to the ranks. A few hours later a motorcyclist arrived bearing a message that basically said, 'You're an idiot. It's not a question of country of origin, but of political allegiance. Your party is the Czech party.' Soon after, he called me on the phone and said, 'This resolution was adopted to deal with traitors in the Polish Communist Party, not militants. There were traitors in the leadership, so the party has been dissolved, and then we'll see.'

I was perplexed. I had already heard talk of a purge in the Yugoslav party, which had almost led to its liquidation, and similar problems in other parties. That was a big deal. On the other hand, though, there was the case of Doriot in France, who went over to the other side bags and baggage. I told myself that if there could be a Doriot in a country like France, where the party was legal, why shouldn't there also be Doriots in a semi-fascist country like Poland? It was the same scenario that was repeated with the Marty affair in 1953. The great mass of militants believed that Marty was a police agent.

The war in Spain also coincided with the Moscow trials. Isaac Kotlarz learned of these in a rather odd way, but it scarcely affected him at first:

> At that time, I didn't yet have the doubts that I felt later. I remember one scene: in May 1937, we were holding the Córdoba front, on a hillside. We were in trenches with the fascists opposite us, quite close. They called out, 'Hey, *los Rojos* [Reds], you know what's going on in Moscow? They're shooting your comrades!' In fact, the great purges had started, and they, the Francoists, were informed of this. But we put it down to bluff.

Could it be that the USSR was not the lighthouse they imagined? It was in Spain that certain militants began to ask themselves this question. Léa Stein, for example:

> In Spain, I met Yugoslavs who had left for the Soviet Union in 1924. Naive as I was, I asked them to describe the magnificent existence they had led there. But they kept quiet. One day, however, one of them, who had been wounded, took me aside and said, 'The USSR isn't like you believe. You can't say, of course, that it's nothing, but it's not what we had hoped it would be.' And he fell silent. 'How so?' I asked. But he wouldn't say any more. People distrusted everyone, they feared denunciations.

Along with his advisers, agents and political commissars, Stalin exported the methods of his dictatorship to Spain. Léo Lev had experience of this. Expelled from the Palestinian Communist Party in 1936, he nonetheless left for Spain and enrolled in the Brigades as 'non-party'. But his past caught up with him.

When I was wounded, I was evacuated to Albacete. I came across a political commissar, a Jew from France, who sharply said to me, 'You've got no business here. Leave the country as soon as you can; go to France!' I didn't understand, thinking that he was referring to my state of health. But he made clear that it wasn't this; information had come from Palestine indicating that I was a doubtful element, who'd been expelled. I understood then what the danger was, and I left.

Despite their bitter experiences, these fighters did not break with Stalinism immediately after the Spanish war. As we have seen, the impending period was hardly propitious for historical reflection, for profound and calm summing-up. Trapped by fascism, they had no other choice at this time than to launch into other combats, and these gave rise to new hopes, a new revolutionary optimism despite the horrors that the Second World War brought. It was Spain, however, that was the starting point of the slow work of doubt, giddiness and subterranean questioning that, for the majority of these militants, led later on to a partial or total challenge to what had been for them an ineradicable credo at the time of their departure for Spain. Léa Stein well describes this path of doubt, after her Yugoslav friends warned her against an idyllic view of Soviet reality:

That set me wondering. I stopped believing blindly. I remained in the party, I obeyed, but I no longer took what I was told for gospel. From that time, I relied on my critical spirit. I was ignorant of all the liquidations and other horrors that were going on then in Spain, but I could see that there were hardly any Soviet soldiers in the country, and couldn't understand why the USSR wasn't more committed. Still today, this remains a mystery for me; could it be that Stalin really wanted the defeat of the republic? He was a communist, after all …

For Isaac Kotlarz, reinterpreting the past went together with a certain bad conscience:

Later on, when I read Hemingway's For Whom the Bell Tolls, I found an enlightenment that did not correspond to the official fables: that reminded me of facts I had heard spoken of in Spain, but which I had not paid attention to at that time. What was said of Marty's role in the International Brigades, the nickname he was given of 'the butcher of Albacete'. In reality, we knew more about this chapter than we wanted to say. But we didn't have the courage to speak; we had sincere discussions only between intimate friends, even if there were basically enough of us who did not agree with these procedures.

We should note here that it was not from contact with Spain, from the relationship with the Spanish people, that this giddiness and unease arose, but rather from the policies followed in Spain by the movement's strategists. Our interviewees are unanimous on this point:

> The Spanish population were not chauvinistic, they welcomed the Brigades with enormous sympathy. I very soon learned Spanish and sought contact with the population, which was easy. In the course of a retreat, I was entrusted with the task of guarding a village shop for a few days, along with a mate. The villagers were hungry. But the little that they had they shared with us; they knew that if the fascists came, those who had helped us would be denounced, that this could cost them dear. But that didn't prevent them at all.

And again: 'The Spanish women had an extraordinary morale and demeanour, whether as fighters or as auxiliaries in the medical services. I found them much stronger than the men!'

Let us leave the realm of analysis for a moment to return to the practical conditions lived by these men who threw themselves into battle. Reaching Republican Spain was not a tea party. As one militant recalls,

> it was quite an adventure. Most people who left for Spain did not have passports. They crossed frontiers illegally, and were often sent back by the police of the countries that they tried to enter. All the police of Europe knew, of course, that there was this movement of volunteers for Spain.

Artur London, in *The Confession*,[7] describes a trajectory of this kind, which in his case led from Moscow to Albacete by way of Finland, Sweden, Denmark, Antwerp, Paris and the mule tracks of the Pyrenees. For some volunteers, the journey took several months, interrupted by imprisonment and expulsions. But the will to struggle against fascism was stronger: clinging to trains, helped by anti-fascist organizations in every country, they almost always ended up reaching their destination.

As Jonas Brodkin recalls,

> Initially it wasn't all that difficult. I was a member of one of the first groups of foreigners to join the Republican camp, at the end of 1936. At that time, the Blum government still turned a blind eye, more or less. In Paris we had a superficial medical examination, our names were put on a list, we were given a drop-off point in Perpignan, a train ticket, and fifty francs for a binge before leaving. In Perpignan, the train emptied out. We slept in abandoned barracks, and the next day reached the border by bus. The man in charge of our group had spoken with the gendarmes and told them he was accompanying eighty Spaniards. The gendarmes didn't make a fuss, and we crossed. As soon as we entered Spain, we sung the 'Internationale'.

Léa Stein's journey was rather more adventurous. One night she crossed the Yugoslav border on foot and reached Austria, then Switzerland and France by a whole range of means of transport. At each frontier, she was awaited by local communist comrades. The network functioned well.

The majority of the militants who arrived in Spain joined the International Brigades. Sometimes they were simply posted to one or other of these; in other cases they had a choice. Each brigade was supposedly 'national', but this national characteristic was quite relative: in most of them there were Spaniards; the German brigade included Hungarians, the Polish brigade Ukrainians and Byelorussians. Right from the start, Jews were scattered through all the Brigades, even if

---

7   Artur London, *The Confession* (New York: Ballantine, 1971).

some were more 'Jewish' than others: the Anglo-American Lincoln brigade, for example, was almost 50 per cent Jewish, and the Polish Dombrowski Brigade likewise.

How did those Jews who had the opportunity of choosing their posting make this choice? The criteria seem to have been very varied: geographical origin, knowledge of languages, affinities of all kinds, the combat reputation of this or than unit. Léo Lev recalls this choice rather maliciously:

> I arrived in Alicante along with my friend Segal. We had both come from Palestine, where we had been expelled from the Palestinian Communist Party. We didn't want to be separated, so I asked Segal: 'What brigade should we enrol in?' He replied, 'Look; we speak Hebrew, Arab and Yiddish. So our only choice is to go to the Germans; after all, in both Yiddish and German *links* is left and *rechts* is right.' That's how we joined the German brigade!

Following the same logic, Jonas Brodkin recalls that a Palestinian Arab was recruited to the Polish brigade because he spoke – of all things – Yiddish; and another because he spoke Hebrew. That could almost be a Jewish joke, but above all it is a precious indication of the strength of Jewish representation in this unit.

Adam Paszt, who spoke Polish, joined the Mickiewicz battalion of the Dombrowski Brigade; Max Technitchek, though originating from a region of Ukraine annexed to Poland after 1918, joined the Balkan brigade which combined Czechs, Yugoslavs, Bulgarians, etc. In the 1930s he was active in the Czech Communist Party. Basically, of course, this dispersal of Jewish volunteers, as well as political and military cadres, simply reflected their integration in the different workers' movements and parties (overwhelmingly communist) that were nationally structured. It was only from this point of view that there was any 'Jewish problem'.

It is appropriate here to mention a certain paradox. Even if, as we have seen, the Yiddishland revolutionaries found themselves doubly concerned by the fascist threat, and even if the specifically Jewish dimension of their commitment in the Spanish war is self-evident,

THE SPANISH SKY 119

it was also in this struggle that their projection on the terrain of revolutionary universalism, the human universalism that we also call internationalism, was most apparent, most spectacular and most strong. Commitment to Spain was based on notions and emotions that directly appealed to a universalist political and human consciousness, a concept of the unity of the European – if not world – revolutionary struggle that is quite remarkable.

Many of these combatants, too, would not basically consider themselves – and were not considered – as specifically Jewish, but simply as communists, revolutionaries. This was the case, for example, with Artur London, who was on André Marty's general staff, and many other political and military cadres of the Brigades, including the hero of the defence of Madrid, General Kléber (Manfred Zalmanovitch Stern).[8] On the other hand, there was also a red thread of Jewish involvement in this war, as shown by other indications as well.

Among the first foreigners who took up arms against the putschist officers, well before the creation of the International Brigades, were a group of Jewish athletes who had just arrived in Barcelona to take part in the 'Olympiads of sport and culture' due to open in the Catalan capital on 18 July. This festival was conceived as the democratic and anti-fascist response to the great Olympic spectacle staged by the Nazis in Berlin. The Olympiads were organized by workers' organizations, for the most part communist. The working-class Jewish associations that were very active in Poland, France and Belgium were deeply involved, in particular the YASK, controlled by the communists. There was something deeply significant about the immediate commitment of these Yiddish athletes, who had never touched a gun in their lives, but who exchanged the cancelled football match in Barcelona for the barricades. One of these novices in street fighting, who hastily learned to use a rifle in the lorry taking him to Lerida, the first front in the fighting, was Emmanuel Mink, later the last commander of the Jewish Botwin Company.

---

8   On Kléber, cf. Sidonie Gross, 'Manfred Stern alias Emilio Kléber: Histoire d'une vie', in Stéfanie Prezioso, Jean Batou, and Ami-Jacques Rapin, *Tant pis si la lutte est cruelle: Volontaires internationaux contre Franco* (Paris: Syllepse, 2008).

The creation of this company, in December 1937, is clearly the most striking illustration of the existence of this 'Jewish thread' in the involvement of our witnesses in Spain. Many of them volunteered specifically for this brigade. One of them, Shlomo Szlein, recalls the conditions in which it was created, within the Palafox Battalion of the Dombrowski Brigade:

At the end of 1937 there was a certain ferment among the Jewish volunteers in different brigades; the idea of creating a Jewish unit was in the air. A meeting was held, for Jews from Poland, France, Palestine, etc. Opinions were divided: some people thought that the Brigades should maintain the same structures as the parties, organized on a territorial basis; others argued that the participation of Jews in the anti-fascist combat in Spain should be emphasized, and a Jewish unit created for this purpose. In the end it was the second point of view that prevailed, and the Botwin Company was established. We were encouraged in this by Luigi Longo, among others, the inspector general of the Brigades (known as 'Gallo' during the Spanish war). We began to publish a newspaper in Yiddish, with very rudimentary material that a correspondent of the *Naïe presse* in Paris had brought. The Jewish workers' cultural organizations gave us considerable support.

A solemn order of the day was adopted by the commander and the political commissar of the Dombrowski Brigade, announcing,

In the struggle for your freedom and our own, the anti-fascists of all countries have come to each others' aid. Among the volunteers in the International Brigades, and the Dombrowski Brigade in particular, Jewish volunteers have always distinguished themselves by their heroism, their combative spirit and their devotion to the struggle against fascism. Outside Madrid, in Guadalajara, Brunete and Zaragoza, everywhere that our brigade found itself engaged in the struggle against fascism, mortal enemy of humanity, Jewish volunteers were in the front line, giving an example of anti-fascist heroism and consciousness. By emphasizing their large number and the importance of Jewish volunteers in the Dombrowski Brigade, so as to commemorate also the

memory of Jewish fighters who fell for liberty, we have decided that
the 2 Company of the heroic Polish Palafox Battalion should become a
Jewish company under the name of Naftali Botwin.[9]

Botwin was a young Jewish militant from Poland who had been shot
in 1925 for killing a provocateur.

The Botwin Company was far from including all the Jewish fighters in the Spanish war. Its strength never exceeded a few hundred
fighters. But, as the order of the day announcing its creation clearly
signified, what counted was the symbol represented by the establishment of a Jewish unit. It took part in several deadly battles,
particularly in Extremadura, and then on the Ebro. Dozens of
volunteers in this company fell in the course of these battles. The
company had to be reinforced, particularly by Spaniards. Besides its
activities on the front, it published six issues of a Yiddish-language
newspaper, *Botwin*, as recalled by Shlomo Szlein; composed
songs and chants; and set up a theatre (in Yiddish, naturally) and
even a football team. It was withdrawn from the war in October
1938, along with the rest of the International Brigades. The survivors paraded triumphantly on the Plaça de Catalunya before
leaving the country, but the shadow of defeat was already looming.
Adam Paszt:

> In April 1938 we fell back to Catalonia. Our units had been decimated. I
> was then in the Botwin Company, which had been reinforced by young
> Spanish recruits, college and school students, mostly from the Young
> Socialists, who remained with us to the end. But everyone felt that this
> was the finish, the flow of volunteers had dried up. The offensive on the
> Ebro had been our last victory before the debacle.

For most of the Internationals, the bitterness of defeat was now supplemented by the humiliation of detention. When they crossed the
French frontier, they were disarmed by the Gardes mobiles and transported to what were already called concentration camps: Argelès,

---

9   Diamant, *Combattants juifs dans l'armée républicaine espagnole* (Paris:
Éditions Renouveau, 1979), p. 145.

Gurs, Le Vernet, Saint-Cyprien. When the German armies occupied the southern half of France in November 1942, some were transported to camps in Algeria. Still today, they cannot suppress their hostility to the French authorities who treated them as hardened criminals for having been in the front line of the anti-fascist struggle.

The turpitudes of the French government and the Vichy regime have repressed the memory of this episode of imprisonment of thousands of anti-fascists by the French authorities, even before the outbreak of the Second World War. This is a pity, and there is clearly every reason for our witnesses to dwell on this chapter, when the Spanish defeat was transformed into a calvary in the camps of the French republic, then the État français.

Let us hear, first of all, Isaac Kotlarz:

I left Spain in February 1939, two years after arriving there. The gendarmes divided us into two groups: one was sent to the camp at Saint-Cyprien, the other to that of Argelès. I found myself in the second, right on the beach, where the wind tossed up whirlwinds of sand and the waves came up to our feet. We stayed there until April 1939. There were a hundred thousand people there, most of them Spanish refugees, whole families, living in conditions of absolute destitution. Only at the end of this period did they begin to build huts and install a minimum of sanitation. We ate right in the wind, the sand mixing in with our food. Every night people died. One day a delegation from the PCF arrived, led by a communist deputy. I asked him, 'Comrade, why do I have to stay in this camp? I've got a home in Paris, a job, my papers in order.' He replied, 'No, party members have to stay here and help the non-party people!' Naive that I was, I believed him; in reality, however, we were an embarrassment they could do without, with our possible criticisms. As far as I was concerned, it would have been wrong to make a fuss, I didn't think of raising the least objection. And to think that three times I was allowed out of the camp, for one reason or another! But each time I returned – the sense of discipline! I was a militant of the kind that there were in those days, the old model.

In April 1939 we were transferred to Gurs. At the start, we were treated relatively well: the food was adequate, there were huts, we slept

on straw mattresses. The camp was divided into sections by nationality; there was everyone there: Ukrainians, Byelorussians, Portuguese,
Germans, Italians, etc. We, the Polish Jews, were grouped in Camp G.
Until the war began, life there was almost tolerable; I remember than
on 14 July we were allowed out to see the Tour de France, which was
passing close by. We were guarded by regular soldiers. The commander
agreed that we could go out into the road in front of the camp to stretch
our legs a bit. We got parcels from outside.

We had an intensive cultural activity, a kind of university, with different levels and different subjects taught. Choirs were formed, an Italian
who was an opera singer gave real recitals; there were also orchestras.
We received French newspapers such as *La dépêche de Toulouse*, but
you had to read between the lines. On the other hand, some comrades received papers from the Baltic countries which taught us a lot
of things. We collected information and put together little bulletins in
different languages: in some ways, we were better informed than the
French! Each person cobbled together what he could, to keep occupied:
I still have a little chess set that I made in Gurs, it took me three months!
Other people did wonders with food tins, made locomotives, a miner
made a miniature mine, an Italian a bust of Durutti, the Spanish anarchist. We kept ourselves occupied, but then we were young, we only had
one dream, to leave.

When the war began, the situation rapidly deteriorated; the food
became horrible, mainly what we called 'electric soup', mashed peas in
water, a thin broth that you couldn't digest. Dozens of inmates fell ill,
the ground was muddy, the climate damp; rheumatism and tuberculosis
spread daily.

There were an increasing number of escape attempts. The soldiers
were replaced by Gardes mobiles. I tried my luck in April 1940, with
a handful of mates. There were eight barbed-wire barriers to cross to
get to the main road; one of us got caught in the wire and triggered the
alarm; the guards cried out, 'Who goes there?' and we were caught. We
were placed in a dungeon for two weeks on half-rations, our heads were
shaved, but we weren't beaten. In Gurs, there was violence only towards
those who refused to work; I saw people being dragged to the workplace
by their feet.

Then I was transferred to the Le Vernet camp along with eight hundred others, those who were classified as 'activists'. In Le Vernet there were three blocks: political prisoners in A and B, and in C a whole motley crew, particularly Italians. One of them, for example, bought a little chess set from a mate who had made it out of bones – to present it to the Duce! In block A there was a Pole who managed a very neat escape: every Sunday a priest came to say Mass in the camp, and he served. One fine Sunday after the service, while the priest went for a drink with the commander, he took his soutane and hat and left the camp by the main gate, without being spotted or recognized.

Our situation in Le Vernet was very bad: it was a real military camp, very well guarded, with watchtowers and barbed wire. Very soon we all fell ill, with a kind of dysentery. It was our own brigade doctors – they were prisoners too – who saved us, persuading us to give up part of the food we were given in exchange for rice; thanks to the rice water diet we rapidly recovered. I was fed up, and decided to make a new escape attempt: 'After all, what do I risk?' I told myself. 'If they catch me, they'll put me in the hole for three months. But I'm in prison anyway. So …'

My escape was very simple. We were entitled to receive visits, and one day friends of mine came from Paris to see me. I had noted well before this that there was little check on the visitors when they left the camp: it was clear enough that they weren't detainees. So I smartened myself up, put on a suit that I'd bought in Barcelona, a tie … and calmly left with my friends. I walked seven kilometres, then took a train for Toulouse, where the Polish consulate provided me with papers. Then I only needed to take the train for Paris. Everything would have been perfect if my passport hadn't shown that my first name was Isaac.

There were many political discussions in the camp, and that's when I started to wobble a bit in my convictions. The verdict on the Spanish war was a burning question for all of us. The official explanation that the party gave us was that the action of the Brigades had delayed the outbreak of war, that the struggle of the Spanish people had delayed the advance of Hitler and Mussolini. That wasn't true; people hardly believed it. Quite a large number of comrades began to be fed up with this logic-chopping. I said to my mates, 'That's all well and good; I'm in the history books, but how am I going to get out now?'

For Adam Paszt, the test of the camps was a step on the road to the Soviet Union:

After leaving Spain I was imprisoned in Argelès, then in Gurs. Political work continued there. In Gurs we set up cells; we were in contact with the PCF and studied the official history of the USSR. That was when we learned more about the dissolution of the Polish party. The delegate of the Soviet party to the Polish brigade was imprisoned with us, and explained this to us: he was afraid for his family who were back in Moscow, but after the war he became vice minister of security in Poland. The dissolution of the Polish party was a shock for me and my friends; we were completely disoriented.

I made two attempts to escape. Early in the war, after the defeat of France, life in Gurs became very hard. We suffered terribly from hunger. It got to the point where people sometimes tried to leave the camp at night to find bread and bring it back; the police intercepted them but let them pass, and the bakers gave them bread. We were also helped by organizations connected to the Communist Party. And then, even before the Germans invaded the 'free zone', Gestapo commissions came and interrogated the German anti-fascists held in the camp. Some of them had been condemned to death in Germany, and deportation meant certain death for them. Some people managed to escape, and I went with them. We travelled hundreds of kilometres north, on foot. But it was winter, and we were recaptured. I was locked up in a fortress, in the Pyrenees.

I tried to escape again, with the help of a French NCO who gave me rope and a map. The walls were some twenty metres high. My companions and I descended with the help of the rope, but the guards had heard us; we scattered and I lost a shoe in the thick snow. I threw away the other and went sixty kilometres barefoot. One morning I knocked on the door of a village house and asked if someone could sell me a pair of espadrilles. It was the house of the mayor, and his wife didn't want to sell me anything. A bit further on I tried my luck again, and a woman gave me espadrilles – and food as well – without taking any money. I told her that I was Spanish, but she laughed in my face: 'With your accent ...'

Throughout the region, the gendarmes were on the lookout for us. Besides, the area was infested with young fascists attending a camp not far away. We were captured and taken to the gendarmerie. 'I've got nothing against you,' the officer in command said. 'My son is a prisoner of war in Germany, and I'd like him to escape too. But after all, orders are orders!' As we were drenched through, he lit a fire, ordered an omelette for us and offered us wine. Then we were chained and taken back to the fortress on foot. My feet were bloody. When we reached the destination we were locked up for a month in a kind of cellar, which was freezing cold.

It had been announced in Gurs that we would be transferred to Algeria. It seemed we were to work on the construction of a trans-Saharan railway line. We all refused to leave. That might seem surprising, given the dangers facing us in Europe, yet we had the impression that going off to the unknown Sahara was the most dangerous choice of all: in Europe at least we had friends, networks … A thousand gendarmes had to be mobilized to force the detainees to embark on the ships taking them to Algeria, they had to be chained up. I joined the others only later, after the failure of my second escape.

We were then transferred to Djelfa in the Atlas mountains. We lived in tents, dying of heat in the summer and of cold in the winter. The hunger was particularly terrible. The camp commander was a certain Caboche, a fascist who had been with the French military mission in Poland in 1918. He made no secret of his anti-Semitism, and announced, 'I've been given the mission of destroying you.' But compared with the Germans he was still an angel. All things considered, by transferring us to Algeria against our will, the French authorities saved our lives. We were hungry the whole time. Fortunately we received money from the French Communist Party. A Red Cross representative one day brought me a postal order and said, 'Your girlfriend has sent you money.' I knew very well that was impossible; it was a cover for the party. We used this money to bribe the Arab guards at the camp. They brought us dates hidden in their wide trousers; this was a very nutritious food and saved our lives. I ate half a kilo of dates per day! We rebuilt Communist Party cells, but had very little contact with the outside. We were freed in 1943, after the Anglo-American landings in North Africa. We wrote a letter to the Soviet ambassador in London. Two delegates came to the camp after a while, and proposed that the veterans of the Spanish war should go to the Soviet Union. The majority accepted, including myself, of course. We were looked after by a mixed Anglo-Soviet committee and shipped to the USSR by way of Tunisia, Egypt, Palestine, Jordan, Iraq and Iran. I spent two days in Palestine, in Haifa, where by a remarkable chance I met my sister, who had left Poland in 1936. I was wearing an American uniform and she didn't recognize me. She had married an architect and suggested that I stay there with them – they would find me work, housing. But I refused without hesitating: I wanted to go to the USSR!

Shlomo Szlein's experience was still more gruelling: he was taken prisoner by the Italian fascists, and his Spanish odyssey would last another five years:

With the collapse of the Republican army in February 1939, I was taken prisoner outside Gerona. I was with the rearguard of the Brigades, charged with covering the retreat. We tried to hold a position on the Ter; the Italians attacked from behind and we fell into their hands. I was wounded. Along with two other wounded comrades I was taken to a hospital run by the Italians. We weren't badly treated, but then the German fascists arrived and began to interrogate us. They knew that we were Brigaders, but what they wanted to know is whether we were Jews. We told them that we were Polish, trade union activists, and stuck to this. One day, two young Italian doctors had me and my mate come to a treatment room, supposedly to examine us. One of them took out a pack of cigarettes to offer us one, then stopped himself: 'No, don't smoke,' he said, 'it's Shabbat.' And he showed me a little Hebrew prayer-book. 'Do you think we're here voluntarily?' he said. 'No, we didn't have any choice, we were enlisted while doing our military service.'

Later we were transferred to another hospital, in Aragon. The atmosphere there wasn't good; there were wounded Nationalist soldiers as well as Republican prisoners. A priest came and incited the Spaniards against us: 'How many priests have you shot?' he kept asking. Then there was another hospital again, in Zaragoza, where we were helped by International Red Aid, which operated illicitly. Later I was sent to the fortress of San Pedro de Gardénia, along with my two comrades. There were hundreds of *brigadista* prisoners here. The situation was difficult. The Spanish administration was backed up by a Gestapo unit and an 'anti-Comintern section'. But we were well organized and in touch with the outside.

In 1940 I was transferred to a 'labour battalion' charged with rebuilding the town of Beceite. We were treated like slaves; it was not unusual for the soldiers to shoot at us. We had to go seven kilometres to work on foot. We were dying of hunger. Then I dug tunnels in the mountains, for the army. We worked in the dark, practically without eating. In three weeks, forty of my mates died of typhus. Then I decided to escape, with two other comrades. But our plan was discovered and the soldiers beat us to pulp.

Finally I landed up at the Miranda camp on the Ebro, which had been set up for refugees fleeing France after the Nazi invasion. We, the prisoners of war, were responsible for major works and for the maintenance of the camp, we did the cooking, some people acted as interpreters. There were only two hundred of us among 4,000 refugees, but we ran the camp.

When the Germans arrived close to the Spanish frontier, refugees and prisoners were gripped by despair. But the camp commander knew that without us the camp would fall into anarchy, and gave his word of honour that he would open the gates if the Germans crossed the frontier. But they didn't do this.

Later on, the negotiations that the English and Americans were having with the Francoist authorities with a view to the liberation of prisoners began to bear fruit. Lists of comrades who were 'releasable' were drawn up. As a representative of the Polish prisoners – then of Polish refugees – I was one of the last to leave. But unlike most of the others, I didn't choose to go to London, which was the seat of the provisional Polish government that was hostile to the communists. Among the refugees there was a former police commissioner from Lvov, who had recognized me. I managed to obtain a certificate allowing me to leave for Palestine. The German and Italian detainees were not so lucky; they were handed over to the authorities of their respective countries. That was in 1944.

At the end of this long and painful imprisonment in Spain, Shlomo Szlein's journey reached a fork in the road, both personally and politically. As soon as he could, he left for Palestine, where the former cadre of the Polish Communist Party became a fighter in the Haganah – a transfer of his utopia that was in no way exceptional for Yiddishland revolutionaries in the wake of the Second World War.

Shalom Chiloni, president of the association of International Brigade veterans living in Israel, who similarly 'forked' in the direction of Palestine and Zionism after the war in Spain, believed that this was the real test of faith, the crossroads for these activists. He was a communist when he arrived in Spain, but no longer one when he left and was interned in a French camp. It was clear for him that there was an intimate and direct relationship between the defeat of the Republic, the failure of the Brigades, and the orientation of official communist policy. When he tried to raise these problems among his comrades, he was expelled from the party and isolated. From that time on, he pursued a different 'great dream', militating for a different cause, without having the feeling of reneging on the fundamental aspirations that had led him into the camp of communism, or ceasing to see himself as a 'pioneer' in search of radical solutions to put an end to the misery and discrimination that his people suffered – by participating in the construction of a Jewish state in Palestine. After a career as a high official in Israel, he believes today that the verdict of history vindicates him against those of his comrades who remained loyal to their communist faith after the Spanish defeat: have not many of them ended up, several decades later, following the same path as he and accepting the evidence of the facts by leaving 'socialist' Poland, Romania and Yugoslavia for Israel? Even if it appears paradoxical in more than one respect, he remains convinced today that, for a Jewish revolutionary, the road leading from Albacete to Tel Aviv was more consistent and right than that which led from Madrid in the late 1930s, via Moscow or Paris, to Warsaw in the 1950s.

4.

Silent Starry Night

> The starry night is silent
> and the ice burns like fire.
> Do you remember how I taught you
> to use a pistol?
> > Song of the Warsaw ghetto

From the anti-fascist struggle and the Resistance movements in various European countries, a singular and paradoxical figure emerges: that of the Jewish fighter, whether engaged in the national movements struggling against occupation or waging his own war, the men and women of the Main-d'oeuvre immigrée with their 'unpronounceable' names and the insurgents of the Warsaw ghetto.

A singular figure: the image of the Jew in the face of Nazism that history has retained is not that of the Resistance fighter but that of the victim, the long convoys heading for Auschwitz or Treblinka, the gas chambers and crematoria; while the image of the Resistance is that of patriotic national movements – sometimes to the point of chauvinism: 'To every man his *boche!*'

What, then, is the place among all these stereotypes of those whom the Vichy propagandists called *métèques* ('half-breeds'), the stateless, the cosmopolitan, and whom the Nazi warlords in Poland saw as sheep letting themselves be calmly led to the slaughter? Are these Resistance fighters simply the exception that confirms the rule?

In that case, though, how is it possible that one need only scratch lightly the veneer of 'patriotic resistance' in Paris, from summer 1941 on, and examine more closely its armed actions, to find the indelible mark of the Jewish immigrant worker, the militant of the communist MOI who believed it 'better to fall as a fighter than die as a deportee'? How is it that one need only examine carefully what the 'great patriotic war' declared by Stalin meant behind the German lines, in Byelorussia and the Baltic lands, the partisan struggles in these regions, to find again the trace of the Jewish fighter in flight from the ghetto, the 'Avengers of Vilnius' and other *maquisards* of the Minsk region? How is it that this figure of the Jewish fighter emerges even in the extermination camps: the revolt of the Auschwitz *Sonderkommando* and the rebellions in the camps of Sobibor and Treblinka?[1]

Too often, these acts of resistance are frozen in symbols and epic myths – like that of the Warsaw ghetto uprising. But in this case the legend, with its emotional and spectacular aspects and heroic songs, distorts and conceals the reality. The cult of great heroes, the petrification of the action of the martyrs in rituals of memory, only distance us from reality and lead us onto a terrain of poetic illusion, a cinemascope Resistance, vividly coloured but imaginary.

Beyond the odyssey of people like Léopold Trepper, and the sacrifice of Mordechai Aniélevitch,[2] was there really a Jewish Resistance? How was the action of the Yiddishland revolutionaries continued – or interrupted – by the war? Did the figure of the Jewish combatant acquire a sufficient profile to stand against that of the victim and martyr who accepts his lot as the blow of fate?

This Resistance did exist, and was quite different from the image given by the rose-tinted stereotypes. This is what we learned from our meetings with militants who were engaged on different fronts, from the Bulgarian labour camps to support networks for children in Lyon. Its texture was not that of the heroic gesture immortalized in a snapshot; its constant themes were hunger and fear, missed encounters, tiresome tasks, boredom and greyness, pain and anguish. The

---

1   *Sonderkommando*: the 'special unit' composed of prisoners in the Nazi extermination camps forced to participate in the process of the 'final solution'. [Editors' note.]

2   A militant in Hashomer Hatzaïr, the military commander of the Warsaw ghetto insurrection, who committed suicide when the battle was lost.

individuals whom we interviewed did not conduct Red Orchestras or lead Combat Organizations; they committed themselves to the Resistance without hesitation, in a movement that was quite natural, 'because it had to be done', and they acted anonymously, rarely with any glamour, and with their existence constantly in peril. It is their commitments that made up the everyday Jewish Resistance in its infinite diversity. Their stories recall this Resistance of the shadows.

What was specifically Jewish about this Resistance? Lucien Steinberg reveals this in the book he wrote on the struggle of Jews against Hitler throughout Europe. Recalling that Hitler's war against the Jews was in a certain sense a 'war within the war', he writes,

> Whereas for the non-Jewish individual participation in the Resistance increased the risks of death, for the Jewish individual this very participation gave him an additional chance to survive, more or less great according to circumstance and place ... To sum up, among all the human groups in Hitler's Europe, the Jews were the only ones who were absolutely obliged to disobey his law if they wanted to physically survive.[3]

This remark of a general character, however carefully weighed, does not take account of the conditions and forms of Jewish participation in the Resistance. Fundamentally, the conditions of struggle were different for Jews in the Western countries and in those of the East. The structure of the Jewish population was different, and the conditions in which the 'final solution' was applied were also different – as witness the absence of ghettos in the West. In Eastern Europe, Jews would find themselves tragically isolated, alone in confronting their fate, whether they met this with resignation or armed resistance – a situation that Manès Sperber laconically sums up as follows: 'The ghetto explosions shook up the atmosphere. The Poles slept.'[4] In Western Europe, on the other hand, Jewish resistance was integrated into the

---

3   Lucien Steinberg, *La révolte des justes: Les juifs contre Hitler 1933–1945* (Paris: Fayard, 1970).

4   Manès Sperber, *Qu'une larme dans l'océan* (Paris: Calman-Lévy, 1952), pp. 182–3.

context of national movements: the fighters of the MOI were attached to the France-Tireurs et Partisans Français (FTPF), their leader Louis Gronowski reporting to Jacques Duclos. Yet this combat took different forms according to the particular situation. It was not accidental that a detachment made up exclusively of Jewish fighters was formed within the FTPF-MOI framework in early 1942. Conversely, it was not as a Jew, but as a highly competent military strategist, that Joseph Epstein (Colonel Gilles), a Yiddishland revolutionary, communist, veteran of Spain and escapee from prisoner-of-war camp, became head of the FTPF in Paris in 1943. Similarly in Bulgaria, there were many Jews among the partisans, and they considered themselves first and foremost Bulgarian resisters; there was very little anti-Semitism in Bulgaria before the Second World War.

It could be said that under the German occupation, refusing to wear the yellow star, obtaining false papers and working under a false name was in these circumstances, for a Jew, already an act of resistance, a battle and a challenge to the adversary. One Spanish veteran told us that after escaping from the camp at Le Vernet at the start of the war, he went to Paris 'to melt into the crowd'. We asked him what he had done then – had he joined the Resistance?

Not at all, I led a normal life. I worked throughout the war; I was a winder in a company making electric motors. I passed as a Catalan, I was lucky not to 'look Jewish', as people used to say, or have a typical accent. I went everywhere without papers, I had decided once and for all that this was less dangerous than to show a Polish passport giving my first name as Isaac. I always managed to get by. In the factory, however, there was a bloke who suspected that I wasn't in a regular situation; he was a nasty piece of work, a Croix-de-feu member. One day he called me a 'dirty kike'; it wasn't so much the insult that bothered me, but the danger of word spreading around that I was Jewish. Then one of my mates, an Alsatian who knew that I'd come back from the Spanish war, went up to the Croix-de-feu type and said: 'Drop it, or I'll punch your face in!' So things went quiet. When the Service du Travail Obligatoire [STO] was started, I managed to convince the boss that I couldn't go off to Germany, without going into details.

It goes without saying that the chutzpah and sangfroid that enabled this Jewish man to 'get by' for four years in a Paris occupied by the Germans and patrolled by the French police under their orders was not accidental. The man who waged this 'private' resistance, without a fuss, was a militant who had been prepared politically and psychologically for this dangerous existence by his years of struggle in Poland, France and Spain; but how much less desperate this was than the lot of those thousands of people who unresistingly climbed into the buses taking them to the Vel' d'Hiv on 16–17 July 1942.[5]

Basically, the Nazi racial lunacy condemned all European Jews to the same death sentence, no matter what their origin and their social category. This was particularly apparent after the sadly famous conference at Wannsee on 20 June 1942. Yet not all European Jews were prepared in the same way, by their social background, mental attitude and political convictions, to confront this situation. Thus, while there certainly was in France a Jewish Resistance, or a Jewish dimension of the Resistance with certain specific characteristics, it would be wrong to say that this was the action of French Jews. In these exceptional circumstances, despite themselves, there were Jews on both sides of the barricades, as there had been before the war and would again be after. On the eve of the Second World War there was no such thing as a Jewish community in France, but, as Pierre Vidal-Naquet puts it, 'a *plural* ensemble whose limits and boundaries were strictly speaking indefinable'. Two antagonistic poles, however, openly and bitterly so, were constituted on the one hand by those assimilated dignitaries of whom some even sympathized with the far right, and on the other hand by the lower strata of recent immigrants from Yiddishland who were strongly influenced by radical currents – communist, Bundist, left Poale Zion. Was it by accident that in 1943 one group provided the personnel of the UGIF, a creation of the Gestapo for which it drew up lists of Jewish children, while the other blended into the ranks of armed Resistance in Paris, Lyon, Grenoble, Toulouse and Marseille?

5   The Vélodrome d'Hiver, or Vel' d'Hiv, was an indoor stadium for cycle racing, and the first destination for many of the 13,000 Jews whom the Nazis and French police rounded up on 16–17 July 1942. [Translator's note.]

Nor is it accidental that the Vichy authorities made a distinction that was not simply 'tactical' between Jews who were French by origin and foreign Jewish refugees. If at the start of the war they went beyond the Nazi demands as regards the census, internment and subsequent deportation of the latter group, it required a far stronger pressure of Himmler's men and the collaboration 'ultras' for similar measures to be applied to the former. Enemy number one for Vichy was the immigrant, the 'half-breed', the cosmopolitan whose attachment to the international communist conspiracy was scarcely in doubt.

There was a basic kernel of truth in this madness. It would be hard to imagine the 'Israelite' president of a board of directors, the senior army officer, the business lawyer – 'Israelite' being more respectable than 'Jew', as these dignitaries themselves said – suddenly breaking with all the instilled mental attitudes of respect for authority, administration, legality, etc., and going to throw bombs and derail trains, whereas embarking on Resistance, underground struggle and the hazardous forms of existence this implied represented far less of a rupture for the immigrant from Yiddishland who had worked for years on the black in illegal workshops on the boulevard Poissonière, or the militant who had known the rigours of repression in interwar Poland, or the anti-fascist who had crossed ten frontiers with false papers in order to go and fight in Spain. Besides, there is the question of social and political consciousness. This category of Jews from the East had a far more realistic perception of German fascism than did the dignitaries of the consistory whose response to Kristallnacht had been to minimize the anti-Semitic outrages in Germany. They knew what mass anti-Semitism and the anti-Semitism of the state pogromists could lead to, they or their family had often experienced this in the flesh, they knew that no accommodation or compromise with this barbarism was possible, they perceived the impending confrontation with death in its full dimensions. Those of them who had come from Germany, and those who had been in Spain, had long since known that Hitler wanted war, that his triumph would inevitably lead to a European conflagration; they were the last to fall into the illusion of Munich.

Even in the East, or in Poland, the application of the 'final solution' did not put an end to the conflicts of class and interest that divided the Jewish community. Hannah Arendt was much criticized for having written in her book on the Eichmann trial that the *Judenräte*, the Jewish councils set up in the ghettos by the Nazis, bore a share of responsibility for the fate that befell the ghetto populations. Léon Poliakov considers that, with all the reproaches that can be made against certain of the *Judenrat* leaders, 'historically, the Jewish councils were inevitable'. Gershom Scholem, for his part, resolved the problem by saying that 'among their members, some were monsters and others saints'.

But this problem can be tackled from a different perspective than that of moral or historical responsibility: that of social attitudes. In the Warsaw ghetto, workers either continued to work in the factories set up by the Germans, or if they were unemployed they died of hunger. Those who sat on the *Judenräte* and enjoyed certain privileges from this had not been productive workers before the war, but individuals whose competence in matters of organization, management and administration fitted them for this task. Politically, they were not extremists or radicals, but people from the right-minded middle, the party of common sense, along with a few adventurers; their natural movement was to do everything to 'limit the damage' – even after the Germans had deported four-fifths of the ghetto, and despite alarming news from other ghettoes – rather than preaching revolt. In the few cases where communists or other representatives of radical currents infiltrated the *Judenräte* (as in Minsk), this was to strengthen resistance and not to 'administer' the impossible. Before examining the problem in moral terms, it should first be noted that on the whole, in these exceptional circumstances, social allegiances continued to determine the respective trajectories of both sides; it was not Jewish dignitaries who set up the Combat Organization of the Warsaw ghetto, and it was not class-conscious workers who managed the catastrophe under the vigilant eye of the SS.

In his essay on French Israelites' attitudes towards Nazism from 1930 to 1940, Maurice Rajsfus gives several examples of what he sees as the blindness of the Jewish bourgeoisie in France (also, in some cases, their German counterparts) towards the rise of fascism in Europe.[6] He recalls how, for them in general, the most fearsome enemy was certainly not Mussolini, whose muscular nationalism and sense of order aroused lively sympathy, and not even Hitler, whose ravings were scarcely taken seriously until 1933, and whom they tended to consider even later as a braggart with no future – no, the real enemy was Moscow, the Soviets, the communist movement, the spectre of collectivism. Most often deaf and blind to the coming catastrophe, these worthies prized above all their loyalty to the existing state and its institutions; their patriotism worked overtime, and as French Jews they noisily expressed their concern about the influx of Jewish refugees, even German ones after Hitler's seizure of power in 1933. As for German Jews, they waxed indignant at the campaign to boycott German products launched after Kristallnacht.

Kurt Tucholsky, the radical German-Jewish writer and lucid witness of the Weimar Republic, invented the character of 'Herr Wendriner', one of these Jewish bourgeois content in his skin and in his country, a caricature true to life, like a drawing by Georg Grosz. Herr Wendriner's sleepless nights are filled with stock exchange quotations; his visits to the barber are the occasion for long chauvinist tirades and homilies against the Bolsheviks; when he attends a funeral it is to talk business; and when the time comes to salute by extending one's arm, he salutes like everyone else … Was the attitude towards Nazism of so many Wendriners in France, Germany and Poland anything but the extension of what had seemed to them most 'reasonable' before danger threatened?

The most conscious fraction of the Jewish workers, those most inured to political struggle, reacted differently. For them there was no radical break between pre-war conditions and those of the war: in these aggravated conditions they continued to militate for the same cause.

The odyssey of Pierre Sherf is typical in this respect. Wounded in Spain, he returned to Paris, renewed his contact with the party, and was active until the declaration of war. Then he enlisted in the

6   Rajsfus, *Sois juif et tais-toi!*.

French army, fought and was taken prisoner, spending two years in a POW camp. He was returned to Paris ill and sent to the Val-de-Grâce military hospital, where he was visited by his wife and by comrades already active in the Resistance. So when he returned to civilian life in March 1943, he could immediately 'resume service'; he took part in Resistance work among Romanian immigrants in France, then became a cadre in the underground MOI.

The anti-fascist radicalism of this kind of militant was undivided and complete. What Mélinée Manouchian said of the Armenian Resistance fighters is perfectly applicable here to their Jewish comrades in battle: 'Everything prepared us for an underground existence. Like Marx's proletariat, we had nothing to lose; doubly persecuted, as foreigners and as Communists, we had endurance to pain, and from our childhood no longer feared either cold or hunger.'[7]

Janine Sochachewska, one of the leaders of Jewish resistance in Lyon (the 'La Carmagnole' group), adds,

> I was young, I was strong, I had a moral strength as never before. It was not just the Jewish spark that awoke in me – I am Jewish despite myself, because it is impossible to free yourself from an education, a culture, although my whole life I have been among Poles. I struggled because I was a Communist, and because my country, Poland, was occupied, and because France was occupied.[8]

This statement is an excellent basis for examining the Resistance activity of those eastern Jews who were immigrants in France. They knew very well that it was impossible to make a deal with fascism, and the pact between Stalin and Hitler at the start of the war did not convince them to the contrary.

'Did I agree with the German–Soviet pact? At the bottom of my soul, no,' wrote Louis Gronowski, leader of the MOI:

> I remember my disarray, the inner conflict. This pact was repugnant to me, it went against my sentiments, against everything I had maintained

---

7   *Libération*, 24 June 1975.
8   *Le monde diplomatique*, 26 April 1981.

until then in my statements and writings. For all those years, we had presented Hitlerite Germany as the enemy of humanity and progress, and above all, the enemy of the Jewish people and the Soviet Union. And now the Soviet Union signed a pact with its sworn enemy, permitting the invasion of Poland and even taking part in its partition. It was the collapse of the whole argument forged over these long years. But I was a responsible Communist cadre, and my duty was to overcome my disgust.[9]

And yet, a few days after the signing of the pact, when the front pages of the newspaper displayed the photo of a smiling Stalin alongside Hitler's envoy Ribbentrop and the German army was marching into Poland, Adam Rayski, another cadre of the MOI, wrote in the organization's Yiddish-language paper *Naïe presse*,

Let the name of Adolf Hitler disappear forever! Cursed for always the idea of National Socialism! No one wanted this war except Hitler and his clique ... He will drown in the sea of blood that he is preparing to spill; beneath the ruins of his destruction he will find death.[10]

This was in no way the tone of the PCF, despite the MOI being closely dependent on it; until the end of 1940 the party continued to put forward slogans that were quite ambiguous in the context of the time, such as the 'expropriation without compensation of big Jewish and non-Jewish capitalists to the benefit of the popular collectivity'.

This dilemma facing Jewish communists at the start of the war, this contradiction between their visceral anti-fascism and what was now presented to them as an imperative of realpolitik for the USSR, crops up in the statements of our witnesses: 'When explanations are really needed, when people really look for them, they always end up finding them', Max Technitchek remarks, mentioning the way in which he had to convince himself at this time that once again Stalin was right:

9   Louis Gronowski, *Le dernier grand soir* (Paris: Éditions du Seuil, 1980), p. 117.

10   Adam Rayski, 'Être communiste et juif en France au temps du Pacte germano-soviétique', *Les nouveaux cahiers*, 68, Spring 1982.

At the beginning of the war I found myself, like many foreign refugees in France, enlisted as a 'volunteer' in the French army. I saw the weapons we were given, and understood right away that we were going to lose the war. Rifles dating from before 1914 against Hitler's armies ... I knew that France and England were not prepared for this confrontation. But this only strengthened me in my convictions: the pact between Hitler and Stalin was naturally a shock to me, but I ended up telling myself that basically things were complicated. The Munich agreements had isolated the USSR, and I found it normal that it should try and extract itself from this hornet's nest. Also, I didn't know the secret clauses of the pact that handed part of Poland to the USSR; I felt that France and England dreamed of a war between Germany and the Soviet Union – in short, I ended up considering the signature of the pact as a legitimate tactical manoeuvre on the part of the USSR.

'We were disoriented,' Isaac Kotlarz adds:

On the one hand there was the propaganda of the Communist Party in favour of the German–Soviet pact, on the other hand the Red Army seemed to be on the skids in Finland. After Munich, we no longer placed any trust in the France of Daladier – besides, we had already been well and truly scalded by the non-intervention policy of the Blum government in Spain. France run by people like Weygand and Gamelin meant the victory of confusion: we were well aware that it would all end in catastrophe. Those who were party members were in expectant mood, awaiting instructions.

In actual fact, the unease of these militants would continue until Hitler's invasion of the Soviet Union, which they learned, one of them notes, with a relief that was paradoxical but none the less immense. They had finally found their political compass again, recovered their footing; in short, they would be able to launch all their forces into the struggle against the Nazis without the fear of sinning against the 'line'. Adam Rayski: 'And so, for us to become ourselves once again – that is, Jews, Frenchmen, anti-fascists – we needed Hitler's aggression, termed "criminal", against the "homeland of socialism".'

It is all the more remarkable that, in the depths of their disarray, these combatants began to establish structures and draw up perspectives of action that often set them in the vanguard of the Resistance in France.

Louis Gronowski recalls in his memoirs that while certain leaders of the French Communist Party were engaged in negotiations with the German occupation authorities with a view to obtaining authorization for *L'Humanité* to reappear, immigrant militants began individually to orient themselves towards actions against the occupation. Up to the invasion of the USSR by the German armies, in June 1941, the PCF leadership was opposed to any propaganda against the occupiers, and still more so to any action; but immigrants were already active in sabotage of German airfields and in the mines of the Nord. From autumn 1940, Gronowski says, the political and military apparatus of the MOI was reshaped and ready to act. In July and August 1941, the Jeunesses communistes (JC) organized the first demonstrations against the occupation in Paris. Many young foreign Jewish militants took part in these. One of them, Tyszelman, a very popular figure in the JC, was arrested on 13 August along with a French militant, Gautherot, while taking part in an illegal demonstration; they were shot a few days later, their condemnation proclaimed on Paris walls by one of the first *Bekanntmachungen*, which would be followed by many more. On 23 August, another JC militant, the future Colonel Fabien, shot a German officer at the Barbès metro station. 'I've avenged Titi' (Tyszelman), he cried out. This action was reputedly the first armed initiative against the Germans in France. Fabien was accompanied by another militant whose name proclaimed his foreign origin: Lucien Brustlein.

To be sure, not all these Jewish proletarians and petty artisans from Central and Eastern Europe who found themselves in France under the occupation were engaged in the Resistance to a single man. Tens of thousands of them died together with their families, non-combatant victims, in the death camps. It is their figures, bent, humiliated and starving, and the piles of their dead bodies, that are the essential focus of the historical research, literature and film devoted to the fate of European Jews during the Second World War.

But an active minority struggled and most often continued to struggle. This was not just with the energy of despair, when, as Léon Poliakov puts it, the final solution could no longer be ignored; Jewish resisters began to be active in Paris even before the Vel' d'Hiv round-up and the first deportations. It was particularly when organizations and traditions of struggle already existed that the combat was pursued – or renewed – in new forms.

Some people have maintained that in the face of absolute horror and genocide 'any resistance was impossible' (Hannah Arendt), or again that 'in such circumstances, to die fighting, singing psalms, veiling the gaze of children with one's hand, or screaming with fear and despair, were strictly identical behaviours'.[11] This may be true in relation to the situation of deportees arriving on the ramp at Auschwitz and headed for immediate gassing, but it was certainly not the case for the situation of all Jews in Hitler's Europe. Those who resisted were not simply, as Léon Poliakov writes, exceptions who 'shone with an incomparable brilliance',[12] but rather a category whose behaviour as a minority in the face of adversity had very clear social, cultural and political roots.

They were, moreover, so little the exception that Poliakov himself cites the figure of 15 to 30 per cent of Jews in the French Resistance. Even if this figure is exaggerated, the question that has to be raised is not 'why did so few Jews resist?' but rather 'why, in proportion, were there so few native French in the patriotic Resistance in France, why was the percentage of foreigners so high, particularly that of Jews from Eastern Europe?' As one of their number, a member of the Manouchian group, said shortly before his arrest in late 1943, 'I only did what had to be done; if more people in this country had done as much, the situation would have been quite different.'

The answer to the question raised here can largely be found already in the previous chapters. It remains true that this situation brings to light a strange paradox. In all the European countries occupied by the Nazis, resistance developed on a national basis, rooted in national

---

11   Richard Marienstras, *Être un peuple en diaspora* (Paris: Maspero, 1975), p. 17.

12   Léon Poliakov, *Le bréviaire de la haine: Le 3e Reich et les juifs*, with a preface by François Mauriac (Paris: Calmann-Lévy, 1951), p. 257.

sentiment; it was a patriotic resistance. Yet behind this generally accepted fact – did not Stalin himself put proletarian international-ism in cold storage, proclaiming that this was the time of the great patriotic war and liquidating the Comintern in 1943? – the reality was more complex: first of all, because the struggle of the Resistance was combined, at the national and patriotic level, with the social dimension of the struggle: the hundreds of thousands of workers and peasants who mobilized in Greece, France, Yugoslavia, etc., against the occupier were struggling for the liberation of national ter-ritory, for the defeat of fascism, but also so that 'nothing should be as it was' in their respective countries, in terms of social organiza-tion and political structures; for a world from which the conditions that gave rise to the barbarity of fascism would disappear forever – it was this combination that made for the specifically revolutionary dimension of the Resistance. It is also what explains the tensions and conflicts over strategy that divided the Resistance in each country, leading to a rift within the Resistance in states such as Greece and Yugoslavia, and, in a country like France, to the complex antago-nisms between the different tendencies of which its precarious unity was woven.

We should also note that the patriotism or nationalism of the Resistance was not necessarily the same among those at the top and among those at the bottom. For someone like de Gaulle, it meant above all the *union sacrée* of the nation against the occupier, around leaders determined to restore after the war the traditional forms of 'democracy' and the old order; for a rank-and-file communist mili-tant, it meant above all expelling the occupiers by a mass mobilization, a radical struggle that would sketch the outline of a new world.

Jewish combatants in the Resistance were uprooted émigrés straddling several cultures, swept up by the course of history and nat-urally internationalist; how did they find their place in this patriotic Resistance, and could they find an ideological anchorage? How could they accept, as Jews, the frequent outbursts of chauvinism?

The head of the MOI recalls that it was not always easy, when the organization undertook its first terrorist actions, to convince militants educated in an internationalist spirit that every German soldier was an enemy, a *Boche* that it was legitimate to get rid of. This problem arose also for Max Technitchek, despite his rapid rallying to the new line:

> I was, I believe, a true internationalist. I hated the Nazis not simply because they were anti-Semites, but above all because they were racists in general, despising Slavs and French. On the other hand, however, I was not shocked by the patriotic character of the Resistance. In France, I understood the policy of the national front as a continuation of the Popular Front policy. In order to win, the whole people had to be united, including large fractions of the bourgeoisie. The population had to be mobilized around general themes, such as liberty, independence. And then, if you wanted to mobilize the mass of French people, you had to play on the emotional and patriotic wellsprings, accept saying *Boche* rather than 'Nazi' or 'German'. On condition, of course, that this was understood as just being a tactic, limited in time and adapted to an exceptional situation.

The majority of Jewish Resistance fighters undoubtedly subscribed to the same type of 'realist' argument. They accepted the national patriotic character of the Resistance as a fait accompli, a necessity. Besides, their 'being-in-the-world' as émigrés was infinitely variable: many of them were young people, even adolescents who had arrived in France in early childhood, who spoke French without an accent, knew certain quarters of Paris like the back of their hand, were integrated into groups of young people whom they played sports with, went on excursions with, militated with – in other words, they were young Parisians from the popular quarters, not greatly distinguished from any others, except for the fact of speaking Yiddish at home. These young people who viewed France as their adopted homeland did not feel foreign to the national sentiment that inspired the Resistance. In the streets of occupied Paris, they felt far more at ease than did the older Jewish militants who had gone to school in Poland and could get rid neither of their raucous accent nor of the habit of 'skirting the walls' and furtively turning round to see if they were being followed. If they accepted this national dimension of the Resistance struggle, however, they did not believe that the specific dimension of their Jewish struggle had to disappear.

From the start of the war, the Jewish group of the MOI was the best-structured and most active; it would provide the cadres of the Organisation spéciale, responsible for major acts of terrorism and sabotage; it would also supply almost all the militants of the Travail allemand, the work of propaganda and demoralization among the German troops – work that was extremely dangerous, and internationalist par excellence, carried out for the most part by women. In cafés and other public places frequented by the Wehrmacht, young women who spoke German sought to make contact, starting with an anodyne conversation on how hard times were, the absurdity of the war, by way of which they sought to 'situate' their conversation partner: as a fanatical Nazi, indifferent, former socialist or communist, etc. If the exchange proved positive, the discussion could take a more open turn at the next meeting; sometimes anti-fascist leaflets written in German were scattered, left on cinema seats, in restaurant toilets, etc. This work did indeed bear fruit; groups of German soldiers were formed in contact with the Resistance, information was transmitted, uniforms and weapons supplied to combatants. Sometimes, too, militants of the Travail allemand were denounced to the Gestapo and paid for this activity with their lives. Rachel Schatz, who was active in the Resistance in Lyon, recalls that the Parc de la tête d'or was a favoured place for the Travail allemand: women militants entered into conversation with soldiers, leaving leaflets on the benches and posting stickers:

> One of my friends, too, went to work for the Germans. This was doubly dangerous work. On the one hand, she collected material and information under the cover of 'doing the cleaning'; on the other hand, her Resistance activity required her to hang around in public places with Germans and be taken for a collaborationist, a soldiers' girl, one of those whose heads were shaved at liberation. But she brought round several German soldiers to work with the Resistance.

Throughout the war, in France, the existence of an underground Jewish press in both French and Yiddish, basically initiated by the communists, attests to the existence of a Jewish Resistance. In May 1943 it celebrated the courage of the Warsaw ghetto fighters, whose insurrection had just been crushed. Many other indications also manifest the desire to emphasize the part played in the struggle by Jews. Thus, in 1944, an MOI circular designed for PCF cadres called for the creation of Jewish units with the perspective of the battle for the liberation of Paris. The argument here was particularly clear:

> At this time, the thousands of Jews in the ranks of the Forces Françaises de l'Intérieur [FFI] are seen as French, Polish, etc. citizens, not as Jews. We want to destroy the reactionary and fascist lies that claim Jews cannot be soldiers or fighters. At the same time, we will break the chauvinist and wait-and-see policy of the Jewish reactionaries. [The point is] to show the world that Jews, just like other peoples, have the right to life and happiness.

This was a somewhat premonitory text. After liberation, the desire to wrap the Resistance up for posterity in the tricolour, and affirm its essentially patriotic character to the detriment of its social dimension, often led memoirists and historians to push this *métèque* face of the Resistance into the shadows – the *Mémoires* of Jacques Duclos, and Charles Tillon's book on the Francs-Tireurs et Partisans, scarcely speak of it, just to cite those Resistance leaders who were in direct contact with the action of foreigners, and Jewish partisans in particular, by force of circumstances. Does it damage the patriotic image of the Resistance to accept that during the year 1943 the greater part of partisan actions in Paris were the act of foreigners, activists in the MOI, up to the great raid that came down on them in the autumn? Is it a sin against internationalism to recognize, behind the 'Polish', 'Hungarian', 'Romanian' or 'Czech' partisan, the Yiddishland revolutionary, the traditions of struggle he or she pursued, their culture, their language, and the particular resonance of their name? It was not because, on the infamous *affiche rouge*, the Nazis exposed to public vindictiveness the 'Hungarian Jew' Elek and the 'Polish Jew' Rayman, making their Jewishness an argument against the Resistance as a whole, described as an 'army of crime', that the Jewish dimension of Rayman and Elek's struggle and commitment became a factor best no longer alluded to. The intransigence of their anti-fascism, their courage to act, were clearly rooted in a consciousness for which the communist ideal and the sense of their Jewish identity were indissociable. It was no accident that their action, that of the combatants of the *affiche rouge*, became a symbol of the revolutionary spirit of the Resistance.

In the years after the end of the war this revolutionary spirit of the Resistance continued to disturb, and not only those whom one might logically expect to reject it. In 1951, Artur London, one of the leaders of the MOI, and responsible in particular for the Travail allemand before being deported to Mauthausen, was arrested in Czechoslovakia in the context of the Slansky affair. He was stupefied to hear his interrogator demand that he should acknowledge that the MOI, 'whose three leading figures were Jews', was 'a section of the Trotskyist Fourth International': 'The very fact that despite being Jewish you returned alive [from Mauthausen] is proof of your culpability and proves us right.'[13]

As we have said, not all the Yiddishland militants involved in the Resistance were made of heroic material. They joined the struggle like anyone else, without pretensions, because this commitment struck them as a necessity at the time. Léa Stein, a Yugoslav communist and veteran of Spain, joined the Resistance in France by a circuitous route. In 1938, after being demobilized from the International Brigades (where she was a nurse), she found herself in Paris along with her husband, a *brigadista* of Austrian origin whom she met in Spain. She was pregnant. In early summer 1938, the situation of immigrants in France was aggravated by the new regulation that removed the few rights they had gained under the Popular Front: Léa Stein's husband was assigned residence in a village in the south-west. When the war with Germany broke out, he was arrested along with other German citizens in France, anti-fascists and Jewish refugees included, and interned in a camp in the Pyrenees:

---

13   London, *The Confession*, p. 151.

I was responsible for one newborn baby and I was pregnant again; I heard it said that it was possible to be repatriated to Yugoslavia from Marseille. I had a terrible desire to go home, so I left for Marseille with my baby and a bulging belly; Yugoslav and Italian comrades arranged things for me. In Marseille they were beginning to register Jews; I asked at the Yugoslav consulate for a repatriation certificate, but I was refused this, as I was in their records as a communist. What to do? I feared I would be arrested, so I decided to return to Paris, in the occupied zone. A smuggler got me across the demarcation line. In Paris I made contact again with comrades from the Yugoslav Communist Party, and obtained a foreigner's residence card by using my sister's papers. It was then that the party, knowing that I spoke German, asked me to go and work in the Nazi administrative apparatus.

In the countries of Western Europe, as we have seen, the Jewish Resistance was essentially integrated into the national Resistance, while often asserting its specific character and the special dimension of Jewish struggle against Nazism. In the East it was generally isolated and dramatically alone, even if, in Byelorussia, for example, the Resistance in the ghettos was in contact with Soviet partisans.

The stubborn will to survive, however, could sometimes lead in these exceptional conditions to forms of resistance that were out of the ordinary. Shlomo Strauss was mobilized into the Polish army in 1939.[14] Wounded during the German invasion, he was taken prisoner and interned in a camp. When he learned that the detainees would be divided according to their national origin, he decided to forge a new identity; he was now called Timofei Marko, the illegitimate son of a Ukrainian laundress. He grew a long Cossack moustache to fit the part.

A commission of SS and medics arrived in the camp where he was held and selected a certain number of tall and fair-haired Ukrainians whose 'racial purity' they appreciated. Marko was among these. He was transferred to Austria where he was taught the trade of a turner. His knowledge of German led him to be appointed head of this group of newly promoted 'Aryans'.

---

14   Shlomo Strauss-Marko, *Dam Tahor* (Pure Blood) (Tel Aviv: Or-am, 1978).

At Sankt Pölten, in Austria, Marko established an underground communist cell among his 'compatriots' and made contact with Austrian communists. On the eve of the offensive against the Soviet Union, the Nazis sought to form a volunteer corps from these Ukrainian ex-POWs that would fight alongside them. This was how Marko learned that Hitler was getting ready to unleash hostilities against the Soviet Union. He went to the Soviet consulate in Vienna and conveyed this information. Without much result, it would seem.

Having become a skilled worker, Marko was posted to an aircraft factory at Obergrafendorf, close to Wiener Neustadt. The communist cell that he set up carried out small acts of sabotage. Responsible for all the *Ostarbeiter* (Ukrainians, Byelorussians, Poles, etc.) in the factory, he maintained almost friendly relations with various German officers, who viewed him as a National Socialist. He took advantage of this position to try to improve the situation of the *Ostarbeiter*: abolition of corporal punishment, improvement of rations, etc. He helped some of his fellow workers escape and join the ranks of the Resistance.

Always acting in combination with the Austrian Resistance, Marko obtained and hid the plans of the Rotbach Neuenkirchen underground aircraft factory. But when the Red Army reached Austria, Marko was immediately arrested as a 'collaborator'. Interrogated relentlessly by the NKVD, in a state of exhaustion he signed the paper he was handed. When he said that he was a Polish communist, he was asked to show his card – of an illegal party dissolved by the Comintern years before. He was thrown into prison. In the end, he owed his salvation to chance: a Soviet prisoner of war whom he had helped when working in the aircraft factory. He was then interned in a camp of Soviet prisoners awaiting their repatriation – they would in fact be deported to Siberia. On return to Poland after the war, Strauss-Marko held high office in the police service before emigrating to Israel.

The combativeness of Jewish Resistance fighters was based on a paradoxical and dramatic combination of historical optimism and absolute despair; continuing to trust in the future, the basis of the pre-war revolutionary utopias, their Jewish historical optimism rested on the conviction that at the end of the day barbarism would be conquered and Nazism defeated, that the Jewish people would rise again, that a better world would be born on the ashes of the barbaric empire. Even the fighters of the Warsaw ghetto knew that, if their own battle was a desperate one, Germany had none the less begun to lose the war at Stalingrad; even those condemned to death by the *affiche rouge* knew that a near future would justify them. On the other hand, however, there was the absolute despair of those witnessing a crime that as yet still had no name, that human consciousness and their Jewish consciousness were incapable of conceiving, who witnessed the disappearance of their world. In this dead of night they often had the impression of fighting against phantoms, in an absolute dispro-portion of forces; what could bullets do against a barbarism that the highest reason and historical understanding could not even name, no more than they could conceive the future beyond this catastrophe? That is the despair of the hero of Manès Sperber's novel, at the time when the Nazis had finished razing the Warsaw ghetto:

> He felt free from everything, the gratification of a useless freedom. The freedom to commit destructive acts, to shoot one of these gaping bystanders, to set fire to a cinema filled to bursting, to kill a German officer on the public road, to kill themselves with a bullet to the heart. But there was no freedom to dream of a future, to imagine a different tomorrow. He was not free to escape his helpless being.[15]

Hunted down, cast into illegality, forced to live with false papers, to obtain food and everything else necessary to survive outside the 'normal' circuits, to live underground, the Jews who rejected the law of their persecutors under the occupation were thereby made avail-able for the Resistance; very often, therefore, the step was easily taken, particularly by young people, leading from the refusal to declare oneself at the local police station as a Jew to a more active opposition. In fact, the transition to organized resistance, if synonymous with increased risk, also meant for the new combatant the end of isolation, joining a dynamic collective with means of action and protection at its disposal.

---

15   Sperber, *Qu'une larme dans l'océan*, p. 176.

The derailing of trains, the execution of *collabos* and Nazi offic- ers, the firing of fuel dumps, throwing hand grenades in restaurants, sabotaging of industry and factories working for the occupation, the destruction of electricity pylons – these are well-known images, clichés of Resistance action. There was no action of this type in which Jewish combatants did not take part, which they did not organize, by the dozen, on all fronts, at all levels. It was Jewish partisans who prepared an attack on the German commandant of 'Gross-Paris', von Schaumburg, and then liquidated the organizer of the STO in France, Ritter. It was Epstein, an exceptional military strategist, who perfected in 1943 the tactic of attacks in successive waves against the parades of German troops in the streets of Paris. But the Resistance was also the patient and painstaking work of people like Léa Stein:

> Thanks to my knowledge of German, I managed to enter the *Werbebüro*, the recruitment centre at Pontoise. All the lists of persons due to be requisitioned for work in Germany passed through my hands; I warned the Resistance, or sometimes the interested parties directly – like the baker's son who gave me bread until the end of the war as a token of gratitude. The Germans clearly had no suspicion that I was Jewish. In 1942, however, I felt that things might turn out badly. I had lost my connections with the Yugoslav comrades, most of whom had returned to their country to fight in the ranks of the partisans. I left Pontoise …

The Resistance also included escape attempts from POW camps by the likes of Max Technitchek, where the solidarity of the detainees sought to block the discrimination that victimized Jews:

> After volunteering in the French army, I was taken prisoner at the start of operations and deported to Germany. The Resistance was very well organized in our camp; we had our underground newspapers, we organized all kinds of sabotage, we prepared escapes. I twice tried to flee and was recaptured. I was unlucky, my second escape in particu- lar had been very well prepared; I had money, papers and contacts to cross the frontiers into the 'free zone'. But at Kassel I came up against an

extraordinary control; my papers weren't sufficiently 'solid' and I was sent back to the camp.

Hanna Lévy-Hass, for her part, had never held a gun, yet she played her part in the partisan struggle in Yugoslavia. A secondary school teacher in Montenegro, and a militant in the Communist Party, she was entrusted with a particular mission after the Italian occupation: to teach peasants how to give first aid to the wounded, with the perspective of insurrection:

> It was clear from the start of hostilities that the Yugoslavs were going to rise up. When the generals capitulated, the ordinary soldiers fled back to their villages with their weapons; I saw these Montenegrin peasants returning with full boxes of munitions, I saw women building up stores in the cellars. From the beginning, the occupiers only held the cities. The mountains and villages were controlled by the insurgents who were lacking in everything, even shoes, but ready to fight.
>
> The Italians launched an offensive against the partisans in our region. I found myself in the midst of the battle; the towns and villages were bombed. I saw our first dead; the wounded flooded in. After two weeks we understood that the uprising in Montenegro would be crushed. The partisans fell back, leaving us with the wounded. The Italian army was approaching. We had to evacuate our field hospital. I saw our wounded leave under their own steam, with open wounds; they showed an amazing courage. We took refuge in the mountains, in a kind of citadel where we gathered our wounded, as well as a certain number of wounded Italians. When the Italian army arrived, we passed ourselves off as voluntary nurses acting out of humanitarianism. I spoke Italian; the officers wanted to know where the partisans were, but we kept silent. They took down our names but let us leave. On the plain, we saw the burning villages.

As a Jew, Hanna Lévy-Haas could no longer work as a teacher. After the defeat of the uprising, she found herself confined to the small town of Cetinje:

The Italian occupation was burdensome, but it was nothing compared with that of the Germans, which followed in 1943. When they laid siege to the town there were some thirty Jews there, including elderly and sick. I wanted to join the partisans. But the Jews begged me not to leave: 'If you go,' I was told, 'if one of us disappears, we will all be shot.' I gave in, and a little while after we were locked up in the town prison. We remained there for six months. We had not given up hope, we were still on Montenegrin soil, the Red Army was advancing westward, the Anglo-American armies had landed in Sicily, and the opening of a new western front seemed imminent. And then suddenly, the Germans loaded us into cattle trucks … I arrived in Bergen-Belsen in August 1944.[16]

In the Lyon Resistance, the husband of Rachel Schatz was engaged in activity that she herself defined as 'very dangerous', without going into further detail. But 'you just didn't ask questions'. Her work was to rescue Jewish children, most of whom had come clandestinely from the occupied zone. This was a special commission run by women and linked to the MOI, which took responsibility for this delicate mission in Lyon:

> The first thing was to see to the children whose life was threatened and place them in institutions, basically religious ones, or with peasants. It wasn't easy work; you had to follow rules of strict security; we had false papers, so did the children whom we took to their refuges. Sometimes you had to take the train with a whole group, and it wasn't easy to persuade a young child that he's no longer called Moshe or Yankel, but Jean or Richard. I remember a trip from Lyon to Limoges when I accompanied a group of children; I'd rehearsed them and told them to pretend to be asleep if a police control was carried out on the train. There was indeed a control; I told the gendarmes some story or other, and everything went well. Were they fooled or not? Who knows?
>
> We had set up networks for placing the children almost everywhere

---

16   Lévy-Hass, Hanna, *Journal de Bergen-Belsen 1944–45* (Paris: Éditions du Seuil, 1989).

around Lyon. In the region of Villefranche-sur-Saône, for example, there was a network that operated very well in the surrounding villages, led by a Jew and a non-Jew.

My daughter was ten years old at the time, and also placed away from Lyon by the network. She told me much later that she had been angry at me for devoting my time and energy to other people's children instead of her. She couldn't understand.

Shlomo Shamli, a Bulgarian Jew, left Hachomer Hatzaïr for the Communist Party just after the invasion of Soviet territory by the German armies. In Sofia the communist militants had collected weapons with the prospect of coming battles. Shamli took part in this activity, but Jewish men were soon requisitioned for forced labour by the Bulgarian authorities allied with Germany. He was sent from one camp to another, eventually to one close to the frontier with Greece. Bulgarian Jews were assigned to the construction of roads and railways.

The Communist Party had set up an underground organization in the camp. It developed its propaganda among forced labourers and made contact with partisans in the region. The camp officers were Bulgarian. Shamli was in touch with one of these administrators who was a party member. The others lived in fear of an attack by the partisans.

Dynamite was used for railway construction. Shamli and his comrades got hold of some and passed it to the partisans, along with weapons, clothes and shoes that they obtained in the camp:

In March 1943 we saw trains pass close to the site where we were working, taking Greek Jews to Auschwitz. We managed to get an enormous rock to fall on the tracks. The traffic was interrupted and a train blocked. We stole food from the camp and took it to the deportees in the train, trying also to convince them to escape. But most of them refused, unable to believe that they were being taken to their death. Only fifteen of them listened to us. We hid them in the camp and they later joined the partisans in the mountains.

May 1943 saw the famous – and sadly, exceptional – episode of the demonstration that prevented the deportation of Bulgarian Jews to Auschwitz. When it was announced that Jews would be transported to the Danube ports and from there to the camps, a demonstration was called in Sofia. It was held on 24 May and attracted more than 10,000 people, Jews and non-Jews alike. The police brutally intervened, arresting hundreds of people, including the chief rabbi.

On 25 and 26 May, the Jews were taken to the ports of Lom and Svistov on the Danube, but the Bulgarian authorities were forced to abandon deportation in the face of the growing mobilization of public opinion, particularly inspired by the Orthodox Church, the Writers' Association, lawyers and many personalities from the world of art and entertainment.

Pierre Sherf, in charge of the Romanian 'language group' of the MOI in Paris, saw to the 'little tasks' that made up the everyday activity of the Resistance militant: circulating forged banknotes and ration tickets 'expropriated' by the combatants, manufacturing false documents of all kinds and organizing solidarity with the families of the deported. Then he was entrusted with the task of organizing liaison with MOI groups in the north and east of France, where Polish and Italian miners were particularly active. Rail tracks were sabotaged, electricity lines brought down, German soldiers disarmed and killed, strikes organized in the mines, and so on. Each month, Sherf's partner, who was also his liaison agent, visited groups, delivering political reports, ration cards, weapons, etc. Sometimes Sherf himself visited, sleeping in miners' homes and leaving at daybreak: 'They didn't always know that it was the Communist Party', he says; 'most of them were non-party, or just party sympathizers – but they knew what racism was'. Sometimes, too, he had to decide on a difficult problem, a case of conscience:

> There was a partisan commander in the Briey basin, a Polish Jew, famous for his courage; one day he had two fighters who had refused to take part in an action shot. What should be done? Finally, we expelled him from the party. Later, an MOI leader said that he would have decorated him for his courage then arrested him for his brutality.

During the Paris insurrection, Sherf was a commander in the patriotic militia; then he took part in the liberation of northern France on
the heels of the American army. But in December 1945 he was summoned for still more pressing tasks: Romania was in the process of
swinging to the camp of 'socialism' Stalin-style; the Communist Party
there needed all its cadres.

In countries such as France, the repression that fell on Jews,
including foreigners, was relatively gradual, massive deportations
being preceded by alarm signals of all kinds, discriminatory measures. Militants thus had time to prepare for battle. But in the East, in
Poland in particular, the picture was different; from the very first days
of the German occupation terror reigned across the whole country,
with massive arrests among the leaders of Polish political parties and
the intelligentsia – 180 professors of Cracow university were arrested
and sent to concentration camps. As far as Jews were concerned, the
Nazis consistently applied a policy of isolating them from the rest of
society, starting by imposing the yellow star, then forbidding any collaboration between Jewish and Polish institutions, then encouraging
bands of Polish lumpenproletarians to carry out pogroms, then forbidding Jews to travel by train (January 1940), then sending them to
forced labour camps (from February 1940) – a policy of segregation
that culminated in the construction of ghettoes: the Warsaw ghetto
was established in November 1940.

The Jewish communists, the Bundists and the socialist Zionists
thus found themselves in danger of death by virtue of being Jewish
and revolutionary. Before the question arose of taking part in the
struggle against Nazism, they thought first of all of saving their own
skins. For many of them, salvation lay in the part of Poland occupied
by the Red Army under the clauses of the Molotov–Ribbentrop pact.

This meant a brusque rupture with no return in the existence
of these women and men, a new chapter that opened, despite the
great diversity of their 'Soviet' trajectories: for some, struggle in the
ghettos or in the ranks of partisans in Byelorussia or Lithuania; for
others, deportation to Siberia; for others again, adaptation to the
Soviet system, acquisition of Soviet citizenship, with the benefits
and dangers of such a situation. The testimonies of those who found

themselves caught up in this torment illustrate the contrast between the situation in the West and that created in the East by the German invasion.

When the Wehrmacht fell on Poland, Isaac Safrin, a radical but non-party student, was working during the vacation at a children's home in Warsaw. 'Leave immediately!' his father insisted, 'go to Russia!' He knew that his son had drawn attention to himself at university by virulent articles against the Nazis, published in various political and cultural magazines. Isaac hesitated; his mother was against his leaving, believing that things would soon 'settle down'. But his father insisted: 'Leave. Then at least one of us will survive.' A clear-sighted prediction: Isaac Safrin was the sole survivor.

In the early days of October 1939, Safrin thus left Warsaw in quite adventurous conditions:

> I was asked to accompany handicapped children to the Soviet-occupied zone, and accepted. But I did not have a pass. On the other hand, I did have one for the children, made out in Russian by the Soviet authorities. I thus thought of a ruse. Although I didn't know Russian, I learned by heart the text of the pass and translated it into German. Then I presented myself at the Kommandantur, asked to be received by the major, quickly showed him the document and read it to him in both Russian and German – but adding my own name to it. This worked; we received an official document from the Gestapo authorizing us to leave the part of Poland occupied by the Germans. The officer even said, 'Go, you can take off your armbands [with the star of David], you're not Jews any more, now you're Soviets!' That says something about how good relations still were between Hitler and Stalin.

Late in the night, Safrin and the children arrived at a small town on the Bug; this was the demarcation line. The region was swarming with smugglers, traffickers of all kinds. But the Soviet border guards blocked their passage. There were thousands of refugees there, completely destitute, mostly Jews. Safrin saw a Red Army soldier for the first time in his life:

He wore a curious pointed hat, called after Budenny, which made a big impression on me. I said to myself, 'Perhaps he's got a hidden aerial in it connecting him to the general staff?' It was terribly cold. People were there without any shelter. I wore all three of the jackets I'd taken with me. The smugglers prowled around in search of victims to fleece. In the middle of the night, an old man died. People made preparation to bury him, digging in the ground with bare hands. Then there was a scene engraved forever in my memory. A Bund militant who happened to be there stood up and began to speak. He spoke and spoke, with that rhetoric peculiar to the Bundists. I no longer remember the content of his speech, except for one phrase: '*Die Raten haben uns verraten!*', 'The Soviets have betrayed us!', which he repeated over and over again. The next morning, however, the border was opened and we were able to reach Białystok.

As a Bund militant, Haïm Babic had no illusions about what to expect when the Germans reached Warsaw. In the night of 7–8 September, therefore, he crossed the bridge on the Vistula and headed east – one of thousands fleeing the German advance. The German planes machine-gunned their columns along the roads. When, after several days, he approached the river Bug, people began to turn back: 'The Germans are already there!' Despite this discouragement, Babic continued his route, but a few kilometres from Brest-Litovsk the road was cut; Germans and Poles were still fighting. Along with a group of refugees, he spent the night in a village deserted by its inhabitants, but the next day the Germans who had occupied this ground forced them away:

In no way would we take the road back to Warsaw. So we tried our luck across the fields; we hid. Finally, a demarcation line was established between the zone occupied by the Germans and that which fell to the Soviets. The Soviets took control of Brest-Litovsk, and I was fortunate to land up there at the end of September 1939.

It seems that in the course of this exodus, around 300,000 Jews left the territories occupied by the Germans and fled east. Thousands later returned to the zone occupied by the Germans, deceived by the apparent calm that reigned there, but some 250,000 remained on Soviet territory. Among them were many cadres of the Bund, the left Poale Zion and the former Communist Party; the life of these parties was all the more paralysed.

It may seem strange that a powerful organization such as the Bund, rich in long traditions of underground action, which at the outbreak of the war held seventeen out of twenty seats occupied by Jews on the Warsaw municipal council, found itself caught unawares by the German invasion. Haïm Babic maintains that 'we Bundists had no illusion as to the ability of the Polish army to resist the Wehrmacht'. But the sudden departure of this experienced and courageous militant was in no way surprising, if we remember that he did no more than follow such prestigious leaders as Alter and Erlich – liquidated by Stalin in 1941.

To tell the truth, the disarray of the communists – whose party had been dissolved by Stalin in 1938 – was no less. Yaakov Greenstein, an experienced militant from the Łódź region, also took the road for Białystok thanks to a quite remarkable combination of circumstances:

I was walking in the street [in his home town, Pabianice] when I noticed a comrade, of German origin and a militant in the Young Communists, wearing a swastika armband. I hid myself in a doorway out of fear that he would see me and denounce me, but he did see me and came after me and caught up with me: 'Listen,' he said, 'all the *Volksdeutsche* who do not collaborate with the Nazis will be shot. I don't have a choice, I'll try to do work where I won't dirty my hands. I'm working at the town hall, but at the bottom of my heart I'm still the same. I'll look you up to warn you if you're on their black list; if they don't arrest you tonight, it'll be the night after; you'd better disappear.'

But I didn't know where to go. We discussed it, and finally he made me the following suggestion: 'I'm an interpreter at the town hall. You can turn up there tomorrow morning when it opens, and I'll try and get you a safe conduct to join your girlfriend in Białystok, in the Soviet zone.' I thought about it; the proposal was tempting. On the other hand, the town hall was really the wolf's lair. Finally, I tried my luck. At exactly ten o'clock I was there, and my friend was waiting. 'Here,' he called out to the German soldiers, 'this is a good bloke from the town. He's come to ask for an *Ausweis* to join his wife on the other side of the demarcation line. Can you give it to him?' A German replied, 'As you know him, write out the paper yourself!' We went into an office, and he made out the pass in my name and stamped it. 'Well then,' I said, 'why don't you stamp a dozen blank ones for me, I can make use of them.' And that's what he did. I handed the precious documents to the party comrades and set out for Białystok. Later on, this *Volksdeutsch* comrade provided our friends with many other valuable documents.

Poland was now a country devastated by bombing and terrorized by the occupying forces. The Resistance was divided into groups that were very often hostile to one another, and found extreme difficulties in getting organized. The Jewish militants, in contrast to those fighting in France, most often found themselves cut off from this Resistance, a section of which was vigorously anti-Semitic. The liquidation of Jewish *résistants* by their Polish counterparts that Manès Sperber depicts in his novel *Qu'une larme dans l'océan* is no mere literary device; some of our witnesses were themselves caught up in such 'incidents'. It was precisely here, where the Jewish workers' movement was most solid, most dynamic and most autonomous, that it was most directly affected by the new conditions created by the war. And it was here, in a surprising way, that the Jewish *résistants* found themselves most isolated and most vulnerable.

At the time of the invasion of Poland, the Communist Party no longer existed; it was slowly re-established, in the Warsaw ghetto, among other places. Only in January 1942 did it officially reappear as an underground party under the name of the Polish Workers' Party (PPR): its armed wing was initially called Gwardia Ludowa, later Armia Ludowa. In the Warsaw ghetto, one of the communist groups published from December 1941 a daily paper that lasted until March 1942. The Bund, for its part, re-organized its pre-war security service in April 1940, with a backbone formed of street porters, transport workers and kosher butchers, in order to respond to the anti-Semitic gangs that were organizing pogroms. It was also very active in the Warsaw ghetto, issuing a plethora of publications. One of its opponents from that time, Adolf Berman,[17] a leader of the left Poale Zion, pointed out that with its youth movement Zukunft and what remained of its trade unions, the Bund was the largest organization in the ghetto. But the left Poale Zion was also present in the ghetto, publishing there its paper *Proletariche Gedank*.

In the ghettos, as in the extermination camps to which they were the antechamber, the *résistants* embarked on a race against death. To struggle and resist was the only lucid choice, but this most often meant for the fighters no more than choosing the time and manner of their death. Beyond the immediate outcome of the struggle, which most often was inevitable, their combat was for history, for memory. After the war, historians and the surviving actors themselves studied at length the political and military weight of the Resistance in the countries of Western and Southern Europe, compared to that of the great pitched battles: the question is far from settled. But no one would claim that the revolt of a few hundred insurgents in the Warsaw ghetto in April 1943 influenced the course of the war in any way. The immense importance of this event was in another dimension: a symbol, as is often said, the manifestation par excellence of the will to attest by struggle 'despite everything' – the famous *trotz alledem* of Heinrich Heine, found also from the pens of Rosa Luxemburg and Karl Liebknecht, and again in the famous song of Wolf Biermann. It embodied the will and capacity of human resistance in the face of adversity, despite the extreme disproportion of forces.

It would not be said that the Nazis managed to liquidate the entire Jewish community of Poland in the crematoria of Treblinka without resistance. That was what the Zionist, communist and Bundist militants proclaimed when they united in the Jewish Combat Organization that was formed after the great *akstia*, the raid of July 1942. This affirmation of life by way of a sacrifice and combat with no prospect of victory is a tragic paradox that can only be understood as an act of faith in history, in the capacity of humanity to rise again beyond

---

17   Adolf Avraham Berman, *Bamakom asher yaad Li Hagoral* (Where Fate Placed Me) (Tel Aviv: Hakibbutz Hameukhad, 1978).

barbarism, in the future of the Jewish community of Yiddishland. In his remarkable memoirs and reflections (recorded and transcribed by the Polish journalist Hanna Krall), Marek Edelman,[18] who was a member of the leadership of the Combat Organization, relates the following fact: before the insurrection was launched, some people asked whether a collective suicide in the ghetto would not be a way to alert world opinion and Western governments to the fate of the Jews in Poland. One of their number proposed that all the survivors of the ghetto should force the wall on the 'Aryan' side and wait to be encircled by the Gestapo and executed by machine guns; a woman militant proposed setting fire to the ghetto and letting the wind 'scatter their ashes'. Edelman notes that at the time these proposals were made, they in no way seemed to arise from a pathetic view of history, but were quite simply presented as concrete alternatives.

In order to protest against the indifference of the Western powers to the massacre of the Jews of Eastern Europe, Artur Zygelboïm killed himself in London on 17 December 1943. He was the Bund's representative to the Polish government in exile. His testament bears the mark of a complete despair about the present, a riveting cry directed at world opinion:

> I cannot live while what remains of the Jewish people in Poland, whose representative I am, is being liquidated. My comrades of the Warsaw ghetto have fallen arms in hand in a final heroic combat. I have not been given the chance to die like them, with them. But my place is by their side, in their common graves. By my death, I want to express the strongest possible protest against the passivity with which the world views and tolerates the extermination of the Jewish people. I know that in our day a human life is worth little; but as I have been able to do nothing while alive, perhaps by dying I shall contribute to breaking the indifference of those who may have the possibility of saving in extremis those Polish Jews who still survive.

---

18   Hanna Krall, *Lekhadim et Elohim* (Going before God) (Tel Aviv: Adam, 1981); French translation: *Mémoires du ghetto de Varsovie* (Paris: Éditions du Scribe, 1983).

Curiously, this despair as to the present went together in Zygelboïm's testament with an extraordinary confidence in the future, in particular the future of the Jewish community in Eastern Europe. He wrote, 'I desire that those of the millions of Polish Jews who survive will one day experience liberation, together with the Polish population, in a world of liberty and social equality. I am convinced that such a Poland will come to pass, that such a world will exist.' On the threshold of death, at the very bottom of the abyss, this militant reaffirmed the validity of the utopia of his organization, the Bund, his conviction that his historical perspective was correct.

On the eve of the Warsaw ghetto uprising, the majority of members of the Jewish Combat Organization pronounced in favour of struggle, despite the overwhelming disproportion of forces (they had only a few dozen pistols in poor condition, and some grenades, knives and Molotov cocktails, and their numbers were only around 220, according to Edelman, in contradiction with the exaggerated figures that were subsequently advanced). 'Humanity has already established that to die arms in hand is finer than to die with bare hands', Edelman notes at this point, with the bitter irony that characterizes his memoirs. He also mentions the suicide of Mordechai Aniélévitch, a Zionist militant and commander of the Jewish Combat Organization, along with his eighty comrades, in the final hours of the insurrection, though he does not approve of this symbolic sacrifice: 'This should not have been done. You don't give your life for symbols', he maintains. Edelman, together with a few of his companions, managed to escape from the ghetto through the sewers. He then worked as a doctor in Poland, where he had some trouble in the wake of Jarulewski's *coup d'état* on account of his active sympathy for the Solidarność trade union. Could one imagine a more living embodiment of an act of faith in the future of humanity than the Warsaw ghetto uprising, when the Red Army was still a thousand kilometres from the Polish capital?

We discovered that there was far more truth in the memoirs of an escapee from the ghetto such as Marek Edelman, written without pretension or glamourizing, than in all the epic reconstitutions of this insurrection. Far from being heroic, Edelman explains, life in the ghetto was first and foremost grey and wretched, stunting both minds and bodies. The images retained in his memory – the trade in the 'life numbers' parsimoniously attributed by the Germans, the queues waiting for the trains to Treblinka despite the warnings of the Resistance (at the doors of the wagons bread was distributed to those leaving), the forming of the Jewish Combat Organization by a handful of young people whose combined age was just 110 years – these all created a scandal by giving the lie to prevailing legends. But, Edelman asks, is it an attack on the memory of the ghetto combatants to recall that they were so few in number and that their leader who will be remembered by posterity was the simple son of a fishwife?

The pious discourse about the Holocaust obscures memory, as the only distinction it makes is between the generic category of victims and that of the murderers. This is certainly in part because, at the end of the day, the Nazis reserved the same fate for a banker or a tailor, for the leader of the UGIF, the head of the *Judenrat* in Łódź and Warsaw as for the militants in the underground resistance in the ghettos. But for all that, this sinister democracy of the crematoria does not make an Edelman or an Aniélévitch equal before history with a Rumkowski, the head of the Łódź *Judenrat* who, with the help of his Jewish police, handed over tens of thousands of individuals on whom the deadly trap of the ghetto had closed, in the hope of saving his skin, or even a Czerniaków, the head of the Warsaw ghetto who ended up committing suicide in July 1942 when the Germans launched the first major deportation operation, having administered the ghetto on their behalf since it was established in 1940. These men followed traditions that were totally contradictory, a contradiction continued beyond the Nazi genocide.

In Paris, during the war, Jewish partisans organized commando actions at Jewish workshops in the Faubourg Poissonière, where the bosses prospered from making equipment for the Wehrmacht; some of these combatants were arrested in the course of the actions, denounced by these 'good' Jews, and shot or deported. In the ghettos, the shadow fighters liquidated the most zealous members of the Jewish police or the collaborators of certain *Judenräte*. The leader of the Resistance in Vilnius handed himself in to the Germans under the pressure of his brothers in misfortune. The Judaism of the devout, fuelled basically by incantations and conditioned reflexes, does not like facts of this kind to be remembered. Which is why Hannah Arendt's *Eichmann in Jerusalem* has a sulphurous odour still today.[19]

We have seen, in the revolts of the ghettos and extermination camps (in Sobibor, Treblinka, Auschwitz), rebels whose motivation was above all else the desire to testify for the future, the moral and historical meaning of the action being more important than its tangible result. But such a meaning is not contained in these actions with the same precision and dryness as a military communiqué of the Resistance announcing that in the course of an action a group of partisans has killed so many enemies and taken so many rifles. The uncertain subjective dimension attached to the meaning of actions such as the revolt of the Auschwitz *Sonderkommando* or even the Warsaw ghetto uprising opens the field for deadly clashes between candidates for the moral, historical and political legacy of the action of these combatants, for burning quarrels over interpretation and, let us say frankly, sometimes for the most injurious travesties of reality and distortions of meaning.

For some writers, the Warsaw ghetto uprising was pretty much entirely the work of Zionist militants, and when they took up the gun in April 1943 it was with the thought of their companions 'across the Mediterranean', the happy people making the desert bloom in Eretz Israel; it was to them, the future of the Jewish homeland, that they dedicated their combat and their death in the ghetto. Grayek Chalom, for instance, when he mentions this or that legendary figure of the ghetto uprising – Marek Edelman, Michaël Klebfish, the Bund militants – whose mistake was to be a political opponent of Zionism, shamefully omits to mention their regrettable political

---

19 In particular, the mention in the postscript to *Eichmann in Jerusalem* of the 'role played by Jewish officials', members of the Jewish councils in the parts of Eastern Europe under German administration, aroused very negative reactions, particularly in France and the United States, on the part of representatives of Jewish community organizations as well as of hostile publicists. By openly attacking those who act 'as if there was no difference between helping Jews to emigrate and helping the Nazis to deport them', Arendt put her finger on a wound that was not ready to close.

allegiance.[20] For others, the insurrection was above all the action of communist militants, and clearly the 'sublime heroism' of the combatants was nourished by the Stalingrad victory.[21] For others, again, the uprising was a kind of stoic sacrifice designed to shake the conscience of the world, or else a combat conceived and organized with the perspective of linking up with the partisans in the forests. The list of these disagreements, and the transfiguration of reality that certain heroic visions of history induce, is never-ending and not always disinterested: the few hundred fighters, ragged and starving, armed with knives and home-made revolvers, becoming thousands, their faces lit up with hope by the victories of the Red Army (which, a year later, camped on the banks of the Vistula while the Germans crushed the Warsaw insurrection), or else by the grandiose achievements of the *haloutzim* in Eretz Israel.

A Bund veteran who has lived in Palestine since 1934 expresses indignation at this self-interested partiality of memory:

> In Israel, the establishment is unwilling to recognize the positive work of other currents; you never hear any reference to the Bund in the schools, in discussions of the Warsaw ghetto. And yet, didn't we take part? The engineer Michaël Klebfish, who distinguished himself by making grenades and Molotov cocktails before falling in combat by throwing himself at a machine gun so that others could escape, wasn't he one of ours? And wasn't Artur Zygelboïm one of ours? However, I often remember that at the time many *sabras* were not among those least indifferent to the fate of our brothers in Poland.
>
> One day, I recall, soon after the war, we organized a meeting in Tel Aviv to commemorate the Warsaw ghetto uprising. A woman comrade from the Bund, who had escaped from the ghetto through the sewers, and the former secretary of the tailors' trade union in Poland, Hersh Himmelfarb, were due to speak. Their speeches would be naturally in Yiddish. When Himmelfarb started speaking, he was interrupted by

---

20   Stéphane Grayek Chalom, *L'insurrection du ghetto de Varsovie* (Paris: Foyer ouvrier juif), 1978.

21   David Diamant, *Combattants juifs dans l'armée républicaine espagnole* (Paris: Éditions Renouveau, 1979).

some people who started making a terrible row and finally attacked the podium and threw a flowerpot at his head. The meeting had to be stopped.

By dint of being commemorated, celebrated, recuperated, the Warsaw ghetto uprising often ends up being no more than a lifeless symbol, if not something still worse, an advertisement.[22] These rituals almost lead to the resistance and combats in other ghettos being forgotten, such as those of Lachwa, Tuczyn, Białystok (a week of fighting in August 1943) or Minsk.

The odyssey of the Minsk ghetto combatants is striking in more than one respect. First of all, by the power of the organization that they set up only a few weeks after the Germans had captured the Byelorussian capital in late June 1941; its ramifications extended even into the *Judenrat* appointed by the Nazis. Also by the quality and solidity of the relations it maintained with the non-Jewish Resistance among the Soviet population, including the partisans. And finally by what was the most spectacular exploit of this ghetto Resistance: the rescue of thousands of people, including women and children, who managed to leave the city and join the partisan detachments and 'family camps' in the Byelorussian forests.

Two of our witnesses, Hersh Smolar and Yaakov Greenstein,[23] both experienced communist militants who took refuge on Soviet territory at the time of the invasion of Poland, and were caught in Minsk by the speed of the German advance in June 1941, played a key role in the ghetto Resistance. Smolar was one of its three leaders. He kept a

---

22   A good example can be found in an issue of *Points critiques* (July 1982), the journal of Jewish progressives in Belgium (UPJB). In an article eloquently entitled 'Du bon et du mauvais usage du ghetto de Varsovie', the UPJB expresses indignation that 'the commemoration of the Warsaw ghetto uprising that took place on 18 April ... was transformed in the most anti-democratic way possible into a demonstration of unanimous solidarity by the Jewish community with the present policy of the Israeli government.'

23   Hersh Smolar, *Tokhelet veshivra: Zichnorot shel 'yesek' leshéavar* (Memoirs of a Former 'Yevsek') (University of Tel Aviv, 1979), Chapters 18–24; Yaakov Greenstein, *Oud Mikikar-Hayovel* (A Firebrand from Hayovel Square) (Hakibbutz Hameukhad, 1968).

grip on the many activities of the underground combatants: publication of leaflets and papers, reprinting the broadcasts of Soviet radio (it was a capital offence to possess a radio set in the ghetto), and contact with the outside world, in particular with partisan groups. The ghetto Resistance fighters provided weapons, medicine and uniforms that they took from the Germans to the fighters outside. Yaakov Greenstein gives an insight into these many activities:

> The Resistance was structured into groups that acted according to the rules of strict secrecy. After a certain time, each group was responsible for contact with the partisans in a particular zone. We even had people in the ghetto administration, in the labour office, the housing office, the police. Some of them, working outside the ghetto, were charged by the organization with stealing weapons or printing and radio material. In this way our printer comrades managed to bring a whole secret printing press into the ghetto. But the task that most mobilized our militants was the production of weapons and their acquisition by every means possible.[24]

His wife, Bella, took an active part in this work of 'recovery':

> Bella went to work for a German unit. This unit was in charge of a major Soviet arms depot that had fallen into the hands of the occupiers. Along with other women, Bella had to do cleaning and washing, sometimes even clean weapons. This group of women were charged with stealing weapons, munitions and grenades and bringing them to the ghetto.
>
> Bella did her work well. Each day, on her return from work, she brought precious weapons. We had made special trousers and shoes for her, so that she could hide bullets in them. From time to time, she brought a bundle of firewood: when we untied it, we found machine-gun components and grenades.

The head of the ghetto police, who subsequently joined the Resistance, obtained a false identity paper for Hersh Smolar, in the name of Yefim

---

24   Greenstein, *Oud Mikikar-Hayovel.*

Stolarewitz. These false papers enabled him to move around and also work a bit in the ghetto, so as not to die of hunger. Soon, however, the Nazis were on his track:

> The following night and day until noon, the Gestapo tried by all means to discover a trace of me. After midnight, Gestapo cars arrived in a courtyard that was only three buildings away from the place I was sleeping that night. But I heard the echoes of their automatic weapons, and the cries of despair of the women and children. An ordinary night in the ghetto …
>
> At dawn, I left my hiding-place and made for Moshe Gebeliev's workshop. He was one of the members of the Resistance triumvirate, and I asked him what had happened during the night. That was when I fell into the hands of the ghetto police, who took all the men to the very house which I used for my meetings, the apartment of Nina Lis, our liaison agent with the 'Aryan side'. They ordered us to bring out the bodies of the people who had been killed the previous night and take them to the cemetery.
>
> I was frozen, as if paralysed. I could hardly put one foot in front of the other. At that point I felt a hand on my shoulder pushing me back. I lifted up my eyes and saw Hersh Ruditzer, one of our people who was also a member of the *Judenrat*. He had me accompanied by a ghetto policeman to a house close by, where they explained to me that the Gestapo had been looking in the night for Yefim Stolarewitz, and that, not finding him, they had killed all the inhabitants of the house, including women and children, a total of seventy people. Among them was Nina and her young daughter. The Gestapo had issued an ultimatum: if I was not handed in by midday, the whole ghetto would be liquidated.

The new head of the *Judenrat*, Yoffé (the former head, Eliahou Moushkin, had been hanged), had a clever idea, albeit macabre: he hastily had new papers made in the name of Yefim Stolarewitz, headed for the cemetery where he muddied them with blood from the victims of the previous night's massacre, then took them to the Gestapo chief: 'We found these papers in the pocket of one of the dead men', he said, 'Yefim Stolarewitz is no longer in this world.'

Smolar himself, still well and truly alive, set out to organize the departure of as many people as possible from the ghetto for the zones held by the partisans. These were very active throughout Byelorussia, which was covered with forests and marshes. From July 1941, Stalin had given the order to develop partisan detachments in the enemy's rear. These initially had to provide themselves with weapons taken from the enemy, and food from the peasants, but from 1943 they received logistic support from the Red Army. Liberated zones were formed, and the partisan detachments grew.

In Byelorussia, the Nazis were unable to complete their project of total extermination of Jews, as they had largely managed to do in Ukraine. Many Jews thus joined the partisans' ranks, and family camps were formed under their protection. In 1942, Smolar says, the partisans only accepted people able to bear arms. The ghetto resisters, for their part, supplied weapons bought from Italian soldiers who had been sent to the Russian front. But the successive raids conducted by the Nazis in the ghetto made this kind of activity increasingly difficult. The Resistance's financial resources dwindled, German workshops employed ever fewer Jews, and the resisters no longer had a foothold in the *Judenrat*. The Germans' successive *aktsia* led to the deportation of thousands of people. The Resistance leaders felt the net closing in around them.

They decided then to establish a Jewish base in the forest. At the same time, the leadership of a partisan unit led by a Soviet officer, Semion Gozenko, took the same decision. 'We appointed a builder, Shalom Zorin, as commander of this operation', Smolar explains. 'Our aim was to concentrate in the Zorin base all those we had been able to get out of the ghetto, including women, children and old men. Among those able to fight, many were directed to other partisan units, in the Nalivoki forest.'

Yaakov Greenstein explains that Semion Gozenko, a Ukrainian communist, had been helped to escape by Jews in the ghetto who worked on trash collection. They had hidden him in a cart filled with rubbish. He subsequently became commander of the Ponomarenko brigade, in which Jews were welcomed. He adds,

Zorin was in one of the first groups to escape from the Minsk ghetto and make for the forests. This group was part of the Stalin brigade. Zorin sent a message to the general in command of the brigade, Platon Tcherniagov, asking him whether it was possible to establish Jewish family camps for those unable to fight, under the protection of partisan units in the forests of Nalivoki.

Constantly subject to the threat of German round-ups, living in extraordinarily precarious conditions, suffering from cold, hunger and disease, these refugees did not have an easy life in the family camps. Many failed to survive the test – though a greater number did so than survived the convoys heading for Auschwitz or Treblinka.

Greenstein joined a partisan detachment fighting in the Ivenitz forest. Out of 130 combatants, seventy were Jews from the Minsk ghetto. The first action he took part in was designed to ensure supplies for the unit. At night, the partisans encircled a village whose inhabitants were known for their hostility towards the Resistance. They seized cattle and flour, loaded their booty onto carts and returned to their base across the German lines. He recalls,

We acted in groups of eight to ten people, so as not to be spotted by the Germans. As we operated in villages that were very close to the German garrisons, we conducted operations very quickly so as to get back to the forest before dawn. Each of these expeditions lasted a week. Each region was divided into zones, and each partisan brigade had its zone in which it had the right to draw supplies. The peasants themselves knew which brigade their zone belonged to. In the villages of their zone, the partisans were supposed to behave 'humanely'; that is, only to take what was necessary, not to steal, and to convince the peasants that it was their duty to accept this tribute voluntarily in the fight against the enemy

Every week, representatives of the 'special department' went out to the villages and obtained information about the partisans' behaviour. If it turned out that they had behaved incorrectly, or stolen, their group was severely punished. These rules did not apply to villages hostile to the partisans, those that collaborated with the invaders.

Hersh Smolar, after joining another partisan unit, accompanied the commander to the villages. This time it was no longer a matter of supplies, but rather of propaganda and recruitment:

> Every evening I went with Commander Kasinski to one of the villages. We gathered the young people in one of the shacks and tried to convince them. If they agreed to follow us, we gave them a few hours to make preparations, and returned with them to the base at night. The majority of them came with their weapons. But if they did not show great enthusiasm, if they hesitated or said, 'We'll see, wait a bit', Kasinski declared in a solemn tone, as if giving an order, 'In the name of the Red Army, I declare you mobilized.' Then they all came to the base. Once they arrived in the forest, they asked us to pardon the lack of enthusiasm they had shown, but they did not have any choice. If it was not clearly apparent that they had been 'enrolled by force', the Germans would kill their families.

Charged with directing a small unit of recruits, Smolar was quick to notice their lack of enthusiasm for the partisan life. He soon understood why:

> One day, before midnight, I was standing guard – I did not want to give those placed under my orders the impression that I was privileged, either as leader or as a Jew – and I began to hum a Polish poem by Adam Mickiewicz. And suddenly, without my noticing, all my partisan group got up and stood around me, looking at my face with surprise, but without a word. Then they said, 'Continue, chief, it's very good.' They didn't say 'beautiful', but 'good'.

It turned out that all these partisans were Poles, Catholics, whose parents had been arrested during the terrible year 1937 as 'Polish spies', and who even among the partisans had not dared 'confess' that they were not Byelorussians. After this episode, says Smolar, his relations with his men became excellent.

But the consequences of this forced mobilization appeared very dangerous. Smolar recalls how one day, at the time of the battle of

Stalingrad, his brigade found itself encircled by the Germans while it was attempting to move base. He managed to escape, but lost all his recruits, the Polish peasants, who surrendered to the Germans. When the time came for investigation, explanations were conflicted. The brigade commissar explained that this treason was easily explained by the 'origins' of these young people. 'The apple does not fall far from the tree', he said; in other words, like father, like son. But a Jewish militant blamed those responsible for such a risky operation. At the end of the day, it was decided to regroup the Jewish partisans in a special unit. Smolar was appointed its commissar.

Yaakov Greenstein took part in an attack against a railway hub of strategic importance for the Germans, which was crowned with success:

> Around 800 partisans, the whole brigade, had been mobilized for the operation. We were divided into different groups. My task was to take the station, then to blow up the tracks with dynamite. The brigade took up position, and at midnight exactly we launched an almighty fire. We were deployed over several kilometres. Shouting 'hurrah', we set off to attack the rails. Our shooting and cries from all sides sowed confusion among the Germans, who started running in all directions. Our bullets stung, and their dead and wounded littered the ground all round the railway station. We mined the tracks, lighting fuses that could be seen sparkling into the distance, then we mined the wagons and the locomotives that were in the station. The fire ceased and we withdrew – everything blew up. At dawn we were already 25 kilometres away. Our losses were only one dead and six wounded.

In Byelorussia, the partisans were not just fighting German troops, but also bands of Ukrainian irregulars, 'Vlassovians', the Byelorussian police, and sometimes also Polish partisan units supported by the government in London. Greenstein relates the extermination of a group of fighters belonging to the Zorin detachment by one of these Polish groups. By way of reprisal, he recalls, 'we erupted into their camp, taking them by surprise, so that they surrendered without a single shot being fired. Then we disarmed them, took their officers, and divided their soldiers among our different units'.

Until the Second World War, despite the successive shocks of Hitler's victory, then that of Franco, the defeat of the Popular Front in France and the Moscow trials, the world view of the Yiddishland revolutionaries maintained its unity, a form of cohesion based on confidence in the dialectic of history, the conviction that revolution was the currency of the century. After the war, the picture changed completely. Their world view, their perception of the present and the future, was torn asunder, between two resolutely antagonistic and contradictory poles. On the one side, there was the fact that, at the end of the day, fascism had been defeated and the traditional order in Europe overturned by the presence of the Red Army on half of its territory, and by the existence of powerful mass movements born out of the Resistance in countries such as France, Italy, Yugoslavia, Greece, etc. Revolutionary optimism was thus set to gain a second wind in this situation, in which history seemed to be on the move once more, and the slogan 'never again' was echoed by tens of millions of workers and by thousands of fighters who were still armed. It was in order to take their place in this new rise of seemingly impending revolution that many Jewish militants returned to Poland, Romania and Yugoslavia to take part in the building of the 'new order', and others took up their work again in the workers' organizations of Western Europe.

On the other side, however, there was also the fact that the world from which they had come, their native soil of Yiddishland, had been wiped off the map, and along with it the social, cultural, linguistic and historical fabric of their own existence. An irremediable break, a yawning gulf between past and present, which made them for evermore survivors of a *Yiddishkeit* suspended in the postwar air, more uprooted than the most wretched of the *Luftmenschen* of their buried world had ever been. For them, in particular, nothingness had become, as Adorno put it, a historical category.

'Let a Frenchman try to imagine', wrote Richard Marienstras,[25]

---

25   Marienstras, *Être un peuple en diaspora*, p. 11.

but could he imagine its full consequences, a France wiped off the map, and him finding himself with a handful of French-speakers among men quite ignorant of what had been the collectivity to which he belonged, and whose language, customs, landscape, history, cuisine, institutions, religion and economy defined the concrete modalities of his member-ship of the human race. What then would be his taste for living, what possibility would he have of defining himself otherwise than in the most external fashion with the project of the community in which he found himself?

It was only in the symbolic order, then, that this escapee could try to rebuild a bridge between past and present, to conceive his future beyond the genocide and the eradication of the Yiddish world – for example by rebuilding his existence in Israel.

From this point on, the existence and world view of our witnesses swings between these two poles, at the cost of new and dramatic tensions, new wanderings and new dangers, new disillusions – and without a single one of them being still able to believe that history is governed by reason.

5

The Song of the Revolution Betrayed

> For all my comrades now I sing
> The song of the revolution betrayed
> And for my betrayed comrades I sing
> And sing for my comrades the betrayers
>   Wolf Biermann, 'Song for My Comrades'

The USSR holds a central place in the experience and thoughts of Yiddishland. In contrast to militants of the workers' movement in France, Germany or even post-1918 Poland, they often had a direct knowledge of the Soviet Union. Some of them went there voluntarily, because they believed. Others, despite their doubts about the Soviet regime, went under the pressure of dramatic circumstances. Still today, despite the distance in time and space, the Soviet episode remains the point where their testimonies most radically diverge.

There is basically nothing surprising about this. No historian has yet been able to write about the October Revolution and the Soviet Union without giving vent to his ideological convictions and commitments; and when it comes to analysing the situation of the Jews in the USSR from 1917 to our own day, we are right in the thick of the dispute, where a priori judgements reign supreme.

'The Bolshevik revolution in Russia accomplished much of the destruction of European Jewry that the Nazi counterrevolution in Germany would continue by other means', was the summary verdict of one historian.[1] For another, 'the [Soviet] regime was doing all it could to uproot [anti-Semitic prejudice], until 1939.'[2] 'Owing to the particularity of their social structure, the Jews suffered more than any other nation from the socio-political system introduced by the new regime', was a third writer's judgement.[3]

These dissonant voices suggest the complexity of the problem. The present-day position of Jews in the USSR,[4] the striking and scandalous forms of national discrimination that they suffer, only heighten the weight of passions and ideological prejudices in this debate. Our informants, living in Israel, are no more exempt from this than are others. But they bring the weight of a direct experience, a knowledge of the USSR often gained at the highest cost in their dual quality as Jews and socialist militants. An experience that stretches from the first days of the February Revolution, via the darkest hours of Stalinism, through to the advent of Khrushchev. Their condition as both Jews and revolutionaries throws an often singular light on the course of Soviet history, for instance the story of a socialist Zionist active illegally in the USSR from 1926 to 1955(!), or that of a Yevsektia activist who for several years shared the hopes of those who dreamed of a new Jewish life guided by the principles of communism.[5]

---

1   Gedeon Haganov (Boris Souvarine), 'Le stalinisme et les juifs', *Spartacus*, 32, August 1951, p. 4.

2   Rodinson, *Cult, Ghetto and State*, p. 41.

3   Mikhail Frenkin, 'Some Observations on Russian Jewry and Russia's Political Parties (1917–1921)', *Crossroads* (Jerusalem) 3, 1979.

4   This was written in 1983. [Translator's note.]

5   The Yevsektia grouped the Jewish sections established in 1918 within the Russian (later Soviet) Communist Party. Initially it had an autonomous status and functioned as a Jewish communist organization. Over the years it became simply an apparatus charged with applying the Communist Party's line among Jews. Its tasks included the development of secular education in Yiddish, the promotion of Jewish culture in all its forms, the establishment of Jewish 'councils' and courts (in Yiddish), the formation of Jewish agricultural colonies, etc. It waged a bitter struggle against Zionist organizations and Jewish clericalism. Its leadership was riven by factional struggles that were often intense; these were due among other reasons to the disparate political origins of its leaders, former Bundists or Poale Zion as well as Bolsheviks, and to the necessity of aligning itself to the successive turns made by the party leadership. Its best-known leaders were S. Dimanstein,

When the revolution of February 1917 broke out, Yehoshua Rojanski had been active for several months in Tsaritsyn, where he had set up a small Poale Zion group. The extraordinary events that then shook Russia gave a new impulse to his activities. He published a small paper in Yiddish, *Das Wort*, and a Poale Zion militant was elected to the city council. But the first revolution was only a prelude to new confrontations. Rojanski was attracted to the most radical solutions, and practised his own kind of revolutionary vigilance:

> One day, as I was walking with some comrades by the city warehouses where large amounts of wine and vodka were stored, I noticed a suspicious agitation. Some people who seemed to belong to the bourgeoisie, or at least its lower depths, were strolling around with no apparent object. I soon realized that they were counterrevolutionaries who were preparing to seize the alcohol and distribute it to the soldiers in the barracks, so as to stir up a revolt against the new power. I immediately alerted the city soviet, and half an hour later three lorries of armed men arrived. Together, we emptied out the barrels and poured the wine and vodka into the Volga.

At the end of the month the third congress of Poale Zion was held, to which Rojanski was elected a delegate. It turned out that the small socialist Zionist organization had become a significant force, with 10,000 militants across Russia. But the strategic debates that divided the Russian workers' movement did not spare Poale Zion. The majority of the delegates leant to the Bolshevik side, while others felt more affinity with Menshevism, with others again swinging between the two. Rojanski, for his part, was among those who supported the Bolsheviks, though without abandoning the specific character of Poale Zion. On 28 August 1917, the charismatic founder and leader of Poale Zion, Ber Borochov, arrived at the congress. Its militants had flocked to the railway station and waited for part of the night. In the early hours his train came in. People pressed against each other to

---

M. Rafes, M. Frumkin ('Esther'), M. Litvakov and A. Chemerisky; all were liquidated in the late 1930s on Stalin's orders. The Yevsektia had already been dissolved in 1930.

approach him, threw flowers and urged him to speak. He stood on the platform and exhorted his comrades carried away by the contrary currents of the Russian Revolution to remain united at all costs, not to stand aloof from Russian events but neither to forget the objective of Eretz Israel. 'To my great regret', Rojanski comments,

> the majority of the 250 delegates present did not understand him. The comrades were carried away by the maelstrom of the Russian Revolution, they saw the perspective of world revolution opening, whereas Borochov insisted that Eretz Israel, with its emotional charge, should remain at the heart of our propaganda and our concerns. I agreed with him; I was struggling in Russia, I was ready to go and agitate or fight wherever the party sent me, but my dream remained that of leaving for Israel.

The congress was rudely interrupted by the rebellion of General Kornilov. The delegates rushed to their positions in the civil war that was already beginning. Rojanski was sent on a mission to the Caucasus, among the Jews of the mountains. As against the Bund delegates, those of Poale Zion did not leave the congress of soviets in protest after the Bolshevik insurrection. They did not approve it, but neither did they condemn it, fearing above all that the counterrevolution would make use of divisions in the camp of the workers' parties to raise its head. They demanded the establishment of Jewish sections in the soviets to represent the interests of the Jewish population. This was the position that Rojanski tried to apply in the Caucasus; he saw himself as an ally of the Bolsheviks, though not a supporter. But when Kornilov's troops seized the region they made no distinction between the different varieties of 'Reds', massacring everyone they considered a 'Bolshevik', with a special predilection for Jews. Rojanski made a hasty escape.

Like Rojanski, the great majority of Jews in the tsarist empire had welcomed the February Revolution, often enthusiastically, as it had overthrown their persecutors and abolished the most glaring discriminations that they suffered. Like him, too, many of them found themselves swept along in the maelstrom of Russian politics, the general currents of history beyond the immediate concerns of the Jewish community. The majority of Jews, on the other hand, did not view the October insurrection in a favourable light. It was only natural that the industrial and commercial establishment, and large parts of the intelligentsia as well, should be hostile to a revolution whose programme envisaged their immediate expropriation. But even among the radicals, Jews committed to the progressive and socialist parties, only a minority supported the Bolsheviks; a majority leaned towards the Mensheviks, the Socialist Revolutionaries, or else the Bund and the Zionist parties.

It is certainly true that, as far back as the mid-1880s, Jews occupied a particularly prominent place in the Russian revolutionary movements. In the tsarist prisons they made up around a quarter of the revolutionary militants held. Yet we should not forget that they were represented right across the spectrum of Russian parties, except for the overtly anti-Semitic and ultra-reactionary groups, and provided leading figures for the Socialist Revolutionaries and the very moderate Cadets, the Polish PPS and the different factions of Russian and Polish social democracy.

On the eve of the October Revolution, the majority of Jews involved in political activity did not recognize themselves in the Bolshevik programme, particularly rejecting Lenin's revolutionary defeatism, as did the Bund, the Mensheviks and the Socialist Revolutionaries. Paradoxically, they were most often 'patriotic' and 'defencist'. The gains of the 'democratic' revolution, which were substantial for Jews, seemed to them to be worth defending, even at the cost of continuing the war in increasingly difficult conditions. Emancipated by the fall of tsarism, they tended to a certain degree to identify with the new Russia. It is also interesting to note that the Bolsheviks, constantly denounced by people nostalgic for the good old days as a Jewish party (and indeed there were several Jews among the Bolshevik leaders), never bothered before the revolution to develop any specific activity among the Jewish workers of the Pale of Settlement. For them, starting with Lenin, who constantly repeated this theme in his polemics against the Bund, the role of the revolutionary party was to unite workers over and above national, linguistic or other differences.

Before 1917, the Bolsheviks scarcely published any agitational material in Yiddish, and never bothered to adapt their propaganda to the specific character of the Yiddish working class in the regions where this was concentrated – contrary to the practice of the PPS, despite its very 'national Polish' character.

Thus the Bolsheviks largely left the field open to the Bund, whose influence on the eve of the revolution remained predominant among the Jewish workers of the Pale of Settlement. From 1912, however, the Bund had made common cause with the Mensheviks. During the war it adopted ambiguous positions, or opposing ones, in the debate raging within the international social democratic movement: to rally to the *union sacrée* or maintain an internationalist stance? In Poland, occupied by the Germans and Austrians since 1915, the Jewish population gave a cautious welcome to the occupying forces, who accommodated them to a certain extent. Jewish parties were authorized, including the Bund; certain Bund leaders who remained in Poland sympathized with the German and Austrian Social Democrats who had rallied to support their governments. And in Russia their comrades, like the majority of Menshevik leaders, leant rather to the side of Russian 'patriotism'. A difficult situation, which foreshadowed still more fundamental splits in the course of the revolution. Immediately after October, the Bund came out clearly against the Bolshevik *coup d'état*, thereby influencing a large proportion of the Jewish working class in Russia.

For the Jewish community of the former tsarist empire, the victory of the Bolsheviks and all the consequences that flowed from it brought with them tremendous upheavals, tensions and contradictions that were often insurmountable. It is impossible to understand the consolidation of Soviet power after the revolution, or its victory at the end of the civil war, without relating this to the application of the Bolsheviks' programme – bread, peace and land – which rallied to them the majority of the working class and small peasants. But this programme could not rouse a similarly positive echo in the entire Jewish population. A large proportion of Jewish soldiers mobilized at the front, the victims of constant persecution, certainly welcomed with relief the decision of the new state power to make peace with

Germany, albeit at the price of major territorial concessions; it was clearly not for nothing that many Jews were present on the soldiers' soviets established in the fighting units. But for the Jewish community of Eastern Europe, the peace of Brest-Litovsk (March 1918), followed by the outbreak of civil war in Ukraine, then the independence of Poland and the extension of the civil war to the whole of Russia, were above all synonymous with new difficulties and tragedies, as the social and geographical fabric of Yiddishland was rent asunder. In the same manner, the famous decree on land that roused the enthusiasm of the *muzhikii* could not have the same impact on the Jewish population: scarcely 50,000 Jews worked in agriculture at the time of the revolution, almost entirely in southern Russia.

It was basically on another level that the contradiction erupted that would divide the Jews of Russia. On the one hand, the revolution proclaimed the definitive abolition of all forms of national discrimination; the Soviet government waged an effective struggle against anti-Semitism. The abolition of the Pale of Settlement enabled Jews to move freely across the whole Russian territory; the proclamation of the equality of all citizens opened the doors of the new administration to them; the proclaimed desire of the new power to contribute to the rehabilitation of all cultures and nationalities oppressed by Great Russian chauvinism under the tsarist regime gave them hope for better days for the *yiddische gass*, the 'Jewish street', of Russia. Was not the presence of so many Jews in leading positions in the new state apparatus a tangible guarantee, a deposit on the future? On the other hand, however, it soon turned out that the 'new life' was also synonymous with the destruction of the traditional structures of Jewish communities in Russia. In the 'Jewish street', the construction of the new order involved a bitter struggle against religion, custom, the grip of the rabbis, the permeation of everyday life by the commandments of faith, the influence of bourgeois and Zionist parties that were uniformly denounced as reactionary, the dissolution of the *kehilot*, etc. The entry of Jewish youth and Jewish workers into the fluid world of the revolution, the emergence of a new Jewish culture, secular and progressive, could only happen, in the minds of the new holders of power, at the expense of a radical break with former values, with the communitarian structures bequeathed by a tradition viewed as completely reactionary. In the struggle of the new against the old, Jewish activists (particularly those in the Yevsektia) who by an irony of history were often former Bundists or socialist Zionists were in the front line.

Far more than the reconstruction of everyday life by the builders of communism, however, it was the civil war that would dig the grave of traditional Jewish life. In regions such as Ukraine, Byelorussia, Crimea and the Caucasus, the very fabric of the economic and social existence of Jewish communities was torn to shreds in the course of a merciless confrontation between Reds and Whites – the latter mobilized under the banner 'For Holy Russia, against the Jews!' It was in human lives, first of all, that Jews paid their tribute to this struggle to the death; but the trade and handicrafts from which they basically drew their living was also totally ruined by the end of the civil war, not to speak of the few islands of Jewish agriculture in Ukraine and Crimea.

The events that shook Ukraine in 1918 and 1919 were a particularly striking illustration of the dizzy situation in which Jews were entangled. In November 1917, Petliura and Vinnichenko proclaimed Ukrainian independence – from the Bolsheviks. In the wake of the treaty of Brest-Litovsk, the Germans occupied the country until December 1918, when Petliura regained power. It was in this confused situation that Ukrainian Socialist Revolutionaries and Social Democrats, who formed the backbone of this new power hostile to the Bolshevik revolution, adopted a programme of autonomy for national minorities. This decision applied in particular to the Jews, and the socialist Moishe Zybelfarb became a government minister. All the Jewish workers' parties were represented in the Rada; hundreds of Jewish schools, libraries and theatres developed in Ukraine; and the new Jewish life seemed promised a brilliant future under the sign of cultural autonomy. Soon after the German capitulation, however, civil war broke out, Bolsheviks versus Atamans. The latter, traditional butchers of Jews and impenitent pogromists, vented the same hatred on 'Reds' and 'Yids'. Hundreds of pogroms were inflicted. At least 60,000 Jews – 200,000 according to other figures – lost their lives in Ukraine during the years of civil war. Half a million found themselves destitute. But the most tragic aspect of this episode, as Henri Slovès notes, was that

> the troops of the Ukrainian 'Directorate', presided over by Petliura, held a place of honour in this dismal competition. The same Social Democrats and Socialist Revolutionaries who, the day before, had granted the Jews national autonomy, now organized and led the most bloody pogroms of these atrocious years. The immense pain of the leading milieus of the Jewish community was mixed with a sense of stupor, revolt and deepest bitterness. A whole world of hope collapsed.[6]

It was in the course of the civil war that the attitude of the Jewish community towards Soviet power began to evolve. In the face of the pogroms launched throughout Russia at the instigation of the Whites, the Bolsheviks equated anti-Semitism with counterrevolution and applied the rigours of martial law to pogromists, thus appearing the sole rampart against this rise of horror. Active support for the new power, engagement in the ranks of the revolution, then seemed the only solution for many Jews whose foundations of life had been undermined. Many of them joined the Communist Party during the civil war or shortly after, swelling the ranks of the new administration or enlisting in the Red Army. Mikhail Frenkin points out that 22 per cent of the members of the Soviet administration, the party and the Soviet military apparatus who died in the course of the civil war were Jews – a large number in proportion to Jewish representation in the Soviet population as a whole.[7] He notes that, with a level of education far above the average for Russia at the time, the Jewish community provided very many cadres to both the provincial administrations of the new regime and the army.

This 'revolution in the revolution' exerted a lasting effect on Jewish youth. Esther Rosenthal-Schneidermann, a young communist of Polish origin, arrived in Moscow in 1926 to take part in the first

---

6   Henri Slovès, *L'Etat juif de l'Union soviétique* (Paris: Les presses d'aujo-urd'hui, 1982), pp. 42–3.

7   Frenkin, 'Some Observations on Russian Jewry'.

congress of Jewish activists specializing in the field of education. She recalls her emotion at discovering this aspect of the new reality:

> Up till then, I had never seen a Jew in the role of high official, not to say an official speaking our everyday *mamelosh*, Yiddish. And here on the podium in the congress hall of the People's Commissariat for Education there were top officials speaking Yiddish, in the name of the colossal Soviet power, of Jewish education that the party placed on a footing of equality with the cultural assets of other peoples.

In the party, the proportion of Jews steadily rose from the base to the topmost level. At the tenth congress of the Bolshevik party, in March 1921, ninety-four out of 694 delegates were Jewish (along with 494 Russians, thirty-five Balts, eight Tartars and eight Armenians). In the central committee of the Bolshevik party elected in March 1918, five members out of fifteen were Jewish. Yet these figures should not blind us to the number of Jews who were also irreducible enemies of Bolshevism – anarchists, Socialist Revolutionaries, Mensheviks or Cadets, many of whom would suffer the rigours of Red terror during these years (like Fanny Kaplan, who tried to assassinate Lenin in 1918), while a still larger number took the road of exile.

A substantial sector of the Jewish community, who had been reduced to *Luftmenschen* by the ruin of their *shtetls* under the combined effect of the civil war and War Communism, certainly used the opportunity of the New Economic Policy to resume their traditional activities, often with a certain success. In 1926, Jews made up some 2 per cent of the Soviet population, but 20 per cent of private traders. A still greater number who had been uprooted and suspended in mid-air, as it were, by the overthrow of social and economic conditions, lived from various expedients. In 1927, Kalinin, the president of the central Soviet Executive Committee, noted that between 30 and 40 per cent of the Jewish population were unemployed and living in a state of 'abject poverty'; he added that unemployment reached 70 per cent among Jewish youth. Even if approximate, these figures give the measure of how far the Jewish population of the USSR had suffered from the whirlwind of the revolutionary years. At the same time, however, contradictory tendencies were to be noted. In the mid-1920s, a section of Jewish youth moved into large-scale industry to voluntarily 'proletarianize' themselves, a development that can also be related to directly political factors (was the skilled worker not the pillar of the new regime par excellence?), as well as to social and economic imperatives (if still not sufficiently, workers in large-scale industry ate better than the mass of wretchedly off artisans and hawkers that still remained). In the early 1930s, again, *Tribuna*, the organ of the Geserd,[8] reported the migration of thousands of young Jews from small towns to the industrial centres of Russia, particularly the Urals, where they took occupational training to become skilled workers.

From the end of the civil war on, moreover, the new administration of 'Jewish affairs' established under the aegis of Stalin's commissariat of nationalities sought to define the major lines of the 'conversion' of Jews to productive work. This was particularly to be put into practice by projects for developing Jewish agriculture in Crimea and Ukraine. To this end, the Jewish sections appealed for financial and material support from Jews abroad (particularly in the United States). Various bodies were established to undertake these projects: the Geserd that proceeded from Jewish soviet structures, and the Comerd that was directly attached to government structures. In 1924, some 100,000 new Jewish peasants thus saw themselves allocated plots of land. There was talk of increasing this figure to half a million in a short period of time. In 1928 the project of establishing a Jewish territorial unit in Birobidzhan, in the Soviet Far East, was developed in governmental milieus. The 'reactionary utopia' of the Zionists was now opposed by the perspective of a full expansion of Soviet Jewry, which some people even spoke of as a complete nation. 'Moscow's Palestine' was the dream of the most optimistic. Abroad, bodies charged with

---

8   Geserd: an organization for the settlement of Jewish workers on the land (*Ozet*, in Russian), set up by the Soviet government in 1925. Its initial plan was to settle nearly a million Jews on the land in two years, particularly in Ukraine and Crimea. Its leadership played a key part in developing the project for Birobidzhan. It was dissolved at the end of the Second World War.

supporting the Geserd's activitiy were set up: Ikor in the United States, Frokor in Argentina, and even in Palestine.

Soviet studies in the West today are dominated by the tendency to one-sidedly reinterpret the October Revolution and the 1920s in the USSR in the light of the Stalinist policy of the 1930s and postwar years. The catch-all concept of 'totalitarianism' provides a convenient frame of reference for this. Analyses of the situation of Jews in the USSR are particularly susceptible to this tendency. Most commonly, they ignore the ideological, social and political effects of the attraction that the Russian Revolution exerted on the Jewish populations of Eastern Europe in the 1920s and even in the 1930s, emphasizing rather the social and political repression that struck many Soviet Jewish intellectuals, artists and activists. It is a fact, however, that in the years that followed the October Revolution, all the Jewish socialist parties of the former tsarist empire were riven by a strategic debate in which the issue was whether to rally to the Bolshevik revolution and Soviet power or to reject this 'dictatorship' in favour of a 'democratic' socialism. It is also a fact that large sections of the Bund, Poale Zion and other Jewish socialist organizations such as the Faraynikte rallied to communism,[9] not under the pressure of any kind of repression, but merely under that of a historical situation in which the wind seemed to blow like a storm in the direction of world – or at least European – revolution. No more than a year and a half, for example, passed between the solemn warning of the Bund leader Henryk Erlich, who on 25 October 1917 (7 November by the old calendar) denounced the Bolshevik *coup d'état*, and the second conference of the Bund in March 1919 at which a large majority pronounced in favour of the Soviet dictatorship. In the same way, early 1919 saw a split take place in Poale Zion, the majority of which, supported by the Poale Zion

---

9   The Faraynikte ('unified'): the Unified Jewish Socialist Workers Party, founded in 1917 as the outcome of a fusion between the Zionist Socialist Workers Party and the Jewish Socialist Workers Party, whose members were also known as 'sejmists'. Together with the Kombund (Communist League established by the majority of Bundists in Russia), the Faraynikte formed the Komfarband (Jewish Communist Union) of Ukraine and Byelorussia–Lithuania, which combined with the Yevsektia in 1921 and 1922.

world union, requested membership of the Third International and established a short-lived 'Jewish Communist Party'. Similar developments took place in Ukraine, Byelorussia and Lithuania, where by way of various temporary regroupings, former militants of the Bund, Poale Zion and the Faraynikte sought to construct the foundations of a Jewish communist movement. Even in Poland an ephemeral Kombund appeared like that in Russia, the majority of its militants subsequently joining the Communist Party; the Polish Bund itself adopted the principle of affiliation to the Third International in 1920, though the decision was never put into practice.

This radicalization, however, the turn towards communism of a substantial portion (perhaps the majority) of socialist militants of the former empire, came up against the hyper-Bolshevik intransigence of the leaders of the Russian Communist Party and the International – an intransigence that was actually sectarian and incoherent. On the one hand, genuine national rights for the Jewish population of the Soviet Union were recognized in the wake of the revolution, a recognition applied in practice by the opening of Yiddish-language schools, the publication of books and periodicals in that language, and even the creation, in January 1918, of a sub-commissariat of Jewish affairs in the context of the commissariat of nationalities. But on the other hand, as far as the political organization of Jewish workers and Jewish communists was concerned, Lenin's original conceptions of 1903, the time of the first break with the Bund, continued to prevail: organic unity, the centralization of the party above all else. Thus the communist leaders refused to accept the genuine existence of either the Jewish Communist Party that arose from Poale Zion,[10] or the Ukrainian or Polish Kombund. The militants of these intermediate groupings were summoned to join the 'normal' structures of the Communist Party individually. Any idea of a specific political organization of Jewish workers, which would take into consideration the particularities of their traditions, their language, their form of organization, etc., was rejected as a symptom of nationalist deviation.

---

10   See the passage on Poale Zion in the introduction, pp. 5–6.

The 'Jewish sections' that were then established within the Communist Party and the apparatus of the Soviet state accordingly displayed a fundamentally ambiguous character. Responsible for addressing Jewish workers, organizing them and developing among them a propaganda work written in terms and in a language that they could understand, responsible for raising the consciousness of the Jewish masses, they sanctioned by their very existence the perpetuation of a national dimension of the Jewish problem within the Soviet system. Yet they were conceived as an instrument of integration of the Jewish population into Soviet society, and battled relentlessly against the symptoms of traditional Jewish life: the rabbi, the Jewish middleman and the Zionist were the favoured targets of their propaganda. This bitter struggle to root out particularisms that were seen as outdated made the *yevsek* appear as Russifiers in the eyes of a substantial portion of the Jewish population – even if they carried out their activities in Yiddish.

Simultaneously, though, the *yevsek*, despite proclaiming its 'neutrality' as to the future of Yiddish, was in fact engaged in a struggle against the linguistic assimilation of Jewish workers, active in developing Yiddish schools, press, theatre, etc. And by doing so, it came up against the sensibility of a section of Jewish youth that turned towards large-scale industry and saw their rapid assimilation as 'progressive', a natural and irrevocable process.

Over the years, these contradictions became more flagrant and explosive. The establishment of a federal system in the USSR (in 1922) emphasized the importance and permanence of nations within the union of republics, sanctioning this fact both at the level of Soviet organization and at that of the communist parties. But the Jewish question, because not inscribed in a particular territory, was scarcely affected by the establishment of this new mode of organization. In the context of the Yevsektia, the struggles for influence between those who in the eyes of their opponents were respectively 'assimilators' and 'nationalists', former Bundists, Jewish Bolsheviks, militants of Poale Zion and other *Sejmists*, underlined the incoherence of a policy that lacked direction, swinging between the assertion that 'the Jewish people are faced with an important task, that of preserving their nationality' (Kalinin), and those who never stopped stigmatizing the 'Zionism' rampant in Soviet Jewish institutions.

In 1927, for example, Alexander Chemerisky, secretary of the Yevsektia and a former Bundist who had joined the Communist Party in 1920, wrote that it was necessary to 'declare a merciless war on Yiddishism' and combat the Bund, Zionism and even a Soviet version of Jewish 'nationalism'. It was not the least paradox and incoherence of the situation at this time that all Jewish organizations which called themselves communist and Soviet on an autonomous basis were dissolved in 1923, while the social democratic Poale Zion, the descendant of the fraction of this organization that had refused to adhere to communism in 1919, continued to exist legally until 1928.

It is impossible to understand the scope of subsequent disappointments without stressing how strongly the majority of the Jewish population rallied to the Soviet regime in the course of the civil war, and the attraction that the 'utopia' of the new state power continued to exert on several generations of Jewish socialist militants of Eastern Europe.

Moshe Green, a Bundist militant from Warsaw, had no particular sympathy for Bolshevism. But in 1918 he was mobilized in the army of newly independent Poland, and among the soldiers nationalist sentiments prevailed. When the Soviet–Polish war broke out, he was several times involved in battles against the Red Army, but this war was not his war. In the Minsk region, where a large proportion of the population was Jewish, the Polish soldiers looted Jewish shops and houses and organized pogroms. 'Despite the little sympathy I had for Bolshevism', Green comments, 'I still preferred it to the Polish nationalism whose other face was anti-Semitism. All things considered, then, I would have leaned to the side of Soviet Russia, all the more so as in Poland, too, independence was greeted by a wave of pogroms.'

Solomon Fishkowski, a Poale Zion militant in Kolno, Poland, passionately followed the news from Russia in the German papers that social democratic activists mobilized in the Kaiser's army passed on to him. He enthusiastically welcomed the Russian Revolution. On 1 May 1918 he was arrested while distributing leaflets. He was imprisoned, then enlisted in the Polish army. As a Jew, he was often victimized.

When the Polish–Soviet war broke out he decided to desert and join the Red Army, to rally to this revolution that had proclaimed the end of all discrimination against Jews – a symbolic passage to the 'enemy' for an adolescent who in 1905 had seen the tsar's Cossacks beat his father and leave him for dead, with the loss of an eye, on a country road.

The key element, which really sealed the fate of the Jews of Russia, was the policy of the Bolsheviks. It very soon dealt a mortal blow to the Jewish political and cultural renaissance. In scarcely more than a year or two, the forces of the Jewish community in Russia were liberated by the revolution; then, just as quickly, they were stifled.[11]

So writes a Zionist historian. This unqualified verdict implicitly refers, sure enough, to the destruction of the traditional world of Russian Jews in the course of the revolution and the subsequent civil war, to the ruin of the *shtetl*, then the reconstruction of political structures and a new way of life that ruled out political pluralism, banished the traditional forms of organization of the Jewish community, and promoted a new Jewish culture exclusively oriented to the 'new world'.

It is hard to deny, however, the reality of the Jewish cultural renaissance of the 1920s in the USSR, attested in particular by the remarkable flourishing of Jewish theatre in this period, by an intense and varied production of Yiddish literature, the establishment of Jewish schools, etc. The characteristic of all this renewal and cultural awakening is that it was directly a function of specifically political factors, being to a large degree determined politically and ideologically.

Thus in 1927, *Tribuna* reported the creation of a department of Jewish studies at the Byelorussian cultural institute in Minsk, the establishment of a department of Jewish culture in Kiev, and other similar new projects. The paper also mentioned the creation of a Jewish agricultural school in Novo-Poltakva, the activities of a college for Jewish teachers in Vitebsk, and the foundation at Moscow University of a Jewish scientific society, as well as the opening in Leningrad of a Society for the Study of the History and Economics of

---

11   S. Ettinger, 'Les juifs de Russie à l'époque de la révolution', in Kochan, *Les juifs en Union soviétique*, p. 43.

the Jewish Proletariat. But at the same time, the institutions devoted to Jewish studies dating from the old regime were severely criticized and would soon be suppressed, in particular the Jewish Ethnographic and Historical Society of Leningrad, to whose reputation the work of Simon Dubnow had particularly contributed.

Any judgement made as to the situation of Jews in the 1920s, any comparison between the conditions of their existence before and after the revolution, cannot ignore the global changes affecting this situation. It makes little sense, for example, to write that before the revolution, 'almost all Jewish children attended Jewish schools', and that 'in Ukraine alone, Yiddish was spoken in some 800 schools', whereas in 1932 'there were still 839 primary schools, 59 secondary schools and four teachers' training colleges' designed for Jews.[12] The label 'Jewish school' here, even the criterion of teaching in Yiddish, are an insufficient basis for comparison. The pre-revolutionary schools were almost entirely *heder* that taught the Bible and Talmud; the post-revolutionary schools were secular institutions where a general instruction strongly impregnated with communist ideology was given in Yiddish.

In one sense, the revolutionary upheavals continued transformations that had already begun in the late decades of the nineteenth century among the Jewish communities of Eastern Europe. In the new Russia, the sudden changes introduced by the revolution, and the cataclysms that accompanied them, precipitated the eruption of these communities into modernity and universality, bringing to birth the features of a new Jewish identity in the USSR. But this forced metamorphosis, with all the dramas that accompanied it, is difficult to equate with a simple destruction or 'stifling'. What was now born was a new Jewish culture with a new and radical direction, certainly inflected by the political flux and ideological commandments of the revolution, but far less uniform, 'aligned' and 'instrumentalized' than is often imagined. After 1917 not only was a Jewish theatre in Yiddish established, the Goset, which 'danced on the ruins of the ghetto and

12   *Les juifs en URSS* (Cahiers d'information) (Paris: Bibliothèque contemporaine), p. 21.

the old synagogue', but also a Hebrew theatre, the Habimah, which 'trembled in mystic fear before the omnipresence of God'. The former presented, in an 'explosion of laughter', 'the joy of the newly liberated Jewish people', with pieces by Sholem Aleichem and Isaac Leib Peretz, but also Shakespeare, the specifically Jewish heritage thus linking up with universal culture. This was a politically committed theatre oriented to new aesthetic forms and seeking to 'seize the time' that the Jewish community of the USSR found itself pulled into, to express 'the major trauma represented by the transition from the closed world to the infinite universe'. Religion, rigid morals and traditional life were cast into derision, and the productions emphasized collective action and the movement of the masses. At the same time, however, this rejection of a past 'old in centuries and suffering, rotting and already rotten', was accompanied by a 'self-affirmation', a 'rejection of assimilation' by the new public that recognized itself in this original cultural production. The Habimah, on the other hand, was a theatre oriented towards the traditions of the Jewish people, 'linked to the cultural activities of the Zionist movement'; in 1926, its members took the opportunity of a European tour to leave the USSR.[13]

In the same manner, there existed in the 1920s and up to the great purges of the mid-1930s a Yiddish literature with several rival schools. In the late 1920s, the rise of Yiddish cultural activities in the USSR, and the echo it found among Jewish communities abroad (in Poland, America, etc.), was such that a certain number of leading Yiddish writers, more or less favourable to Bolshevism as the case may be, returned to the USSR: Der Nister, Bergelson, Markish, etc. Throughout these years, Soviet Yiddish literature – like Russian literature, indeed – was riven by sharp quarrels, particularly between champions of a 'proletarian' literature and those who proclaimed the principle of freedom of creation and the autonomy of literature. For the 'proletarians' who stood for a direct and partisan commitment of art in political struggle, their opponents (the majority of Yiddish

---

13   Béatrice Picon-Vallin, *Le théâtre juif soviétique pendant les années 20* (Lausanne: L'âge d'homme, 1973).

writers with a reputation) embodied 'outdated' and 'dangerous' tendencies, from 'passé-ism' to 'neutralism' and even 'chauvinism'. This was a time when hundreds of books were published in Yiddish each year (either original or translations), as well as several literary magazines, but this flourishing should not make us forget the conflicts and debates of a rare violence that consumed Yiddish literary milieus. Here again, the pogroms unleashed between 1930 and 1950 against the representatives of Soviet Jewish culture masked the earlier situation, leading to hasty and often abusive reinterpretations.

In the early 1920s, there was no hesitation in publishing texts by Yiddish writers who had left Russia after the revolution – Peretz Markish, for example. During its early years, the Yevsektia played a very minor role in the field of literature. It did indeed seek to encourage a new type of literary production, written by workers, artisans and peasants, but this did not mean that it boycotted 'non-committed' writers – on condition that they were loyal to the revolution. The periodicals of the Jewish section were not afraid to allow different approaches to literary expression, or to publish the protest of a group of writers who had been attacked by the editorial board.

From 1927, however, the central committee of the Yevsektia began an offensive against 'nationalist' tendencies in Yiddish literature, denouncing the links forged with Yiddish language production abroad. This coincided with the more general turn taken under Stalin's impulse in the party's orientation towards non-Russian peoples. From 1929, the need to introduce class struggle into Yiddish literature was emphasized, and the Yevsektia began to exert a stricter control over literary periodicals and organize campaigns and meetings against writers who did not toe the line.

In practice, the most strident denunciators of 'nationalist' and 'passé-ist' tendencies in Yiddish literature were not Stalinist officials with their minds befogged by Great Russian chauvinism, but rather Jewish writers and activists themselves, generally linked with the famous 'Jewish sections' that saw it as the main duty of artists to make propaganda for the revolution among the masses. The bitter and tragic paradox of this situation is that, before falling under the blind blows of Stalinist repression, several of these people were themselves active agents of an alignment of Yiddish artistic production, the dulling of a literature that was ever more closely under surveillance. 'Yiddish poetry of this time', one specialist later wrote, 'abounded in hymns and paeans to the glory of the party and its leaders, especially Stalin, the building of socialism in town and country and its heroes, the Red Army, the anniversary of the Revolution and 1 May'.[14] In 1929–30, Peretz Markish, a future victim of the 1953 purge, published a number of his poems 'retouched' so as to attract the favours of those governing literature and art in the Soviet apparatus.

The adversaries of Bolshevism are certainly deceiving themselves when, in their stubbornness to lend it Machiavellian intentions *sub specie aeternitatis*, they start from the principle that the Russian communists had well-thought-out plans concerning the 'solution' to the Jewish question at the moment they took power. On the contrary, as shown by all the zigzags and incoherencies of their Jewish policy over the following years, they had no strategic project in this direction, which is in no way surprising if we bear in mind their absence of any previous intervention among the Jewish working class as such, their general underestimation of its national particularities, their contempt for the 'particularism' of the Bund, etc. After the revolution, in fact, their Jewish policy was the result of contradictory pressures, both outside and within the Jewish community of the Soviet Union, with the centre of gravity shifting over the years towards the former – as the genesis of the Birobidzhan project clearly shows. A further contradiction is that the great majority of Old Bolsheviks were foreign to any specifically Jewish life and saw the solution to the Jewish question as a particular and no doubt secondary aspect of the emancipation of man in the new society. The majority of cadres of the Yevsektia, on the other hand, had come from various Jewish socialist parties in which the national dimension of the Jewish question was a central preoccupation. Their 'conversion' to Bolshevism did not prevent them from pursuing, in a certain sense, their political traditions. They were very often placed in a dangerous situation, faced on the one hand with

---

14   Shmeruk Chone, 'La littérature yiddish en Union soviétique', in Kochan, *Les juifs en Union soviétique*, p. 346.

the multiple turns in the party's policy on the national question, and on the other hand with the contradictory aspirations of the 'Jewish street'. When the Yevsektia and its apparatus were dissolved in 1930, these contradictions, far from being resolved, were in the process of growing still more explosive.

The problem of the Yiddish language was one of the factors on which these difficulties and uncertainties focused. Was it only a means of diffusing communist ideas among the Jewish masses, or was it also a vehicle of culture, a value 'in itself', its defence and promotion an integral part of the struggle of Jewish workers for their emancipation? Fundamentally, raising these questions means questioning the purposes of the Yevsektia itself. It is interesting to note how, at the same time (in 1926), two Yevsektia militants reacted differently to these very questions.

The first, Hersh Smolar, attended that year's national congress of the Yevsektia. Esther Frumkin, the legendary Bundist leader who became a communist, delivered a speech there that was a bitter disappointment for the young *yevsek*: she stood for 'neutralism' concerning the future of the Jewish communities in the USSR, whether they would assimilate or maintain their national identity; the guiding thread of her speech was simply the general aspiration to build socialism. But then, Smolar asked, what was the object of all our Jewish work? How to mobilize Jewish activists for a militancy that was often difficult, if the only prospect their leaders proposed to them followed the continuing line of 'the experience of generations of Jewish revolutionaries'? In order to base her 'neutralist' perspective on the Jewish future, Esther resorted to a simple image:

Do you really think that, in a boot factory, each worker could be imbued with enthusiasm for his task for the sole reason that he was convinced that men will have an eternal need for boots? And if it turns out that man no longer needs boots in the future, will his enthusiasm diminish because of this?[15]

15   Smolar, *Tokhelet veshivra*, pp. 63–4.

Quite differently from Smolar, Esther Rosenthal-Schneidermann was shocked by the 'nationalist rush' of one leader of the Jewish Komsomol sections, Herschl Bril, who declared with no beating about the bush that it was time to develop a Yiddish-language activity among all the young Jewish 'pioneers' in the USSR:

> I felt that there was something not quite right here: develop Yiddish-language activity among all the Jewish pioneers? Without exception? Wasn't this extremism? Should this rule be applied even to children from assimilated families who did not speak Yiddish? After all, there were very many of these in the USSR.[16]

These contradictions show the ambiguity of the new Jewish culture promoted by the revolution. Most often, this culture was marked by a rather one-sided and hasty voluntarism, of which 'Yiddishism' and its excesses were one aspect. Starting from the correct idea that Yiddish was the common tongue of the mass of the Jewish working population in Russia, this ended up making a kind of fetish of it, opposing it to Hebrew, which was viewed likewise one-sidedly as the language of rabbis and Zionists, the vehicle of superstitions and illusions. Sometimes, this pre-eminence of Yiddish was even imposed mechanically, as the vehicle for Jewish culture, over Russian that had become at the turn of the century the language of culture for a certain number of Jewish intellectuals.

This hasty voluntarism had still more serious consequences in the field of social and political life. Under War Communism, the traditional *shtetl* artisan who struggled to survive and employed a single worker was often stigmatized as a vile exploiter; all those who lived or had lived from a plurality of those 'jobs' created by tradition and the practice of religion, from the rabbi to the circumciser, the marriage-broker to the synagogue warden, were designated as pillars of superstition, vestiges of a shameful past. The anti-religious propaganda of the Soviet state, conducted in the 'Jewish street' by the young activists of the Yevsektia, did not bother with nuances and didactic concerns.

---

16   Rosenthal-Schneidermann, *Naftoulei Derakhim*, pp. 54–5.

In the synagogues were created cultural circles; on the dates of religious festivals were held meetings, which denounced outdated beliefs and celebrated the cult of the revolution.

It is possible to cite many examples of the sectarian and over-hasty manner in which the struggle against the old in the 'Jewish street' was conducted – particularly on the part of old Jewish Bolsheviks. Dimanstein, for example, the head of the Yevsektia, said that he was 'outraged' by the existence of a Jewish theatre in Hebrew, the Habimah:

> It is immediately apparent to all, not only communists but even Jewish democrats, that Habimah is a caprice of the Jewish bourgeoisie. It is not a theatre in any specific language, but a theatre on nationalist lines, a representative of the bourgeoisie that seeks to use theatrical means to revive a dead language, to bring Jews back into the orbit of absurd religious beliefs, to detach them from the masses and hinder the development of their class consciousness. We have a Jewish theatre. But the fact is that Hebrew is a dead language. If the corpse delays the funeral, it starts stinking! If the bourgeoisie are so set on their free national self-determination, let them do so on their own behalf. They should be grateful to us that the Cheka has not yet closed this establishment.

This judgement without appeal is a good example of a way of thinking that paid no heed to nuances, equating a language (which, despite not being practised in everyday life by the Jewish community, was nonetheless an ineradicable component of its culture) with religion, as a simple vestige of the past and opiate of the masses, and thereby a rearguard battle action of the bourgeoisie.

The same schematism was found in the Jewish press. *Tribuna* constantly developed the familiar themes of anti-religious propaganda, denouncing a rabbi who was so bold as to join a local *kholkoz* in Byelorussia,[17] stigmatizing a teacher who had organized a *minyan* to pray for his sick daughter and another who had eaten matzos in front of his pupils at Passover time, celebrating the transformation of the great synagogue in Leningrad into a cultural centre, describing the

---

17   *Kholkoz*: collective farm.

organization of 'anti-religious Saturdays devoted to voluntary work' (*subbotniks*) in Jewish villages, or proudly proclaiming that 'pork has become commonplace in Jewish life' – now being raised in Jewish agricultural settlements.

Thus the new Jewish culture often appeared, particularly to those sectors of the population most attached to traditional forms of existence, as no more than background music to the Sovietization of their existence. The promotion of this culture and, to a certain extent, of a new Jewish national sentiment went together at this time with a growing social differentiation among the Soviet Jewish population: between those strata who, for better or worse, sought to maintain their position in the traditional sectors of activity of 'middlemen', and those who swelled the growing ranks of the industrial proletariat. In 1935, around a million Soviet Jews were wage-earners, over half of these being manual workers. Between 1926 and 1935, the number of these wage-earners had grown by two and a half times, and the number of manual workers by three times. Which means, as John Bunzl notes, that 'the greater part of the "unproductive" population was in fact proletarianized. However, the specificity of the Jewish problem continued to exist. Its basis was the existence of a non-integrated and unassimilated population, a problem still awaiting a solution'.[18] An ensuing political differentiation, broadly speaking, divided a large fraction of Jewish youth won to revolutionary ideas, who sometimes tended to assimilate to the general Soviet population by way of the factory, the Komsomol, the university, etc. and were sometimes to be found in the ranks of the Jewish sections, from those sectors that remained hostile or 'neutral' towards the Soviet regime.

The first Soviet years of Solomon Fishkowski are a good example of what this integration of tens of thousands of young Jews by the revolution could mean.

When Fishkowski deserted from the Polish army on 2 July 1920 and reached the Soviet lines, he discovered a Red Army that was 'waging a holy war in rags'. The first Russian soldiers that he met led

---

18   John Bunzl, *Klassenkampf in der Diaspora* (Vienna: Europaverlag, 1975), p. 143.

him to the commissar of their unit, and Fishkowski showed his card as a member of Poale Zion: 'He's one of us', the commissar called out to the Red soldiers, 'don't take anything off him!' The commissar had been wounded in the leg and moved with difficulty; he asked Fishkowski to help him, and Fishkowski asked to be accepted in his forces. 'That's not possible', said the commissar. 'I have to send you to headquarters.'

Like all Polish soldiers, Fishkowski had a good uniform made of solid cloth. The Red soldiers, many of whom did not even have boots, cast envious looks at him. On the way to the headquarters, the soldier accompanying him took his trousers and boots, offering him in exchange his own raggedy trousers full of fleas. 'I wasn't annoyed', Fishkowski says today, 'the Red Army was lacking in everything – it had rushed forward and the supplies hadn't followed; the soldiers' rations were dried herrings and stale bread. Whereas we Poles were equipped and fed by the Western powers'.

In the middle of the night, Fishkowski and his 'guide' arrived at a farm where everyone was asleep. They stopped there to get a bit of rest, while the rumble of battle could be heard close by. When Fishkowski awoke in the morning, his accompanier had disappeared along with his papers. During the night the zone had fallen into the hands of the Whites; one of their officers arrived at the farm, took Fishkowski for a lost Polish soldier and went off with his coat. 'These Russians are all bandits!' Fishkowski said to himself. He continued on foot towards Slonin, digging up potatoes from the fields to assuage his hunger. When he reached the town he bartered his tunic for two bits of bread. Weakened by his wandering, he fell sick. A typhus epidemic was ravaging the whole of Byelorussia. He was hospitalized in Minsk; he saw people die all around him, and still remembers the corpses that were brought in their sheets to lie on the floor of the public rooms. His fever made him delirious, and he asked, 'Why are people allowed to die like this in a communist country, why are they living in such destitution, while in Poland we have everything we need?' Nurses and doctors put his words down to fever.

Fishkowski gradually got better. He asked to join the Red Army but was sent to a camp at Tambov, where peasants hostile to Bolshevik policy were detained along with Socialist Revolutionaries and especially Polish prisoners of war. There was terrible famine, and every day bloody brawls between Socialist Revolutionaries and communists. Fishkowski went to the party office and complained, among other things, of not being allowed out of the camp, despite being a convinced communist. The party officials told him, 'Organize a communist group in the camp.' 'If you want me to do this', he replied, 'you'll have to let some of the detainees out so that they can work in the environs and earn a bit of money; we've got nothing, not even salt or matches'. Fishkowski formed a group of thirty men in the camp, all communists. They developed propaganda in support of the new regime among Polish prisoners, while at the same time they appealed to the highest party bodies in Byelorussia, denouncing the situation in the camp. They also wrote to Dzerzhinsky, head of the Cheka, and his wife, who headed the 'Polish bureau' at the central committee of the Bolshevik Party.

Fishkowski fell ill again and was hospitalized once more. One day, an officer sent by Dzerzhinsky turned up at the hospital and asked, 'Bring me this Fishkowski, dead or alive!' Fishkowski got up with difficulty and was immediately taken by car to the camp. The whole complement was on the parade ground and the officer (Markevitch, a Polish member of the Cheka) was addressing them. He paid homage to the revolutionary vigilance of Fishkowski, who had drawn the attention of the authorities to the scandal of the conditions of existence in this camp, and accused the camp commander of corruption and stealing food. On Dzerzhinsky's order, the commander was arrested and the camp opened up. 'You can go where you want', Markevitch declared to the Polish prisoners. Fishkowski again went to the party office and requested clothing and food for the Poles. Tukachevsky, then military head of the region, had a uniform sent for each of the prisoners, and on 1 May 1921 they paraded alongside the Red Army at Tambov. Fishkowski was called on to speak, but once on the platform he was overcome by emotion and could not say a word. When peace was concluded with Poland he was sent to Moscow, where he was involved with the repatriation of Polish prisoners.

In 1922 he was enlisted in the Red Army as a *politruk*, political commissar. He soon found himself at loggerheads with an officer from the old regime, a colonel who got drunk and beat the soldiers. These complained to Fishkowski, who, unafraid to go beyond his rights, had the officer thrown into prison. 'I was a revolutionary first and foremost', he says, 'the soldiers trusted me.' The next day, the divisional commissar summoned him and gave him a lecture. Instead of sending the colonel to prison right away, he should have referred the matter to his superiors. In Trotsky's army, the effort was to establish the commanders' authority, to establish discipline. Fishkowski was himself condemned to two weeks in prison. 'Don't worry, you won't have to do it', the company commissar whispered to him, but the colonel tirelessly wove intrigues against him and Fishkowski was recalled to Moscow, reporting to General Mutalov who was close to Trotsky. He was again appointed political commissar, and even secretary of his unit's party committee, a highly trusted unit that guarded the platform where Lenin and Trotsky sat on the anniversary celebrations of the revolution in 1923. On other occasions his unit was charged with seeing to the security of the same leaders when they took a rest outside Moscow. Disguised as fishermen, they accompanied Trotsky to the lakes he had chosen for recreation.

Towards the end of 1923, Fishkowski enrolled as a student at the University of the West in Moscow, organized by the Comintern. As he recalls,

> Those were the most difficult years in the USSR. The railway stations were full of homeless people; you came across many abandoned children in the streets, kids who had run away from orphanages. I proposed to organize an association to support these children at the university, and several students joined this. We established dormitories for children, set up workshops where they could learn a trade, and were like parents to them.

The University of the West had students from all four corners of the world. Fishkowski organized a group of activists who went into the streets to look for abandoned children. They brought them in, washed them, fed them, educated them – in short, made 'pioneers' of them. 'This is an activity I am still proud of today', says Fishkowski, remembering a great festival where the orchestra formed by these children performed and they were solemnly presented with the pioneer banner. 'The wife of Kalinin, the USSR state president, and the former Bundist leader Esther Frumkin took part in the ceremony.' After university Fishkowski went to work as a locksmith in a Moscow factory. But his career as a Bolshevik took a new turn in 1927 when he refused to vote for a motion condemning the left opposition.

While Fishkowski 'proletarianized' himself, tens of thousands of Soviet Jews entertained the new hope of returning to the land. Yet it is certainly the fate of the various projects to create a Jewish peasantry and develop a Jewish 'region' that most strikingly illustrates the inconsistency of the new state's Jewish policy. In 1923 the 'Crimean project' took shape, with the establishment of Jewish settlements in southern Ukraine and around the Sea of Azov. Supported by the Soviet state, by structures especially created for this purpose (Geserd and Comerd) and by foreign aid, the aim was to create from scratch a Jewish peasantry that in a few years would be several hundred thousand strong. In the mind of Kalinin, who vigorously supported this initiative, it was not just a question of finding a solution to the misery and unemployment of thousands of Jewish *Luftmenschen*, but rather a project with the perspective of the 'national self-preservation' of Soviet Jews, encouraging an initiative based on the 'aspiration [of the Jewish population] to rediscover their national place within the Soviet Union'. In the same way, the old (Jewish) Bolshevik Larin, who oversaw the implementation of the project, emphasized the direct relationship that existed between 'the establishment of Jews in agriculture' and the preparation of the 'foundations of a Jewish state entity'. Such 'nationalist' proclamations were certainly not to everyone's taste, and they were opposed as 'petty-bourgeois pressure' and a nationalism 'disguised in Soviet colours' – especially by activists in the Yevsektia.

It soon appeared, however, that this Crimean project held a real attraction for the Jewish population, besides making an impression beyond Soviet frontiers. The lands that the Soviet state allocated to the new colonists were located in a region close to the old centres of

Jewish life, they were generally quite fertile, and the project registered positive results. The great plan to harness hundreds of thousands of Jews to agricultural production then presented itself as a revolutionary, Soviet alternative to a Zionist colonization chained to the cart of imperialism. The year 1928 saw an astonishing event in which a group of seventy people arrived in Odessa from Palestine to found a peasant community in Crimea. These repentant Zionists made much noise in the Jewish Soviet press about the economic crisis and rampant unemployment in Palestine, as well as the persecution suffered there by revolutionary militants. Very soon, however, the Crimean project would be cut short by a singular initiative that emanated directly from the highest spheres of the Soviet apparatus: the prospect of establishing a Jewish 'territorial unit' on the borders of Manchuria, in Birobidzhan. In 1927, a scientific expedition was sent to explore this remote and deserted land, and in 1928 the principle of Jewish colonization in Birobidzhan was decreed.

Quite contrary to Crimea, this region, 10,000 kilometres away from the traditional centres of Jewish life, had nothing that could spontaneously attract the population. The Birobidzhan project very soon appeared as a competitor to Crimean colonization; the propaganda around the creation of a 'homeland' for Jews in Birobidzhan tended to overshadow the real achievements made in Crimea. 'Between champions of the "Crimean project" and supporters of Birobidzhan', Henri Slovès remarks,[19] 'a competition developed that was basically silent and concealed, but sometimes open and bitter'. Leading Jewish communists openly opposed the project of colonization in Birobidzhan; many Yevsektia militants from Byelorussia responded to the launching of this project by stepping up their own activity in their traditional sites of intervention.

The Birobidzhan perspective was dominated by a gaping contradiction that condemned it to failure: from the standpoint of the Soviet government, the haste with which it was put into operation was basically not a function of concern to bring a solution to the difficulties that the Jewish population suffered. It was inspired above all

19   Henri Slovès, *L'Etat juif de l'Union soviétique*, p. 123.

by strategic considerations, by the desire to protect an open frontier that was vulnerable to the possible pressure of Japanese imperialism. The Soviet state could be assured of the loyalty of Jews who, inspired by a pioneer spirit, would settle in these virgin lands. It might even be that in the minds of certain leaders (Stalin?), this military calculation was accompanied by a rather Machiavellian idea of creating on the Far Eastern borders of the USSR a kind of distant red ghetto that would concentrate part of a Jewish intelligentsia that was too freethinking.

At all events, the future 'autonomous region' of Birobidzhan was founded on the basis of a radical misunderstanding. To mobilize even a few thousand pioneers for this perilous adventure, to motivate Soviet Jewish institutions, to 'export' for Jewish communities abroad a positive image of this project, it was necessary to base it on a grandiose perspective of the national flourishing of Jews in the USSR, to present Birobidzhan from the start as a completely Jewish territory in the making, and – why not? – as the future Jewish state. But this new (and surprising) Soviet 'territorialism' came up against powerful traditions in Bolshevik tradition, starting with Lenin's old analyses (themselves inspired by the works of Karl Kautsky and Otto Bauer), which absolutely rejected the idea that the Jewish question could be considered a national problem in the classical sense that Marxists gave to this term. Besides, the notion of this Jewish 'territory' and its 'autonomy' conjured up old spectres against which the *yevseks* had always furiously battled: that of 'national and cultural autonomy', the battle-cry of the Bund before 1914, that of the necessity of a Jewish territory that even socialist Zionist currents had insisted on, active particularly in the south of Russia before the First World War before being drowned in the flux of the revolution. The historical perspective in which the Birobidzhan project was developed, and the 'liberal' and extensive conception of the prerogatives of national minorities that inspired it, thus created a palpable unease among a Jewish communist apparatus for whom Bolshevism and 'petty-bourgeois nationalism' were resolutely antagonistic notions. When Stalin launched an attack on all 'nationalist deviations' in the late 1920s – actually enshrining the official renascence of Great Russian chauvinism under the banner of Bolshevism – the disease could now only be compensated by discipline, the spirit of submission that became an iron rule in the party and Soviet administration, supplanting any free confrontation of ideas. As one specialist notes, the *yevseks* now found themselves constrained to practise a kind of 'acrobatics', political and theoretical, forced on the one hand to remain faithful to the 'anti-nationalist' positions of communist doctrine, and on the other to 'bank on the dream of Jewish colonization', like Professor Josef Liberberg, the first president of the Birobidzhan executive committee, who hoped to transform this remote territory into a centre of Jewish cultural life. *Tribuna*, for its part, had to perform theoretical gymnastics to 'demonstrate' that the development of the Birobidzhan project had 'nothing to do with territorialism', that the Jewish workers who went to settle there, 'overcoming the greatest difficulties', did not seek 'a country for themselves', 'a new homeland', since, as everyone knew, the USSR as a whole was this 'homeland'. Former members of Poale Zion were mobilized to explain in the newspaper's columns the difference between the Birobidzhan project and Zionism.

These contradictions explain why, until the purges of 1936–8 drowned the 'dream' in blood, the Birobidzhan project was never really consistent. Faced with an extremely hostile environment, a climate that was baking in summer and glacial in winter, the first waves of immigrants hardly withstood the adversity; 950 settlers arrived in 1928, but 600 left again the same year; 1,875 arrived in 1929, and 1,125 left the same year. By the end of 1933, some 19,635 people had migrated to Birobidzhan, but 11,450 had returned. The support that the Soviet government extended to the colonists was no match for the difficulties they encountered, and most often ill-adapted to the geographical and climatic conditions. Besides, with the exception of certain Jewish intellectuals and a number of Yevsektia cadres, those who left for Birobidzhan were not the most motivated sectors, those with the firm political consciousness required for the enterprise: skilled workers and young communists were too indispensable in their existing work or political positions; basically, the calls to depart for the distant Jewish territory were addressed to elements whose social insertion was essential – which helps to explain the high number of defections in the wake of contact with the hostile reality of the new 'homeland'.

Two of our informants had personal experience of the Birobidzhan project, a disconcerting one in both cases. Esther Rosenthal-Schneidermann, director of the education commission of the Yevsektia in Kiev and a member of the Jewish Cultural Institute, volunteered to go to Birobidzhan in 1935. As a party cadre, she had to obtain authorization from her superiors in the hierarchy. She recalls her conversation with one of these:

> The director of the culture and propaganda commission of the central committee of the Ukrainian Communist Party was an Armenian, Comrade Petrosian. His words to me were 100 per cent Zionist: 'At last,' he said, 'the time has come for the Jewish people to construct a home of their own, after two thousand years of exile.' Then this appa-ratchik, a leading figure in the Ukrainian Communist Party, blessed me with a biblical quotation. And though I was a communist who still saw Zionism as a reactionary movement, I was overwhelmed with joy. In the eyes of the comrades to whom I reported this conversation, all declared enemies of Zionism, Petrosian was seen as a tremendous figure. And who could remain indifferent to the expansionary perspec-tives of Birobidzhan that the highest state bodies promised? For me, the preparations for the move were a festival, I was madly excited during the long journey, and convinced that we had a great national mission.[20]

In 1928, it was suggested to Hersh Smolar that he leave for Birobidzhan as Komsomol secretary. He explains,

> I had just returned from a mission to the Jewish townships in Podolia, and found there Jewish youngsters condemned to a desperate situa-tion: young unemployed not knowing how to spend their days. At the meetings I took part in, they threatened to make a fuss, to tell people that they weren't good-for-nothings. Were they prepared to go to Birobidzhan? I asked. They all looked at me as if my question was in

---

20   Rosenthal-Schneidermann, *Naftoulei Derakhim*, p. 170.

rather poor taste. Yet there was so much for these young people to do in Birobidzhan. 'Naturally,' I continued, 'on condition that as well as the promise of finding work there, they were offered a popular mobilizing slogan, which could convince them that their national and social rights were viewed on an equal footing with those of others ...' But I suddenly remained petrified in mid-sentence, unable to utter a further word. From the podium, Comrade Esther called out the wounding words: 'I thought that I heard something like a belch in the middle of your speech, bringing up the nationalist dish that you swallowed without properly digesting it. You're not actually proposing to organize *halutzim* [Zionist pioneers] for Birobidzhan?'[21]

Early in 1931, the region was opened for immigration: the first families arrived, along with their children. In the same year, confirming the prognosis of the Kremlin strategists, the Japanese invaded Manchuria. The decision was taken to increase Jewish immigration to Birobidzhan by 35 per cent, while the Crimean project was finally liquidated. In 1934, Birobidzhan officially became the 'Jewish autonomous region', but despite the efforts of the Soviet government and bodies such as the Geserd, despite such prestige projects as the opening of technical colleges, the creation of a high-class Yiddish theatre, the intensification of propaganda in favour of Birobidzhan designed for foreigners, and the mobilization of leading Yiddish artists for this new Jewish homeland, the immigration quotas were not fulfilled. At the end of 1937 there were at most 20,000 Jews in the autonomous region. As Henri Slovès wrote, 'the realization of the "Far East project" was carried out under the sign of day-to-day politics, without a spark, without imagination and without soul'.[22] Reality clearly decided between those who, like Kalinin, believed that Birobidzhan was called to be 'the most important if not the only guardian of social and national Jewish culture', and those who saw in the idea no more than a new form of Zionism without a future. Right from the early 1930s, it was clear that the establishment of the Birobidzhan project was cut off from the

---

21   Hersh Smolar, *Heichan ata khaver Sidorov* (Where Are You, Comrade Sidorov?) (Tel Aviv: Am oved, 1973), pp. 68–9.

22   Slovès, *L'état juif de l'Union soviétique*, p. 125.

aspirations of the Jewish population of the USSR. And the further the Soviet Union travelled down the Stalinist road, the more the development of the 'autonomous region' became an instrumentalization of the Jewish problem in the USSR, for purposes quite alien to this question. Bureaucracy devoured utopia.

Stalin's policy as this took shape in the late 1920s, in the context of the restoration of Great Russian chauvinism under cover of the struggle against 'nationalism', tended to repress the specific character of the Jewish problem in the Soviet Union and destroy the structures that were the expression of this. From the mid-1930s, terror became the pivot of the system, striking first and foremost at communists and intellectuals – and among these at Jews in particular, who held pride of place in the great trials of 1936–8. In the end, it was a policy that increasingly turned out to be openly anti-Jewish and anti-Semitic, leading up to a renewed climate of pogrom and anti-Jewish hysteria in the years from 1947 to 1953, with the doctors' trial and the assassination of Soviet Jewish writers such as Markish, Bergelson and Fefer.

The break represented by Stalinist policy was heralded by certain measures, events and changes whose coherence and import were not immediately apparent. It imposed itself bit by bit, in subtler forms than incitement to pogrom. We may see the suppression of Poale Zion – a party that loudly proclaimed its loyalty to the Soviet system, and whose Polish branch practised an almost unconditional pro-Soviet policy – as an advance sign of this. We should also recall that Stalin, the 'specialist' in the national question in the wake of the publication in 1912 of his *Marxism and the National Question*, had never completely settled accounts with the national obscurantism that had poisoned the social atmosphere under the old regime – in contrast to Lenin, who had a horror of racism and denounced national prejudices throughout his life. In 1907, Stalin was highly amused by the joke of a certain comrade Alexinski who, noting that Jews were particularly numerous among the Mensheviks, suggested that it would perhaps be time to 'conduct a pogrom in the party'. When the factional struggle broke out in the mid-1920s, opposing Stalin and Bukharin to the left led by Trotsky and Radek, soon joined by Zinoviev and Kamenev, the latter were amazed to discover that Stalin and his clique had no hesitation, in the heat of the battle, in coming out with sly allusions to their enemies' 'exotic' origins and drawing on chauvinist prejudices that remained anchored in the consciousness of Soviet workers – a particularly painful discovery for these universalist and assimilated Jews, the majority of whom did not speak a single word of Yiddish and were totally indifferent to Jewish religion and culture. Hersh Smolar, a devoted Stalinist at this time, gives an example of these practices that would have a rich future:

> This was the time of bitter struggle between the different factions within the Bolshevik Party. The unified opposition of Trotsky, Zinoviev and Kamenev took the offensive against Stalin. I attended a meeting of activists of the Moscow division of the party. Molotov gave an introductory speech, and a number of opposition delegates took part in the discussion. The intervention of one of these speakers has remained engraved in my memory: he drew the attention of those present to the fact that the only Moscow factory in which the opposition had a majority was one with people 'foreign to us'. An awkward silence descended on the hall, then someone called out: 'See what depths they descend to!'
>
> The factory where the opposition had a majority, in fact, was a clothing factory that particularly employed Jewish tailors. These were Jews from America, who, as a way of expressing their support for the October Revolution, had collected the funds needed to equip a whole factory, and had come to Russia with these machines to work there and endure hunger into the bargain. And it was these workers who were pointed out as 'foreign to us'.[23]

From the early 1930s the Jewish sections were suppressed, while Jewish institutions, press, literature and, of course, the Jewish 'window' of Soviet policy, Birobidzhan, were placed under an ever closer and more brutal guardianship. The period of 'autonomy' was followed by that of alignment; the bodies and structures supposed to guarantee the autonomous expression and action of the Jewish masses were

---

23   Smolar, *Heichan ata khaver Sidorov*, pp. 168–9.

reduced to mere cogs. *Tribuna*, the organ of the Geserd, which in its early years (it was founded in 1927) distinguished itself by a certain freedom of tone, a pluralism that allowed it to publish an uncritical obituary of the Zionist publicist Ahad Ha'am, who was far from being a 'fellow traveller', or praise for the martyr of the Bund, Hersh Lekert, gradually became an aligned Soviet organ. It vigorously championed the 'de-kulakizing' of Jewish villages in Crimea and Ukraine, preferred portraits of Stalin to any other illustrations, and attacked Zionists in the manner that culminated in the rhetoric of Prosecutor Vyshinsky at the Moscow trials (jackals, vipers, etc.).

In a paradoxical sense, Birobidzhan, which was raised to the dignity of a 'republic' in 1936 (with an effort made in the mid-1930s to increase Jewish emigration there, spurred by praise from Jewish writers and artists, and the opening of secondary schools and a prestigious theatre), became over the years a stage set, an export product, a flag designed to fly abroad, as Henri Slovès notes.

When the mass terror erupted in 1936, however, Birobidzhan would be the stage of frightful liquidations, a real pogrom against Jewish communists, the pioneers of this 'centre of Jewish culture'. From one day to the next, Professor Liberberg, president of the republic's executive committee, disappeared; a few months later, a newspaper revealed that he had been 'unmasked' as a 'cowardly counterrevolutionary and Trotskyist, a bourgeois nationalist'; in 1937 and 1938, his successors experienced the same fate. In all the regions where a Jewish population was concentrated, thousands of activists of the Jewish sections, party militants, journalists of the Yiddish press and other writers were arrested; among many others, such major figures as Isaac Babel and Osip Mandelstam vanished in the maelstrom. As both potential 'petty-bourgeois nationalists' and a national group strongly represented in Soviet institutions, Jews paid doubly throughout these terrible years; the majority of cadres of the Jewish sections, the Geserd, and the political apparatus of Birobidzhan, were *gewesene*, former militants of the Bund, Poale Zion or Faraynikte, a retrospective crime that condemned them to the scaffold amid the outrage of the official press. This was a time when no Bundist could be anything but a 'social fascist', no Zionist – even if socialist or communist – anything but

a running dog of British imperialism; a time when, adding the gro-
tesque to the tragic, the aligned Yiddish press joined in concert to cry
for death against the comrades of yesterday, when Jewish communist
cadres who had not yet succumbed to the purges redoubled their zeal
against 'Trotskyists' and other 'Mensheviks' in the hope of escaping
the rigours of the terror – most often without success. Like so many
others, Dimanstein, an old Bolshevik and former head of the Jewish
commission; Litvakov, former director of the newspaper *Emes* and
grand vizier of Soviet Yiddish letters; Larin, president of the Geserd,
all disappeared, while the odd Kaganovitch (Stalin's 'intimate friend')
or Yaroslavsky continued to serve the dictator as a Jewish front.

The pogrom extended to institutions. The Geserd and the Comerd
were liquidated; *Emes* and *Tribuna* were suppressed; hundreds of
Jewish schools closed, particularly in Ukraine; all Jewish life was
viewed a priori as poisoned with nationalism, the entire 'Jewish street'
suspect; the terror broke its spine. In all regions of strong Jewish
concentration, a process of 'de-Yiddishization' was undertaken,
unprecedented in its brutality – not excluding Birobidzhan, where
the status of Yiddish as an official language had been proclaimed with
drums and cymbals just a few years before. In schools and government bodies, even in the courts, where Yiddish was well established,
it was replaced by Russian. In this way, by the end of the 1930s the
entire 'national' and 'democratic' gains of the Jewish population had
been reduced to nothing.

But it was not only in the sphere of 'national' culture and politics
that Soviet Jews were struck full on by the terror that Stalin unleashed
in these years. More frequently still, it was quite simply as communists, revolutionary militants opposed to the 'new course' embarked
on by the winners of the factional struggle that had raged from 1924
to 1927 (building of socialism in one country, forced collectivization,
restoration of traditional values, bureaucratization of Soviet institutions, etc.). Thus Solomon Fishkowski, branded a Trotskyist, followed
the way of the cross that led him to Vorkuta.

In 1927, Fishkowski was arrested and condemned to three years
in prison on account of his membership of the opposition. He was
deported to Ufa, in Bachkiria. In prison, militants representing

different tendencies of the opposition coexisted. Leaflets were circulated, discussions flared up as to the strategy to adopt towards the Stalin faction that was consolidating its power. The majority of Fishkowski's fellow captives were champions of extreme measures: they refused any compromise, and one of them set fire to his cell. They were then deported to a camp further east. Fishkowski, who remained at Ufa, started a hunger strike and was sent to hospital. Various documents from the opposition leaders then began circulating among the detainees. Some believed in rallying behind Stalin under certain conditions, others in pursuing the struggle. Radek, in particular, had written a text in which he proposed an end to the struggle, on condition that the faction in power accept the principle of elections in the party, the soviets and the trade unions. A GPU officer brought Fishkowski this document and said to him,[24] 'Read this text and tell us what you think of it. We will communicate your reply to Moscow and wait for directives.' Fishkowski reflected, then responded to the officer: 'I agree with Radek on the principle of elections, in the party and the trade unions, but not in the soviets. In the present situation, the balance would risk swaying to the side of counterrevolution.' These words were transmitted to Moscow, and the telegraphic reply was not long delayed: 'Transfer him to the isolator at Tobolsk' – the centre with the largest concentration of political prisoners. There Fishkowski rubbed shoulders with several leading figures of the opposition, such as the Georgian Midvan, and several intellectuals and artists imprisoned on account of their sympathies for the left. The regime in the isolator was relatively liberal: political and cultural discussions were regular, visitors could be received, the detainees went out for walks, and all kinds of books circulated. The cell of sixteen persons in which Fishkowski found himself was for him like a new university, where many languages were spoken.

After his three years' imprisonment, Fishkowski was released. But in 1935 he was arrested again, stripped of his citizenship and sent to the Kolyma camp in Siberia. He remained there until 1939. 'How many times did I closely escape death in these years?' he wonders today:

---

24   The GPU was subsequently renamed the NKVD, then KGB.

From the very first days, in the railway wagons taking us to Kolyma, some of my companions died. When we arrived, I was in a pitiful state and the KGB doctors saved my life by evacuating me to Marinsk. But in 1937 Yezhov's policy was introduced, aiming at the systematic extermination of hundreds of thousands of prisoners, and I was deported to the Far North. We were housed there in underground shelters. Those unable to work received 300 grams a day of a bread saturated with water; they steadily declined, and when they were moribund they were sent to the 'camp of the dead'; that was particularly the case with the elderly. My luck was to still be in the prime of life. I worked as a carpenter and so received one kilo of bread per day. We were constantly transferred from one place to another, with never a shelter above our heads. That was the most terrible: the cold, the snow, the rain.

In Vorkuta, I carried enormous sacks of coal that were transferred from rafts onto smaller boats. This involved walking with our loads on very thin planks. We often stumbled, and many people drowned. We no longer even knew the names of those who perished; each person was totally indifferent to the life of others. One person fell, and the administration brought another.

I stumbled on one occasion. I clung to the plank and the others pulled me up, but I was drenched and fell ill. I was transferred to the hospital; alongside me was a Polish officer who died. Hearing that I was originally from Poland, he asked me to let his family know where and in what conditions he had died – if ever I returned to Warsaw. But I did not even have a scrap of paper, and forgot his name.

Once, in the camp, I suggested that those able to do so should help the old men to fulfil their norms. But no one wanted to. The old fell like flies. When I was not working, I sculpted little chess sets in wood to exchange them for a bit of bread. One day, in the hut, when I found myself in the company of a Polish poet who was reciting pieces by Mickiewicz, the camp commander came in. 'What are you doing there?' he asked. 'You see, I'm sculpting a chess set; if you like, I'll make you one for two kilos of bread.' 'So, you're engaged in trade?' he replied. And the next day he had me sent off to the camp of the dead. This meant crossing the river, which was half frozen. Those too weak to continue were beaten and left in the frozen water.

When we reached our destination, we discovered a gathering of moribund who were trying to keep warm, seated around stoves in underground shelters. They got up to allow us to warm ourselves. I understood then that I had to leave this place as quickly as possible if I wanted to stay alive. I didn't want to die without anyone knowing where or how. One day, in the taiga, I heard hammer blows and human voices; it was a mission of geological prospectors from Leningrad. I asked them to send a letter to my mother in Poland, so that she would know where I was. They did this, and six months later I received her reply.

Fishkowski volunteered to work on the construction of a camp intended for women. He felled immense trees, and a more experienced prisoner showed him how to fulfil the norm of four cubic metres a day.

Freed in late 1939, Fishkowski worked in Bachkiria until 1945 in conditions that he says were hardly better than those of the Siberian camps. When the Nazis invaded the Soviet Union, he volunteered for the front, but his request was refused, in view of his past. In 1946 he returned to Poland, where for the same reasons he was treated as suspect. In the 1960s he began to harass the Soviet authorities with requests for rehabilitation and recognition of services rendered. In 1967 he won his case, after travelling to Moscow to assert his rights. In 1970 he left Poland for Israel. Now approaching 84, he still views himself as a revolutionary.

The prevailing discourse on 'totalitarianism' generally assimilates Nazi and Stalinist anti-Semitism, viewing them as equivalent and basically sharing the same features. But this taste for 'round numbers' and short cuts only leads to error, as shown by all the accounts we have received, particularly those bearing on the period of the Second World War. At no moment, even in the worst days of Stalinist repression, under Yezhov in the late 1930s or under Beria in the early 1950s, did Stalinism practise the kind of racial discrimination and repression that the Nazis had made a precept, the very pivot of their system. Hundreds of thousands of Jews were liquidated, including the likes of Radek, Zinoviev, Litvakov and Dimanstein, Babel and Markish, but this was in the context of a terror whose guiding thread was not basically a racial lunacy but a political and social counterrevolution. On the other side of the barricade, there were also murderers and accomplices with names such as Kaganovitch and Ehrenburg. There were also, during the Second World War, dozens of Jewish Soviet generals, Jewish 'heroes of the Soviet Union', even until 1939 a Jewish foreign minister, and so on. This is not a matter of 'relativizing' or half-excusing the anti-Semitism restored by Stalin, which should be unremittingly denounced, in its past and its present effects, as one of the most criminal historic regressions of the century. But it is important to understand that fundamentally anti-Semitism fulfilled different functions in the Nazi and the Stalinist systems – even if it is true that, in the wake of the Nazi–Soviet pact, Stalin handed over to Hitler German and Austrian Jewish communists; even if his blind and criminal policy at the start of the Second World War cost the lives of hundreds of thousands of Jews in Poland, Ukraine, Lithuania and Byelorussia; even if it is highly likely that, as several historians have noted, Stalin was preparing in his final year a pogrom against Soviet Jews of a scope that would have even surpassed in horror for them that of 1937.

It was in the first months of the Second World War that the majority of our witnesses (non-Soviet Jews) discovered Soviet reality, most often by force of circumstance and in dramatic conditions. As militants trained in the school of the debates that shook the socialist camp in the interwar years, they had long since taken sides as far as the USSR was concerned, generally forming an image of it in very contrasting colours, fuelled by propaganda and counterpropaganda, dreams and polemics – in short, an image coloured by their political commitment. For most of them, this was a positive image. The encounter, or rather the collision, between this preconceived stereotype and the reality was thus a crucial experience for them, a shock that they would not forget. Adam Paszt, a veteran of the Spanish war who had spent a long period interned by the French, first in the Pyrenees and then in Algeria, chose, in the midst of the Second World War, what he considered to be 'freedom', and went to the USSR. He describes the successive surprises that awaited him:

After our long odyssey by way of Egypt, Palestine, Jordan, Iraq and Iran, we crossed the Caspian Sea by boat and landed on Soviet soil. This was in summer 1943. The schools were empty and we were put up in these, alongside Russian prisoners who had been freed by the Americans in Tunisia and returned to the USSR by the same route as ourselves. As veterans of Spain we were euphoric, but they were very sad. During the first night, they all disappeared. It was explained to us that they had to undergo various interrogations before returning to civilian life; no doubt they were all sent to concentration camps.

We were very well fed, but we rapidly perceived that this was far from being the common lot. One day we came across children who were rummaging in dustbins. We started speaking with them, and it turned out that one of them was Spanish, one of the many orphans of the Spanish war who had been sent to the USSR. He had been placed in a children's home and run away. Life there was terrible, he said, he would rather die than remain. We began to care for him, to comfort him. But suddenly he disappeared. Those in charge of our group gave us a good dressing-down.

A train equipped with sleeping cars was set aside to take us to Moscow. At this time that was an unheard-of luxury. And on top of it all, we were abundantly supplied with food. The train stopped at Kuybyshev, where we were told it would stay for the day before leaving for Moscow in the evening. Then a railway employee arrived and said to us, 'Why wait all day here? There are three carriages about to leave for Moscow, why not change trains?' We were quite content, followed his advice and climbed into the carriages, cattle trucks with the sign: 'eight horses or sixteen persons'. We were in such haste to reach Moscow.

Well, it is hardly credible, but it took us a month to arrive! That man had made us get on one of those wandering trains that travelled the Soviet rail network, spending three days here, three days there. We rapidly exhausted our stock of provisions, we had no more money, we were weak with hunger. It was clear that the railway employee had sold our places in the sleeping car on the black market – for a fortune!

When we finally arrived in Moscow, we were almost dead with weakness. The people responsible for meeting us, who had expected us a month ago, had not been surprised: they thought we had been sent to a camp on higher instructions. There were some seventy of us embarked on this unlikely adventure, which had begun to shake a bit our faith in the Soviet Union. Other shocks and disillusions would follow. I remember that just before we arrived at Kuybyshev, we witnessed a scene that amazed us: everywhere that the train stopped there were peasants selling odds and ends to travellers, little cakes, pâtés, etc. And suddenly we heard one of them cry out, screaming and whimpering – a young officer had just stolen his cakes before hastily climbing back on the train. That was inconceivable for us: a Red Army officer stealing …

At this time, Paszt's voluntary departure for the USSR remained a fairly exceptional phenomenon. But there were tens of thousands – communist militants like Yaakov Greenstein, Bronia Zelmanowicz and Irena Gefon; Poale Zion militants like David Grynberg; non-party student radicals like Isaac Safrin and veteran Bundists such as Haïm Babic – who hastily fled to the eastern part of Poland occupied by the Soviets in autumn 1939. Their testimonies bear the mark of a tension between two factors: on the one hand, the Soviet reality that they discovered was no 'normal' reality; it was that of a region that had just been 'conquered' by the Soviet army and was overrun by hundreds of thousands of Jewish and Polish refugees. Later, it was that of a country surprised by war and ravaged by its horrors. On the other hand, however, it was that of a country which, by opening its borders to them, had saved their lives, even if some of their number had to pay a very high price for this salvation. Their stories bear the mark of these two factors, in large part contradictory, and the tension that arose from this.

The first stopping point for many of these refugees in their Soviet journey was either Białystok or Brest-Litovsk. Yaakov Greenstein:

The situation in Białystok was amazing. There were tens of thousands of Jewish refugees from Poland, who on the one hand danced in the streets with Red Army soldiers and on the other hand created total anarchy simply by their presence, sleeping in the streets and living in deplorable hygienic conditions. Initially, the Soviet authorities asked those willing to do so to adopt Soviet nationality and go and work further east on Soviet territory. But the majority of these refugees refused. They had fled from the Germans but this did not mean they were admirers of the Soviet state. They told themselves that if they accepted a Soviet passport they would be buried in the depths of this country and never be able to leave. That was clearly not my case. I had a heavy heart because my whole family were still in Poland, I didn't want to stay on Polish soil, and my companion and I had arrived with all our illusions about the USSR: we wanted to work there, to 'build socialism'.

A certain number of Jewish refugees, on the other hand, when they had the impression that the situation had stabilized in the part of Poland occupied by the Germans, wanted to return home. In the Soviet part, the living standard rapidly fell to that of the USSR as a whole, very low; the refugees were hungry and unable to resume their usual activities, and whole trainloads returned to the German-occupied zone. The Russians couldn't believe their eyes. They said, 'You fled from the Nazis and now you're going back? Aren't you happy with us?' Even some German officers asked them when they crossed the provisional frontier, 'Why are you coming back? You're going to your death!'

The majority of refugees, however, remained in the Soviet part. Those who volunteered for work were sent in convoys to the Urals or elsewhere. Those unwilling to move were assembled one day by NKVD troops and sent to Siberia, where they met the same fate as everyone else deported there, Ukrainians, Russians or others. From that point of view, it would be wrong to believe that this was a measure directed against Jews in particular; it was quite simply the common lot.

Bronia Zelmanowicz, when she arrived at Białystok, had only one concern, to resume her political activity. She set up along with old comrades an association of former political prisoners in Poland, and presented herself to the Soviet authorities as an ex-member of the Communist Party in Poland. In retrospect, she still trembles at the 'gaffe' that she made at that time. Very soon, all the refugees who had played a role of any importance in the party dissolved in 1938 disappeared. She owed her own salvation to the mere chance of having been a 'small fish' who slipped through the net of Stalinist vindictiveness towards Polish communists. Along with a friend, she volunteered to go and work in construction, somewhere in the Urals.

Haïm Babic, who had no particular sympathy for the Soviet regime, was one of many who waited to see how the war would develop. As a refugee in Brest-Litovsk, he had not the least intention of adopting Soviet nationality, nor of volunteering to go and work in the Soviet interior; there were hundreds of thousands like him. But the Soviet authorities decided otherwise:

> I remained at Brest-Litovsk until the end of May 1940. My wife, who was then pregnant, managed to join me there. I worked in a furniture factory. On 29 May, we were woken up in the middle of the night, and had to prepare to leave immediately. The authorities had decided to deport all the Polish Jews from that region. We were transported east of the Urals, in the Tavda region, a camp in the heart of the forest. The reception awaiting us was rather chilling: 'You can forget the past. Your home, your Poland, you will never see again. You are here for eternity. If you work, you'll live; if you don't work, you'll die!' Indeed, work and life there were very hard. Fortunately, we remained there only fifteen months. Then the agreement was made between Sikorski and the Soviet authorities, under the terms of which we were released.

David Grynberg experienced the same bitterness: 'In autumn 1939 I reached Brest-Litovsk as a refugee. One fine day, the Soviet authorities carried out a major raid among the refugees and sent them to the east. I found myself in Siberia, in a village, under close surveillance by the NKVD.'

David Sztokfisz, on the other hand, also a militant from Poale Zion, slipped through the net and was taken on to work in a Red Army canteen, before volunteering to work in Kiev, where he found a job in his own trade, as a typographer. The still young Isaac Safrin, for his part, unwittingly played Candide in the land of the Soviets:

> When I arrived on Soviet territory I did not know a word of Russian, and knew very little about Soviet life in general. One of the first days, therefore, I boarded a train, believing that under socialism all public

transport was free. When the conductor arrived and asked for my ticket, I was flabbergasted. I tried to explain myself, and the whole compartment exploded in laughter – I could have died of shame.

As Adam Paszt's story shows, discovery of the backwardness and poverty of the USSR, of mentalities still heavily permeated by the centuries-old traditions of old Russia, was a big shock for our informants. The USSR of 1941 was so different from the rose-coloured images of Soviet propaganda ... Irène Gefon, also a refugee in Białystok, fled the city when the Germans attacked on 22 June 1941, along with her husband, their baby, 'a backpack and a pair of shoes'. They boarded a train stuffed with refugees, en route to Tashkent. Along the way the train was bombed, and Gefon's husband and baby were killed. After eleven days' journey in a goods wagon, she finally reached her destination:

I worked for the ministry of health in Karakalpakia, an autonomous region in Uzbekistan, populated basically by Uzbeks and Kazakhs, though there were also Russians and Ukrainians. It was a rather backward region; either the houses didn't have running water, or it was only on every other day; toilets were a rarity, and it was a privilege to work at the ministry, which had them. The Soviet state had done very good things in this country, in terms of health and the struggle against illiteracy. My boss, a woman, was among the first thousand doctors to have obtained their qualifications under the Soviet power. They were sent to the Asiatic provinces. This woman told me that, in the beginning, the local people didn't allow doctors to approach the sick. Malaria was endemic there. I saw some remarkable things: a mother, for example, whose own son was a doctor, but who thought that if a child didn't have lice, that meant it was ill!

David Sztokfisz, when he arrived in the USSR, was no unqualified supporter of the Soviet regime, but he did 'expect something of this country all the same', an expectation that would basically remain unfulfilled:

When I was working in Kiev, I saw convoys of refugees from Poland pass; they were being sent to Siberia or elsewhere. They called out: 'Long live Stalin!' This is easy to explain; they had arrived in the USSR without anything, barefoot, and this country had taken them in. The disappointment came bit by bit, when I saw everything that was lacking, the queues – the bane of the country. I saw the deceptions, such as the complaint books in each shop, which were said to be a tool for the NKVD. I did not think I was arriving in paradise, but I imagined all the same that it would be better than Poland had been between the wars. But it was worse than this capitalist and fascist Poland; in Poland, at least you could cry out. Meeting the Russian people, on the other hand, was a revelation. We arrived in the USSR on 7 November, the anniversary of the revolution. There were big festivities in Kiev. I saw Khrushchev, who was party secretary for Ukraine at this time, reviewing the parade. We were immediately spotted as refugees from Poland, and people, whether Jews or goyim, took us from one house to another, offering us food and drink, and asking us questions about Poland. When we told them that you could eat there perfectly normally, they didn't believe us. How could things be better in a capitalist country than in the homeland of socialism?

Even those who learned to get by, or were lucky, had moments of stupefaction in the course of what could be called their process of re-socialization to Soviet reality. Isaac Safrin, for example, was surprised to discover that he was 'illiterate'. Having decided to 'play the game' in the country that had opened its doors to him, and perhaps fearing exile in the Urals or Siberia, he requested Soviet nationality and prepared to settle in Ukraine. When he turned up at the local militia office to register, the following scene took place. 'Did you attend primary school?' he was asked by the militiaman on duty, through an interpreter.

'Yes.'
  'Secondary school?'
  'Yes.'
  'University?'

'Yes.'

'Do you speak Russian?'

'No.'

'Ukrainian?'

'No.'

'What languages do you speak?'

'Polish, German, Yiddish.'

And without hesitation, the militiaman wrote on his identity card 'illiterate', meaning that he didn't speak Russian. 'I kept this document for years,' Safrin adds, 'when I had finished my medical studies and was a Soviet officer'.

In Magnitogorsk, Bronia Zelmanowicz underwent a hard apprentice-ship in the life of a Soviet proletarian. She arrived there on 1 January 1940 and experienced both the cold and collective life in a barracks of twenty persons. In the daytime, she learned the trade of building worker, while in the evenings she learned Russian, along with lectures in civic instruction in which the refugees were taught the beauties of the Soviet constitution. She cut down on sleep in order to pass an exam in bookkeeping.

From June 1941 on, the existence of our informants was dominated by the course of the war, caught up in the chaos that was general, with all the ups and downs of this exceptional period. Through the different individual experiences, however, different and divergent attitudes took shape. This disparity in reactions and behaviour was made possible by the development of Stalin's policy, the paradoxes and contradictions that it underwent. The years 1939 and 1940 brought a temporary end to the mass terror, but also the dark hours of the Nazi–Soviet act, with Stalin handing over Poland to Hitler and the impending tragedy of the Jews of Eastern Europe. But it also meant that the Soviet Union opened its borders to the flow of Jewish refugees from Poland. Hence the cry heard from more than one of our informants: 'Stalin was a criminal, but it was the Soviet Union that saved my life, while my whole family, who stayed in Poland, were exterminated by the Nazis.' The years of war saw the proclamation of national unity under the banner of patriotic struggle, the reactivation of the old values of eternal Russia as a bulwark against the invader, the struggle for the national soil rather than for socialism. Threatened with extermination by the Nazis, the Jews who then lived on Soviet soil saw the Stalin regime as the only rampart able to protect them against barbarism. The dictator and generalissimo took advantage of this forced rapprochement and, not without political considerations, relaxed the bridle of the struggle against 'nationalism'. Synagogues were reopened and Yiddish newspapers and theatre experienced an upsurge of life, in those zones that did not fall into the hands of the Nazis. Sure of the loyalty of Soviet Jews, Stalin controlled at a distance the establishment of a Jewish Anti-fascist Committee headed by all the famous names of the Soviet Jewish intelligentsia (its president was the actor Solomon Mikhoels, while Ilya Ehrenburg was one of its most active publicists), whose principal task was to develop support for the USSR at war among Jewish communities abroad, and especially in America.

At the same time, however, the brutality and bureaucratic violence that had become the 'natural' modes of expression of the Soviet system could not be denied: In August 1941, Stalin personally gave the order to execute two historical leaders of the Bund, Victor Alter and Henryk Erlich, shortly after Soviet officials had offered them the presidency of a World Jewish Committee that they then envisaged setting up. However, with the outcome of the battle for Moscow still uncertain, Stalin, envisaging the possibility of a major defeat for the Soviet regime, did not want to take the risk of leaving the field open for his irreducible former enemies. In the same way, all the militants of the Bund and other Polish Jewish socialist parties who were refugees in the USSR were considered a priori political adversaries – particularly when they refused to adopt Soviet nationality – and treated accordingly. It was this double game of the bureaucracy that constituted the backdrop to the often divergent attitudes of our informants.

Despite his 'illiteracy', Isaac Safrin was permitted to enrol at the University of Minsk, where he graduated in medicine. Initially shocked by the manner in which the Soviet administration 'colonized' the part of Poland that the USSR had annexed, he soon 'adapted' and 'integrated':

I was treated as a regular Soviet citizen. I learned Russian by deciphering the posters in the streets and reading *Pravda* every day. The Jews from Poland were very well looked on; people knew what they had endured in Poland, and therefore that the great majority of them were favourable to the Soviet regime. I carefully read the *Pravda* editorials, knew what I should say and what it was better not to say. I assiduously followed the obligatory lectures in Marxism–Leninism and learned the key words of official phraseology. And then the mass terror had stopped after the years 1937–8, the climate had changed a little, and people spoke discreetly of the terrible time of the 'Yezhovshina' … On the evening of 21 June my friends had organized a little party, and we went to bed rather drunk in the early hours of the morning. An hour later, we were woken up by the catastrophe: the Germans had just attacked. At ten o'clock, I went to enrol in the Red Army.

Thus, despite the difficulties with which he was faced, and all the dangers he would have to confront, this young Jewish intellectual from Warsaw found new roots in the USSR struggling against fascism, voluntarily joining a combat that became a fundamental aspect of his existence. Paradoxically, these terrible years of war remain in his memory the 'best' years of his life, those in which it appeared to him that the course of his own life meshed with the highest and most just values, in which he felt in harmony with himself as never before. The situation was quite different for Haïm Babic, for whom this Soviet episode was simply a long succession of inconvenience and tragedies, a terrible exile in a hostile land:

Summer 1941. The country in chaos. The Germans were advancing, we were caught up in the exodus of all those fleeing to the east. Not without difficulty, I reached Astrakhan together with my wife and children, on the shore of the Caspian Sea. Astrakhan was a cul-de-sac, and millions of refugees found themselves there. I found work in a factory; we were housed in a collective apartment. We had only a single room. Another family was also piled into this apartment, as well as sixteen other workers.

That was when my wife died. I found myself along with a two-year-old son and a daughter of two and a half months. The Germans were approaching Astrakhan along the Volga; we had to flee again. The trains were simply stormed. Together with the family that shared the collective apartment with us, we decided to leave, whatever the cost. I established myself at the station, determined not to move until I had obtained tickets. German aircraft began to bombard the city; the crowd fled from the station in panic, but I stayed there and got the tickets.

We travelled thousands of kilometres from there, to central Russia. I had friends on a *kolkhoz* who took us in and helped us. My children were looked after by the family who had left Astrakhan with me. They stayed with them for many years.

In spring 1943 the troubles began again. My friends and I had refused to adopt Soviet nationality. We were arrested and subjected to all kinds of pressure. I was told that my children would be taken away, that I could no longer claim to be their father. I gave in. I remained on the *kolkhoz* until early 1945. Some of my friends then enlisted as volunteers in the Polish army. I would have done the same, if I hadn't had the children. When these friends returned to Poland, in 1945, they sent us papers to allow us to join them. But the local police began to suspect us of being spies. The political police had us under constant surveillance. Finally, in January and February 1945, the first arrests among Polish refugees began. All the men were rapidly arrested. We were accused of counterrevolutionary activity under Article 58, Paragraphs 10 and 11, of the penal code.

I was the main accused, the presumed inspirer of the 'conspiracy'. I underwent a terrible interrogation, a real nightmare. For seven days and seven nights I had to remain motionless, sitting in the same place, without eating or sleeping. When I agreed to sign my 'confession', I was allowed to sleep for an hour and a half on a bench, in the examining magistrate's office. I was condemned to six years in camp, and my comrades to four or five years.

I spent almost the whole of my term in a camp close to Ulyanovsk, then at Sarov, between Kazan' and Gorki. Sarov was a secret camp, a sealed-off town 'for special purpose', and I suspect that atomic weapons were manufactured there. When I left, I was made to sign a document undertaking not to reveal anything of my stay at this strategic site, under penalty of a new condemnation to twenty-five years in the camp.

In any case, instead of releasing me after my six years I was sent to Kolyma, the 'island' at the far end of Siberia. I remained there for four years. After the death of Stalin, under Khrushchev and Malenkov, it was the common prisoners who were released first.

I was freed in 1953, along with a group of Soviet soldiers whose only misdeed was to fall prisoner to the Germans during the war. Although my passport did not authorize me to travel unrestrictedly across the USSR, I reached Riga, where I remained for two and a half years. I dreamed of returning to Poland and renewing my Polish citizenship. Finally, however, my children who were already in Israel moved heaven and earth to have me allowed to join them; they even wrote to the Supreme Soviet. In 1956, I received papers permitting me to travel to Israel, and on 6 July 1956 I landed at the port of Haifa.

David Grynberg, likewise a refugee in Brest-Litovsk in autumn 1939, was deported east, like tens of thousands of Polish Jews who had arrived on Soviet territory. It was an experience that he recalls with bitterness:

In Siberia, I worked in a village where we were under close surveillance by the NKVD. It is hardly credible, but out of the meagre wage that I then earned, I had to pay 25 per cent back to the NKVD for this surveillance cost! I cut trees in the forest as one of a small group of five men. Among us was a boy of seventeen, a student in a rabbinical school. He was very pious and reluctant to work on Saturday. He came up to me and said, 'Try to arrange this with the others. They can do my norm on Saturday, and I'll work on Sunday.' The others meant the common prisoners, robbers, not Jews. The work was very hard; you had to saw the wood, pile it up. We were very poorly fed … Well, not only did they agree that he shouldn't work on Saturday, they did not want him to make up on the Sunday. But he wouldn't hear of it, and insisted on fulfilling his norm on Sunday.

One day, we were not paid as we expected. We were owed a month's wages, which was enormous for all of us. How were we going to feed ourselves? We sat down outside the offices of the municipality and crossed our arms. A party official came out, furious, and shouted, 'What's this? A strike? You know what this can cost you?' 'No,' we replied, 'it's not a strike, but we don't have any food, we can't work.' 'All right,' he said, 'go to work, you'll be paid tonight.' And so we were.

How did the 'great patriotic war' decreed by Stalin transform a Jewish student from Warsaw into a Soviet army officer? What Isaac Safrin describes is a bumpy and perilous trajectory:

It was a total mess. I was appointed to a battalion of elite marksmen, whereas I'd never held a rifle in my life. The Germans dropped parachutists in our rear, and the rout began. I was with a friend, Natek; we decided not to separate, no matter what happened. We retreated more than a thousand kilometres, a good part on foot. On the roads we came across brigands of all kinds, common criminals who had escaped from prison. The Germans bombed the roads, the villages. Everywhere there were wounded and dead. As a doctor, I had the rank of captain. In all the villages the peasants gave us a good welcome, waiting for us on the roadside with jugs of water, giving us food and hiding the wounded.

One day we reached a town that was a major communications hub. The loudspeakers installed in the streets broadcast an order of the day from Stalin, commanding all soldiers of the Soviet army to hold their ground and not retreat any further. We presented ourselves at the local command post. The commandant questioned us and soon understood from our manner of speaking that we were not Russian. He checked our documents and said, 'Good, I'll send you further east.' We began to protest: hadn't Stalin said that we had to stand and fight where we were, to die if need be, etc. We wanted to settle accounts with the Nazis. Then the officer, a major, suddenly said, 'Do you speak Yiddish?' And he began to explain to us in Yiddish, 'We are close to evacuating the town. With your dreadful Russian and your accent, you won't last three days in this town that you don't know, the Germans will kill you right away.' But we insisted, 'No, Comrade Stalin said that …' Then he came out with this wonderful phrase that I have never forgotten: 'Khaver Stalin hat *euch* nicht gemeint!' – 'Comrade Stalin spoke very well, but it wasn't you in particular that he had in mind! You'll be far more useful in the rear, as a doctor and a teacher!' (my friend Natek was a linguist, a literary man; now he teaches at the institute of German literature at the University of Copenhagen). And then the major had had enough of discussing with these two obstinate characters looking for heroism; he had his adjutant remove our weapons, and the matter was settled.

We resumed our retreat, travelling in cattle wagons and covered with vermin – *tanketski* was the name we gave to the fleas, which were invulnerable. We saw both the best and the worst: a Jewish military pharmacist who, when our train had been bombed, leaving many wounded, refused to open his pharmacy because he did not have orders to do so; who, when we were dying of hunger, 'swapped' a superb Waterman pen that I had from my parents against a hunk of bread; Jewish pilots, whom we met by chance, and who gave us food just like that, out of pure 'Yiddish internationalism'; good Soviet citizens in Perm (then named Molotov) who denounced us to the NKVD because we spoke Polish in a tram – so we had to be spies; peasant Old Believers who hid us, fed us, clothed us and even insisted on washing our feet. When we asked them why they were doing this, they answered, 'Our son is at the front, we would like him to be treated the same if he needed it.' In the Urals we met peasants who didn't know what a Jew was and made fun of us like crazy. One day, we were staying with a woman in this region, and we heard on the radio that a Jewish Anti-fascist Committee had just been set up. Ilya Ehrenburg made a great speech, very emotional, and we began to cry. The woman didn't understand what had affected us, and we had to explain to her that it was because he was Jewish.

One day, I received a summons to the party's military department in Molotov. I was received by a senior officer who asked me if I spoke German. I replied in the affirmative, we chatted, he asked for information on my life and offered me tea and little cakes. He sent me to a language institute where an examiner verified that I spoke fluent German. Then he received me a second time, we chatted again, I showed him photos of my parents, he again offered me tea, cakes, and suddenly came the confidential question: 'Suppose that we parachuted you behind enemy lines, that you were captured, that the Nazis rounded up your whole family and said to you, "Either you work for us, or we'll kill you all." What would you do?'

I replied, 'If I begin to give you a great speech, to swear that I'd never betray the USSR, etc., you'll reply that I'm a great hero – here in your office. And if I tell you that I place the life of my parents above all else, you'll say that I'm a traitor. So my reply is: I don't know, if that happens, I'd just have to see.' And he said: 'That's the right answer.'

I expected in the next few weeks to be summoned to leave on a mission. But in the end that didn't happen. It was considered that I'd render greater service by continuing to work as a doctor. I worked in Perm until the end of 1943, then I was sent to train as a surgeon in Moscow. Later I returned to Byelorussia where I had quite high responsibilities in the health service as a surgeon.

Safrin's story shows up the deep ambivalence of feelings and behaviour on the part of the Soviet population towards foreigners in the course of the war – even if for a Polish Jew these reactions were more often matter for divine surprise than for disappointment. The majority of our other testimonies follow similar lines. As Bronia Zelmanowicz notes,

I never saw people display such warmth. When we arrived in Magnitogorsk, lacking everything, we were feted and invited everywhere; people gave us the best that they had. Later on, when we fled before the German advance, the Russians helped us, encouraged us, sympathized with us: 'These poor people, they don't have a home.' And they gave us food and drink.

Soon after, however, she recalls several anti-Semitic incidents:

When we were fleeing from Kalinin, which was threatened by the Germans, everyone was hungry and exhausted, and remarks about Jews started flying around. We couldn't stay there; we left right away. Later on, I took refuge in a small town in the Altai. I remember having had a discussion with a girl Komsomol militant who was a relentless anti-Semite and kept repeating that the Jews never worked, that they always managed things so as not to make war. I went to complain to the local party secretary, but he gave me this disarming reply: 'What do you want? Stalin proclaimed that the Russian people would be victorious because they are a heroic people; this poor girl clearly misinterpreted his statements and deduced that other peoples are less so ...'

Many of our informants were struck by the revival of cultural activities, even of national assertion, on the part of the Jewish community, which was encouraged by the regime in the course of the war. During her wanderings across the USSR, Bronia Zelmanowicz visited Moscow; by day she perused the museums, discovered the Yiddish theatre, admired the extraordinary talent of Mikhoels in *Tevye the Dairyman* by Sholem Aleichem, while she slept at night in railway waiting-rooms. She also remembers a speech by Mikhoels on the radio, in the name of the Jewish Anti-fascist Committee, and a book signing by the poet Bergelson.

In the same way, towards the end of the war, Isaac Safrin, overcome by homesickness and Jewish identity, set out through the streets of Moscow to find a synagogue:

> It was Yom Kippur, there was a crowd, and some people had to remain in the street. They included many Jews from Poland who were exchanging news, talking about the Warsaw ghetto uprising, the extermination of the Jews, the death camps. But there were also several Russian Jews who did not know either how to pray or how to read the prayer books, who had certainly never set foot in a synagogue before. They had come because they were moved by a sense of belonging that had been revivified by events. There were also French officers from the Normandie-Niémen air force squadron, Americans, British, Czechs from the Svoboda army. I experienced very strongly the feeling of belonging to the Jewish community – a feeling I had not experienced for a long time.

It is true that for the six years of its existence, 1942–8, the Jewish Anti-fascist Committee stood at the centre of an intense reactivation of Jewish life. Mikhoels and Itzik Fefer were not the only writers or artists who visited Great Britain and the United States, where they collected funds for the USSR at war; the committee also looked after Jewish escapees from the extermination policy conducted by the Nazis in the occupied zones, and after the war found itself at the centre of a vigorous reassertion of Jewish identity; the bearers of these new currents took advantage of the official assertion, often repeated, that the Soviet Union had been alone among the Allies in acting consistently to rescue Jews from the Nazi genocide.

The champions of this renewal of Jewish identity in the USSR believed they could found great hopes on the complete reversal of the Soviet attitude towards the project of creating a Jewish state in Palestine, a perspective of which the USSR became the most ardent advocate in the United Nations. They felt their struggle legitimized by the immense losses experienced by the Jewish communities of the Soviet Union in the course of the war, by the remarkable role played by Jews in the ranks of the Red Army and the Soviet partisans; they felt encouraged by the renascence, in the wake of the war, of the 'Crimean project' of developing Jewish agriculture and the new waves of migration to Birobidzhan. Beyond the calamities of the war, the idea of a Jewish 'home' permitting the survivors to finally live in peace and assert their identity regained its hold. Thus the poet Itzik Fefer proposed the calling of a world Jewish congress 'to discuss the necessity of pursuing the struggle against fascism, taking measures throughout the world against anti-Semitism and dealing with the question of Palestine', considering that the creation of a Jewish state in Palestine should not just be the business of Zionists, but that of 'the Jewish people as a whole'.

These proposals, however, that aimed to associate Soviet Jews with the renaissance of the Jewish people globally after the Hitlerite genocide, were more than the Stalin regime could tolerate, alarmed as it was by the triumphant welcome that Moscow Jews extended to the first Israeli ambassador, Golda Meir, on 16 October 1948. In the same year, the Jewish Anti-fascist Committee was dissolved. In December 1948 and January 1949, practically all prominent Jewish writers, artists and scientists were arrested; as early as January 1948, Mikhoels died in a 'traffic accident', which was soon seen to be a cold-blooded murder orchestrated by the Kremlin.

In the same way as Stalin had 'punished' the Tartars, Volga Germans and Chechens, along with other small nationalities accused of having shown weakness towards the Nazis – by deporting them en bloc to inhospitable regions where tens of thousands of them died – so he embarked in 1948 on the struggle against Jewish 'cosmopolitanism'. Jewish newspapers, libraries and theatres were closed. A new wave of oppression broke on Birobidzhan, presented as the centre of a vast 'cosmopolitan' conspiracy; the entire Communist Party leadership there was purged. Even in the Soviet dictionary, the word 'cosmopolitan' was given a new meaning; instead of 'an individual who considers the whole world as his homeland' (the 1931 definition), this was now 'an individual deprived of patriotic sentiment, detached from the interests of his homeland, a stranger to his own people with a disdainful attitude towards its culture' (the 1949 definition). The official press poured scorn on 'vagabonds without passports', people 'without family or roots', always in anti-Semitic tones. Condemned to death by the verdict of a show trial, David Bergelson, David Hofstein, Peretz Markish, Leib Kvitko, Itzik Fefer and other Jewish writers were executed in August 1952. Der Nister died in prison. Several others spent long years in labour camps.

The anti-Jewish campaign culminated in 1953, with the fabrication of the famous 'doctors' plot'. Eminences of Soviet medicine, for the most part Jews, were accused of plotting to kill Stalin. Imprisoned and threatened with a trial, they owed their salvation to Stalin's death the same year. Charges against them were dropped by Khrushchev, and the affair was denounced as a pure machination on the part of the state security services.

It was at the same time that Birobidzhan, in the wake of a new pogrom, was frozen into the image of a papier-mâché 'Jewish state': a 'state' with a (meagre) Yiddish press and a Jewish 'folklore' designed for export – but a Jewish state almost without Jews. In 1959, 8.8 per cent of the Birobidzhan population were Jewish, as against 78.2 per cent who were Russian. Russified and brought into line, Birobidzhan today is thus a Soviet region like any other.

David Grynberg, a friend of Peretz Markish, witnessed the liquidation of the hopes that Soviet Jews had placed in the renewal of their culture:

In 1945, I found myself in Moscow. I was active in the Polish Patriots Committee, which was involved, among other things, with the repatriation of Polish refugees in the USSR. Shortly before the committee ceased activity and we left for Poland, we organized a small party. I proposed inviting Peretz Markish, but one of the other leading figures on the committee, Kinderman, an apparatchik was opposed. 'Why invite a Jewish author?' he said, 'we're a committee of Polish patriots, not a Jewish committee!' 'True,' I replied, 'but just look around you: there are fifty people here and hardly three that are not Jewish.' The discussion continued, and in the end I won the day.

For two hours, Markish read from his writings. I remember particularly a short story, or a fragment of a longer tale, which told of a Jewish soldier in the Red Army who reached a devastated village in Ukraine. He entered the synagogue that had been set on fire, and noticed on the ground a Torah that was partly burned. This sad spectacle revived his Jewish consciousness.

Peretz Markish was arrested shortly after. I also remember attending at the end of the war a meeting at which Mikhoels spoke, to a Jewish audience. He spoke Russian. I was sitting next to Markish, I leaned towards him and asked, 'But why does he just speak Russian? Why doesn't he also speak Yiddish?' 'An excellent question,' Markish replied, 'but why not ask him?' I didn't do so, afraid of getting involved in artists' quarrels.

I shall never forget the last words that Markish spoke to me. 'Don't go into the water shivering like an old Jew, throw yourself straight into the current, and you'll find that you're swimming!' At that time, I didn't grasp very well what he meant to say. I believe I understand today.

The failure of Soviet policy towards the Jews was not the product of some metaphysical necessity, a basic opposition between communism and the assertion of national identity on the part of one of the peoples most oppressed by tsarism; nor was it the product of an ineradicable propensity to anti-Semitism on the part of the Russian people. It followed from the application of a reactionary policy that broke fundamentally with the programme of the October Revolution, a process whose fundamental stages we have followed here. It was particularly on the question of nationalities that this policy exerted its pernicious effects. The paradox of this situation is that three-quarters of a century after the overthrow of the last tsar, the Jewish question, which in the early years of Soviet Russia did not present itself as a 'classic' national question, a problem of national oppression 'like the others', increasingly tends to fit into this dimension and this dimension alone.

In the 1920s, in fact, the massive rallying of Jewish communists in the USSR to the Soviet regime, along with the concern for the national dimension of the Jewish problem adopted by the Soviet authorities, mapped out the prospect of a positive, non-coercive integration of Jews into the Soviet system. This integration could fit into a double process that was in no way contradictory, but rather dialectical: on the one hand, the establishment of organizations to enable the free assertion of Jewish identity, and of the national dimension of this identity in the context of a society whose conscious aim was to build a society without exploitation or oppression; on the other hand, the assimilation, by the natural play of economic and social processes, of a part of the Jewish population in the broader national ensembles (not just Russian) within which the Jewish communities lived. We should note, moreover, that this second factor, this natural tendency to assimilation of a fraction of the Jewish population into the social and national environment (a tendency expressed not only in the favourable conditions of France in the nineteenth and twentieth centuries, as well as those of Germany in the late nineteenth and early twentieth, but even in the unfavourable conditions of tsarist Russia or Poland between the wars) is precisely what defines the originality of the Jewish national question in the contemporary world. In this sense, it is a well-known fact that the development or acceleration that Jewish assimilation underwent in the USSR in the 1920s (and, indeed, even later) was simply the continuation of a phenomenon bound up with the rise of the industrial world, a phenomenon that emerged in the nineteenth century with the expansion of capitalism and the birth of bourgeois democracy in such countries as France and Britain. In these countries, this process of voluntary integration of Jews has always been celebrated, including by those directly involved, as a historical progress and a natural evolution inscribed in the course of things. Where Soviet Russia is concerned, therefore, it is paradoxical to ascribe this assimilation, as certain people do, entirely to a discriminatory policy. The most evident facts, moreover, speak against this thesis freighted with ideological a prioris. You can close synagogues or ban the use of Hebrew, but it is far more difficult to compel Soviet Jews to marry non-Jews; these mixed marriages are a good indication of this process of 'natural' assimilation, in a country such as the USSR as much as in the United States. It was not only in the 1920s and 1930s that the number of mixed marriages took a great leap forward compared with the time when this type of union was obstructed by the anti-Jewish discrimination of the old regime. Still today, amid the renaissance of Jewish identity, a renaissance directed against the Soviet state and the constraints it imposes, this figure remains high. A study conducted in the towns of Byelorussia in 1975, for example, showed that 34.3 per cent of Jewish men and 23.3 per cent of Jewish women married someone of a different nationality. In this sense, it is misguided to completely blame the Stalinist or post-Stalinist policy of forced Russification and struggle against Jewish 'nationalism' for the fall registered in the practice of Jewish religion or in the use of the Yiddish language. Without this either excusing or explaining in any way a retrograde policy, we have also to take into account the effects of the integration of Jews into a modern society which, with all its bureaucratic and Stalinist deformations, remains 'open' in terms of the evolution of its general social and demographic currents. This is a self-evident truth rejected only by certain Jewish zealots who are quite prepared to say that the greatest danger that threatens Jews today is not the action of the combined forces of anti-Semitism across the world, but rather 'assimilation'. In this sense, their 'historical' perspective can only be the building of new ghettoes, spiritual and otherwise, in the USSR and elsewhere, satellite ghettoes around the militarist and paranoid super-ghetto that is the state of Israel. In this sense, they can only wax nostalgic for an age when, in the tsarist empire, for example, a 'holocaust' of this kind scarcely threatened Jews enclosed in the Pale of Settlement ...

In this sense, too, we have to say, the discriminatory policy of the Soviet state towards Jews considered as a nationality admirably complements Zionist propaganda. It is no accident that the only emigration visa that Jews (declared as such) obtain in the USSR (with increasing difficulty, we must say) is one to leave for Israel. In this way, the idea is reinforced in the eyes of the Soviet population that every Jew in the USSR is potentially an Israeli citizen, so that the Soviet authorities are right in mistrusting a community that, apart from its official nationality, bears another homeland in its heart. And it is no accident, either, that the state of Israel and Zionist propaganda have made the fate of Soviet Jews into a warhorse, not neglecting any effort to lead them to emigrate to Israel, and Israel alone. Austrian newspapers (Jews emigrating from the USSR pass through Vienna) periodically publish stories on the way in which the new arrivals, as soon as their plane touches down on Austrian soil, are 'looked after' by officials of the Jewish Agency,[25] 'kidnapped', some people say, and isolated from the rest of the world to be 'convinced' that Israel is the only solution for them. There are also tales of the *Rückwanderer* from Vienna, those Soviet Jews disappointed by the Israeli 'miracle' who returned to Vienna under their own steam and remain there in a state of suspension, without jobs or future. 'In Russia', they say, 'they call us Jews. In Israel, they call us Russians'. Foreign currency, therefore, for the Soviet authorities in their global dealings with the White House, and publicity for Israeli authorities more punctilious about human rights in Odessa than in Beirut, the Soviet Jews seem increasingly to be both stake and victims in a political game with endless proliferations, cynical calculations in which every factor is taken into account except their own interests.

Last but not least, the paradox of the rebirth of Jewish culture in the USSR (which also illustrates its limitations) is that it makes a complete break with the modern Yiddish culture that arose in the late nineteenth century in Eastern Europe and developed above all

---

25   The Jewish Agency: a Zionist body set up in 1929, which after the founding of the state of Israel in 1948 was transformed into a government organization charged with Jewish immigration to Israel.

by adapting to the new realities of revolutionary Russia; as a return to the religious and mystical roots of Jewish identity by way of unconditional adhesion to Zionism, this renewal has the Hebrew language as its vehicle and the Talmud and Bible as its sources. The Soviet *haloutzim* do not give a fig for Sholem Aleichem or Peretz Markish. As for those who, not sharing the enthusiasm for the sands of the Negev, 'take advantage' of the chance of being Jewish to go and live their lives far from Andropov's rule in Brooklyn or Montmartre, more Russians in exile than Jews *en galout*, they clearly attract the aggressive displeasure of the Zionist establishment and its institutions.

6.

I Am Tired of Defeats

I am tired of defeats,
and still more tired
of friends who, after each defeat, explain
that 'basically, it was a victory'

Erich Fried

As we said, our choice to interview only former Yiddishland militants living in Israel was in part arbitrary; the same task could have been undertaken in Paris or New York. On the other hand, however, the particular situation of our informants brings out one essential factor: the gaping, radical break between the world that they lost and the arrogant new Sparta within whose walls they have chosen to live. If there is one place in the world where one might expect to find a memorial, a monument to pay homage to their combat, it is certainly the state that claims to inherit the spiritual traditions and struggles of the Jewish people. But this is in no way the case: the state of Israel, expression of triumphant Zionism, has carved on the pillars of the rebuilt Temple the principles of a Manichean view of the world, a system of thought founded on simple oppositions, a binary metaphysics: just as the world is divided in two, Jews and *goyim*, so Jewish history is likewise dichotomous. On the one hand are the people of Israel issuing from Abraham and indissolubly linked to their country, their land; beyond the Roman catastrophe, the continuity of this unity between people and land is symbolically ensured both by the inexhaustible 'burning desire to return to Zion' and by the maintenance of a Jewish presence, no matter how weak, in Eretz Israel. In this sense, Zionism does no more than close a tragic parenthesis. On the other hand, diaspora and exile (*galout*) have simply been a long suffering, an endless diversion from the true history of the Jewish people.

This view of the world classifies Jews themselves into two exclusive categories: Jews of Israel and Jews of the diaspora. In their faith and temperament, the former are the heirs of the Ancestor of Zion, the mythical warrior who made a last suicidal stand at Masada: peasant warriors who made the desert bloom and dispersed the Arab 'gangs', muscular *haloutz* who conquered the land with plough and rifle, unstayed by any obstacle. As for the latter, the Jews of exile, in this representation they are often not far removed from the typical caricature of anti-Semitic propaganda: rootless, cowardly, servile and manipulative, intellectuals greedy for the recognition of the *goyim* or traders hungry for profit, bent over by two thousand years of humiliation, who respond to offence by bending their spine still further.[1] As taught in Israeli primary schools, thousands of these Jews degraded by the spirit of the diaspora were led to the gas chambers like cattle to the slaughter.

Is it necessary to underline that this Manichean system can only find room for the Yiddishland revolutionaries at the price of a complete repression of their own history. Their view of the world did not divide the universe into Jews and non-Jews, but above all into exploiters and exploited; all of them waged a bitter struggle against

---

1   This image is part of the Freudian psyche, as well as of Zionist ideology:

> At that point I was brought up against the event in my youth whose power was still being shown in all these emotions and dreams. I may have been ten or twelve years old, when my father began to take me with him on his walks and reveal to me in his talk his views upon things in the world we live in. Thus it was, on one such occasion, that he told me a story to show me how much better things were now than they had been in his days. 'When I was a young man,' he said, 'I went for a walk one Saturday in the streets of your birthplace; I was well dressed, and had a new fur cap on my head. A Christian came up to me and with a single blow knocked off my cap into the mud and shouted: "Jew! Get off the pavement!"' 'And what did you do?' I asked. 'I went into the roadway and picked up my cap,' was his quiet reply.
>
> Sigmund Freud, *The Interpretation of Dreams*, Standard Edition, vol. 4 (London: Hogarth Press, 1953) p. 197.

every kind of nationalism; and even those who campaigned for a 'territorial', 'national' or 'nationalitarian' solution to the Jewish question rejected in horror any perspective of colonial conquest under the patronage of some empire or other (whether Turkish, British, etc.), at the expense of another people. It was only on the eve of the Second World War that the one revolutionary movement most ambiguous on this question, the left Poale Zion, chose to rally to the World Zionist Organization, to the detriment of the affinities that had traditionally linked it to the communist movement.

It is also very hard for Zionist ideology to find place for the Bundist militants who organized self-defence against the pogromists in 1905, the Jewish communists who went off to fight in Spain in 1936, in the category of the 'little' Jew of the *galout* that it forged for the needs of its cause. Thus official history as written in Israel divides these undesirables into two categories: those who did not exist, whose epic will always be a blank page for the children of this country, and the renegades, the Jews who went over to the other camp, 'self-hating Jews', as the English expression has it. The Bundists and territorialists belong to the former category; the unrepentant communists, Trotskyists and anarchists to the latter.

Why, then, did these combatants, these men and women whose story is so mercilessly rejected by their adoptive country, choose despite all this to go and live there? How do they feel in a society that generally amounts to a living derision and denial of everything for which they struggled? These questions bring up another: why, in 1925, in 1945 or in 1968, did they leave their native Poland, Yugoslavia or Romania? As we shall see, the conditions in which they left their 'world of yesterday' behind, a world that either persecuted them or collapsed in whole swathes, say more than one might believe about their conversion to the reality of Israel.

A minority, among those individuals we interviewed, emigrated to Palestine well before the catastrophe, in the early decades of the century. Their motivations are deeply different from those of the militants who reached Palestine or rallied to the Hebrew state after the Second World War. Certain informants even made one return journey or more between Europe and Palestine before settling there definitively. Nor should we underestimate the role of chance that often governed these itineraries. Leo Lev, born in Ostrowiecz in Poland, arrived in Palestine in 1922; here chance took the form of paternal authority:

> I was a member of the Young Communists. At the age of fifteen I began work as a carpenter. Along with two other comrades I decided to leave for the Soviet Union. But where to find the money needed for the journey? So I went to my father and said to him, 'I want to go to Warsaw to improve my work as a carpenter.' He suspected there was something else I was hiding, but didn't let on, replying instead, 'You have a brother in Palestine, why don't you go and join him?' I agreed, and he gave me the money. I was firmly decided to go to Warsaw and then on to Moscow. But in the end I wasn't able to, it was stronger than me, I didn't have the heart to deceive him, so I went to Palestine.

Leo Lev's brother worked in a *kvoutsa* near Afoula.[2] Leo joined him, but bloody confrontations soon broke out in the region between Jewish colonists and Arab sharecroppers. It was a period when the Zionist institutions were acquiring large tracts of land, sold to them very often by Arab absentee landlords. The main victims of this colonization were Arab fellahin, poor sharecroppers who had lived on these lands and farmed them for generations. The new owners expelled them with the collaboration of the British police. It was not easy for them to find new work in the towns. The nascent class of Arab capitalists was unable to stand up to the expansion of Jewish industry, which had far greater financial and technical resources. The dominant Zionist policy of 'worker colonization', on the other hand, was distinguished from classical colonialism by the fact that it rejected the massive exploitation of indigenous labour power in favour of an economic apartheid summed up in the slogan *Avoda ivrit* ('Jewish labour').[3]

---

2   *Kvoutsa*: a small association of pioneers, ancestor of the kibbutz.
3   Cf. Nathan Weinstock, *Zionism: False Messiah*, translated by Alan Adler (London: Pluto, 1987).

In the wake of the purchase of land in the Jezreel valley, not far from Afoula, by the Jewish National Fund, the arrival of Jewish colonists came up against a strong resistance on the part of the expelled fellahin; the British police intervened on the side of the Zionists and, as Leo Lev reports, an Arab was killed in the course of these confrontations. Leo's brother left the *kvoutsa* with the words 'I won't stay here if they're spilling Arab blood!' Leo followed him and settled in Tel Aviv, where he took up his old trade as a carpenter; he made contact with communists there, and soon after joined the Palestinian Communist Party.

Yaakov Lurié arrived in Palestine from Poland in 1925. He was sixteen years old. He practised all trades imaginable: in Tel Aviv he carted gravel and led camels; unemployment drove him to Afoula, where he took part in drainage work. He joined his brother on a kibbutz near Jerusalem, then returned to Tel Aviv where he worked for a while as a porter. After that he worked on the roads, improving the highway from Jaffa via Ramallah to Latrun.

As a communist sympathizer, Lurié attended the Unity ('Ihoud') clubs founded by the Palestinian Communist Party (PKP) in 1926, where left-oriented workers would meet together in the main Palestinian cities. There he made the acquaintance of a certain Leopold Trepper, who ran the club in Tel Aviv. The origin of these clubs is significant in itself: they were founded following the expulsion from the Histadrut of the 'workers' faction' inspired by the communists. In fact, these had campaigned for the Histadrut to be opened to Arabs, a claim that came up against the Zionist optic according to which the dual objective of this unusual 'trade union federation' was the promotion of the Jewish economy and the promotion of Jewish labour, implying an active boycott of Arab work and goods by the *yishuv* – the Jewish community in Palestine. In the Unity clubs, on the other hand, communists sought to bring together Jewish and Arab workers, just as they campaigned for a trade union federation on a class rather than a national basis.

The PKP is today a forgotten presence not only in the memory of the international communist movement, but also in the history of contemporary progressive movements in the Middle East. Throughout its existence it had to face extraordinary difficulties, being subjected to a manifold repression as well as external pressures that did not help much in furthering its struggle. The general orientations that it sought to apply, however, sometimes with a certain success, mark out an alternative for the Middle East and Palestine that would have spared both Arab and Jewish populations of the region countless tragedies and hundreds of thousands of unnecessary deaths: the alternative of a society in which the Arab and Jewish workers and peasants of Palestine would live on a basis of equality. Relegated by the 'verdict of history' to the shelf of lost utopias, this perspective can only be rehabilitated a posteriori – but also for the future – via the bloody blind alleys into which the triumph of Zionism cast the two national communities of the region.

Founded in the early 1920s by various groupings issuing from the left Poale Zion, the PKP was immediately subject to violent repression on the part of the British authorities. In 1921, the MOPS (Party of Socialist Workers), its original core, was dissolved, the majority of its leaders being imprisoned or forced to take refuge in the Soviet Union. In 1924, the young PKP joined the Third International.

It is interesting to note that at its origin the PKP recruited the majority of its militants from the activists of left Zionist parties. These had in fact been educated in Europe in a Marxist perspective, with the principles of class struggle and internationalism grafted onto a Zionist project. But the collision on the ground between these principles and the reality of the Zionist enterprise to which their parties willy-nilly had to accommodate often made them deeply uneasy. This was the case with Leopold Trepper, who, as a militant in Hachomer Hatzaïr, made his *aliyah* in the early 1920s but soon noticed how the Arab agricultural workers were over-exploited by big Jewish landowners:

> One evening I was talking to my friends: 'If the landowners call themselves Zionists, why do they only use Arab labour?' 'Because it's cheaper.' 'Why is that?' 'It's simple. The Histadrut – the General Federation of Jewish Workers – admits only Jews, and requires employers to pay a minimum wage. So the employers prefer to hire Arabs, who aren't protected by any union.'

This discovery profoundly troubled my serene idealism. As a young immigrant, I had come to Palestine to build a new world, and I was beginning to realize that the Zionist bourgeoisie, imbued with its privileges, was trying to perpetuate the very social relations we wanted to abolish. I was discovering the class struggle here, under the cloak of Jewish national unity.[4]

In early 1925, Trepper joined the PKP.

It certainly took a great deal of courage in the Palestine of the 1920s, a singular determination, to militate against the current in the name of the communist cause. As we shall see, the British authorities did not shy from using the brutal methods towards anti-colonialist militants that the French *paras* would systematically employ in Algeria a few decades later. The Jewish institutions, moreover, if not the *yishuv* as a whole, voluntarily joined the British police in this witch-hunt.

Yaakov Lurié, too, was known for his ties with the Communist Party. He was active in the Palestinian Geserd, and wanted to leave for Birobidzhan. The police harassed him and found ever new pretexts to arrest him. The British authorities and the Histadrut demanded that he should announce in the press that he was not a communist. He refused. From 1933, the Histadrut, which controlled the key sectors of the country's economy, put him on its blacklist; he could no longer find work. Along with a group of communist militants he tried to establish a construction business. But he was not left in peace, and had to leave Tel Aviv for Haifa. There he found work with an Arab, and later, by means of *protektsia* (bribery), he was admitted to Solel Bonè, the Histadrut's construction company. But he was denounced and had to leave again.

In 1937, on the eve of the Jewish Pesach, he was once more in Tel Aviv, where he had found a job with a matzo manufacturer. But the police did not let up. On 30 April they came to arrest him at home; he escaped over the rooftops and hid with neighbours, managing to get back to Haifa, where his mother was waiting with a suitcase.

---

4   Leopold Trepper, *The Great Game* (New York: McGraw Hill, 1979), p. 16.

Leo Lev stresses the isolation of communist militants, the ostracism that they faced even from the Zionist far left, with whom common actions remained the exception:

> We had very bad relations with the left Poale Zion, inasmuch as they also presented themselves as communists; this rivalry even extended to denouncing our comrades to the British authorities. I remember a typical incident that took place in 1928 or 1929. Jabotinsky had come to Palestine for a speaking tour. The day before he was to hold a meeting in Tel Aviv, activists from Brit Trumpledor (Btar) attacked a small gathering of Poale Zion militants who had come to watch a show in Yiddish, in a cabin by the sea that was used as the Poale Zion offices. I was then in the Young Communists in Tel Aviv, and when I went home, a comrade told me of this raid. We decided to react by calling workers to assemble the next day at Kikar Magen David Adom (Star of David Square), where Jabotinsky was to hold his meeting. Before he could utter the words 'Greetings to you Tel Aviv, blue and white city ...' his voice was drowned by shouts and insults: the police intervened and arrests were made.

This isolation in the Jewish milieu was only one of the obstacles that the young PKP had to face. It was handicapped from the start by the great difficulty it had in gaining a foothold among Arab workers, only a very small minority of whom formed a proletariat in the modern sense of the term, in a Palestine that was increasingly becoming the theatre of bloody confrontations between the two communities. Besides, like all communist parties, it was subject from the late 1920s to the iron rule of Stalin's policies, and forced to follow all the zigzags of the Comintern line. Moscow's heavy-handed interference would have particularly damaging consequences in Palestine.

In 1929, Arab riots against the Jews broke out in Jerusalem, Hebron and Safed. The leadership of the Third International, then at the height of the delirium of the 'third period',[5] interpreted the riots as an anti-imperialist uprising, the expression of an awakening of Arab national

---

5   According to this new course inaugurated the year before, the stabilization phase of capitalism under way since 1923–4 was over and a new phase of acute social and political convulsions had begun.

consciousness in the Middle East. It was accordingly urgent, Moscow decided, to Arabize the PKP, starting with its leadership.

The PKP leaders – also the founders of the communist movement in the Middle East: Wolf Averbuch, Joseph Berger-Barzilai, Nahoum Lesinski and Moshe Kupermann – were summoned to Moscow between 1929 and 1932; all were liquidated during the great purges or later, with the exception of Berger-Barzilai, who by a miracle survived his deportation to Siberia. In this sense, the tragedy of the Palestinian Communist Party was matched only by that of the Polish. The Comintern decided that the old central committee of the PKP was to be replaced by a new one with an Arab majority. Given that the great majority of the party's trained and experienced cadres were Jews, this instruction amounted to disarming and weakening it.

In fact, says Leo Lev, the 1929 riots were a more complex phenomenon than either the Zionist or the Comintern legends have it:

> The confrontations that took place in August 1929 are traditionally described in Israel as Arab pogroms in which the Jews were innocent victims, but the reality was not so simple. There were provocations on both sides; there were already at the time, in an embryonic state, groups such as Gush Emunim and other followers of Rabbi Levinger. I was in Jerusalem at the time. The party organized protection for certain Arab villages, and for Arab workers in the city. The day after the events, thinking the whole affair was over, the Arab workers came to work, particularly those in the building trade. It was that day, around midday, that some of them were victims of a terrible pogrom near the Zion cinema; that wasn't the only case when Arabs were beaten in the course of these events. The Haganah was then the dominant force, but you could not say that it was responsible. Was it the work of a group of uncontrolled Jewish activists, extremists of the Betar – a group that committed several provocations at that time? I don't know.

In this difficult context, the bureaucratic Arabization of the party leadership only added to the disorientation, contributing nothing to transforming the PKP from a basically Jewish party to an Arab–Jewish organization. Leo Lev bitterly recalls this period:

That was when the idea began to take hold that the Jewish community would only play a subordinate role in the revolutionary process in the Middle East; it was only a single step from this to the idea that Jews in the party were only a support force, a step that certain people rapidly took. The debate over the respective role of Jews and Arabs in the revolutionary process was to shake the party for long years, and divided it. The fact remains that, during the whole of this period of 'Arabization' of the party, Jews continued to constitute a very large majority.

Yankel Taut and his partner Trude arrived in Palestine with the fifth wave of immigration (1932–9) that was the consequence of the rise of fascism and the economic crisis that severely affected the Jewish communities of Central and Eastern Europe. In the late 1920s they had met in the Berlin Young Communists. They left Germany in haste, a few months after Hitler came to power. Neither of them had the least affinity with Palestine: Yankel was an *Ostjude* of Polish origin, whose parents had settled in Berlin on the eve of the First World War. He was an opposition communist who sympathized with Trotskyism, and Zionism was quite foreign to him. Trude, for her part, came from an old Berlin social democrat family and was not even Jewish. For each of them, Palestine was simply an accidental and temporary place of refuge. Yankel Taut:

> My situation in Germany was extremely precarious, I couldn't work, not having regular papers, and no longer had organized contacts with dissident communists. So I left for Denmark in early 1934, with a false passport. I made contact with Trotskyist German émigrés and joined up with them politically. But my situation in Denmark remained uncertain; I was not, properly speaking, a political refugee for the Danish government, inasmuch as I was not a German citizen but Polish. In principle, I was supposed to return to Poland. I risked being expelled from Denmark, and wondered what to do. Then, one fine day, one of the comrades suggested, 'Why don't you go to Palestine? You're Jewish, after all ...' I was somewhat bowled over by his proposal: 'But I'm not a Zionist, what do you want me to do there?' I replied. 'Don't worry,' he reassured me, not at all impressed by this argument, 'you'll

only stay there a few years until things are sorted out, then you can come back.'

In a certain sense, this suggestion was a relief. I scarcely had a choice, and one of the group's leaders, a man who was an authority for me, gave me his blessing for this way of escaping danger. I obtained the certificates needed for emigration through the Zionist organizations, worked – that was compulsory – on a farm for six months, and left for Palestine in June 1934.

It was quite by chance that Yankel met up again with Trude in the 'promised land'.

Quite astonished, I said to her: 'Trude! What are you doing here? Are you visiting friends?' 'And what about you?' she replied, 'have you become a Zionist?' 'Not on my life, but at least I'm Jewish!' 'Well, what does it matter? Aren't we communists, internationalists?'

Yankel and Trude were far from being the only communists who found refuge in Palestine. All the tendencies of the German left were represented there. The majority of these political émigrés of the fifth *aliyah* left Palestine after a few years, generally for America, unless they had been converted to Zionism in the meantime.

Yankel Taut, for his part, was the exception that confirms the rule. He struck roots in Palestine without renouncing his revolutionary convictions and becoming a Zionist. He first of all linked up with a small Brandlerite group, before leaving them on account of their refusal to distance themselves from the USSR. He then formed a small Trotskyist core that, in good times and bad, continued through the 'wilderness years' of the 1940s and 1950s:

In principle we were against Zionism, against any Jewish *aliyah*, for a congress of workers of the Arab East, for a socialist Arab East. Our position was clearly difficult, given that we were a Jewish group with no organized contact with Arab workers, and also because we could not deny the fact that after 1933 many German Jews came to Palestine because they had no choice – that was something I had experienced

myself. We were in touch, through the intermediary of some British soldiers, with small Trotskyist groups in Cairo and Alexandria, and in this
way we had an indirect relationship with the international Trotskyist
movement.

It was no easy job to be a Trotskyist militant in Palestine at this
time. Not only was the group illegal in the eyes of the British police
and damned by the Zionists, but it was also under threat from the
Stalinized PKP, which viewed sympathizers of the left opposition as
'agents of imperialism', even of the Gestapo.

Shortly before the war, several militants of this group were arrested
and imprisoned. Jakob Moneta, who returned to West Germany after
the war and became a leader of the powerful engineering workers'
union, was one of them:

> A few months after leaving the kibbutz, two months before the outbreak
> of the Second World War, I was arrested and interned along with two
> other comrades who, like me, had been expelled from the kibbutz. By a
> simple administrative procedure, without the least legal judgment, we
> were sentenced to twelve months in prison, which could be renewed at
> the authorities' pleasure. That was our first contact with British imperi-
> alism, which viewed non-Zionist Jews as a danger.
>
> At the police station in Haifa some thirty detainees were piled into
> a single cell. We were so tightly packed that we couldn't even lie down
> to sleep. At night we lay on thin mattresses that some detainees had
> made by collecting rags; during the day, we remained sitting on the con-
> crete floor along with common prisoners, some of whom suffered from
> advanced tuberculosis, venereal disease, scabies or lice. In this prison
> there was no difference between Jews and Arabs, or between political
> and common prisoners. The cell didn't have chairs or a table. In one
> corner there was an open bucket to piss in.
>
> After a few days we were transferred to the fortress of St John of Acre.
> One night I found myself together with an Arab 'gang' – today we would
> say Resistance fighters. Their morale and the passionate way they dis-
> cussed, their combativeness, impressed me greatly. Some of them had
> been condemned to death and were executed.

A bit later, one of the guards informed me that we were going to have a medical inspection and had to reply 'Yes, sir!' to the questions we were asked. We formed up in a line and an army doctor passed us in review, asking: 'Everything all right?' 'Yes, sir', we replied in chorus. The medical inspection was over.

After these twelve months of imprisonment, our sentence was automatically renewed for a further twelve months. In the meantime we had been transferred to Sarafand, then to Mashka, where we found the secretary of the PKP, Meir Slonim, who had spent six years without trial or judgment. The left inmates of the camp, along with Arab prisoners who had been interned by the thousand, organized a hunger strike in order to finally obtain a proper legal hearing. We were force-fed, but after a week we were promised that a commission would examine our cases.

My internment lasted two years and three months, and by the end of this time not only had I learned languages and taken part in organizing a 'university' in the camp, I had also learned what the initials 'CID' (Criminal Investigation Department) meant. I had never heard of this body before my arrest. It meant people who drove splinters of wood under the nails of prisoners, who burned the soles of their feet, who hung them by the hands until they screamed with pain – all this to extract confessions. I learned that democratic imperialism, in its battle to preserve its empire, is no more gentle than fascism that sets out to conquer a new empire.

Three months after the Nazi invasion of the Soviet Union, I finally appeared before the British commission of inquiry. Sir Hartley Shawcross, an English lawyer born in Giessen, who in 1945 was to become a Labour Member of Parliament, then head British prosecutor at the International Military Tribunal of Nuremberg, was the chair of the commission. He rightly wanted to know what I was charged with, and was totally surprised, even indignant, both by the 'evidence' presented by the police and by my advocate, the eminent Jewish Arabist Goitein. Shawcross ordered my release.

During the two years and three months of my internment, only one of my cousins dared to visit me, just once. Anyone who requested this was warned by the CID that by doing so they put themselves at considerable risk.

After my liberation, I was still subjected to police surveillance for a long while, which did not stop me from making contact for the first time with militants of the Arab left, some of whom became personal friends. During the war, by way of [British] Marxist soldiers who were sympathizers, we made contact with the Egyptian literary magazine *Megalla Gedidah* (The New Journal). We embarked on a political discussion with its editors. Some of them took part in the first big mass strike of Arab workers, in 1947.[6]

At the end of the war, Jakob Moneta prepared to return to Germany. He could see no further prospects for internationalist political work in a Palestine prey to conflicting terrorisms. In the wake of the massacres of Arab civilians that sealed the victory of the Haganah and Irgun, he could not tolerate seeing 'Jews become pogromists', witnessing the desperate flight of Arabs who left in a diaspora 'like the Jews nineteen hundred years earlier'. He hoped, on the other hand, that German history, in the aftermath of defeat, would take a revolutionary turn, as it had following the collapse of the *Kaiserreich* in November 1918.

Moshe Green, a Bundist militant from Warsaw, found himself unemployed when his employer went bankrupt in the early 1930s. He survived by working as a blacksmith, but could see no future prospects in Poland and decided in 1934 to join his family who had already settled in Palestine. Life there was scarcely any easier for him, all the less so as he was unwilling to renounce his Bundist convictions:

> I worked at all kinds of jobs: as a labourer with locksmiths and black-smiths, I picked oranges on the plantations, etc. It was haphazard work, and more often than not I was unemployed. I could have done the same as other people, take out a Mapaï card, go to the soup kitchen, and right away I'd have had a good job. But that would have gone against my conscience: those who turned their coats in order to improve their conditions we called 'sold souls'. Even if I had hardly any contact with the Polish Bund (apart from corresponding with my brother-in-law who was still in Poland), I remained loyal in myself. I felt no affinity with

---

6   Jakob Moneta, 'Mehr Gewalt für die Ohnmächtigen', *Kursbuch*, 51, 1977.

the other parties. I was against the battle that the Zionists were waging for *kibuch ha'avoda* ('Jewish labour'). I believed that everyone had the right to work and that those who lived in the same land should have the same rights, that an Arab who lived in this country should have the same rights as a citizen as I did. Besides, when their own interests were involved, didn't the Zionist orange grove proprietors employ Arab workers who cost less than Jews?

The years 1936–9 were marked in Palestine by the rise of anti-colonialist sentiment among the Arab population,[7] years of revolt directed not in an indistinct fashion against the Jewish population, as in 1929, but essentially against the British administration and Zionist colonization. The roots of the revolt were many. First of all, there was the context of the growing struggles in the Middle East against the British and French, particularly in Egypt and Syria. In Palestine, the scale of the new Jewish immigration of the 'fifth *aliyah*' and the effects of the economic depression that struck in 1935 were simply the last straw; unemployment among Arab workers rose very rapidly. On top of this, the Zionist organizations strictly opposed the prospect put forward by the Arab parties of a 'replacement of the (British) mandate regime by a government appointed by representatives of the majority of the population'.

In October 1933, an Arab general strike was launched. A demonstration was held in Jerusalem outside the seat of the British administration and violent clashes broke out when the police intervened. The conflict spread to Jaffa, Nablus and Haifa. In November 1935, a shipment of arms destined for the Haganah was discovered by the police in the port of Jaffa. The reaction of the Arab community was very sharp, leading to new demonstrations joined by the Palestinian Communist Party.

In April 1936, Arab nationalists established a National Committee that called for a general strike. It demanded a halt to Jewish immigration, the banning of land sales to Jews, and the establishment of a representative national government. The movement rapidly spread to

---

7   Cf. Weinstock, *Zionism: False Messiah.*

the whole country. The strike lasted six months and was accompanied by the development of a guerrilla movement in the mountain regions. Groups of Arab combatants derailed trains, dynamited roads, sabotaged the pipeline of the Iraq Petroleum Company and attacked British transports and Jewish colonies.

It is quite restrictive and highly partial to reduce this movement, as official Zionist history does, to a new wave of 'riots', even 'pogroms'. It took the British many months and considerable resources to deal with it: some 20,000 to 30,000 men. The feudal leaders of the Arab national movement were overshadowed by the movement itself and threatened by its radicalism, and they negotiated a truce with the British. But in July 1937 the revolt flared up again, with guerrilla fighters seizing the old city of Jerusalem and the mountains in the centre of Palestine, as well as Galilee, Hebron, Beersheba and Gaza. This time, seventeen battalions of British infantry were needed to crush the movement, supported by aircraft.

The Achilles heel of the Arab national movement then in full swing was its feudal leadership: simultaneously heads of clans and party leaders, behind their nationalist professions of faith these chiefs hid their transactions with the Zionists to whom they sold their lands, and their arrangements with the British authorities. The Grand Mufti of Jerusalem, as the Zionists never tire of repeating, leaned ever more to the side of Hitler's Germany. In actual fact, it was the Zionists who benefited most from the Arab revolt. The general strike enabled the Jewish sector to extend its economic grip, at a time when Jews from Germany brought substantial capital with them to Palestine. In this phase, the military collaboration between the *yishuv* and the British became closer in the face of the common enemy. Jewish enrolment in the police was stepped up, to the point where in 1939 there were 21,000 Jewish policemen, a figure representing more than 5 per cent of the Jewish population of Palestine at that date. Special mixed commandos (made up of British and Jews) were set up by Captain Wingate, whose deputy was Moshe Dayan. They operated by night against Arab villages, killing activists in the national movement and spreading terror among the population. At this time, both the Haganah and the 'revisionist' Irgun (closely tied to the Italian fascists until 1935) were armed and trained by the British. From 1937, the Irgun special-ized in terrorist operations against Arab civilians: bombs in markets and raids on buses and on businesses employing Arab labour.

Shortly before the creation of the state of Israel, Yankel Taut, then a skilled worker at the large petrol refinery in Haifa, witnessed one of these terrorist actions conducted by Zionist groups. By a miracle he escaped death in the course of the incidents that followed:

> In 1946–7, the situation began to grow tense throughout the region. The refinery was a large site that was being considerably extended. Between 1,500 and 2,000 people worked there permanently: Jews and Arabs. At the same time, the British troops were gradually beginning to withdraw. In their camps and on their bases they employed many Arab workers, who found themselves unemployed. Each morning, at the gates of the refinery, several dozen turned up in the hope of employment on the site for a day or two. And each morning, too, a lorry brought two large tanks of milk that were unloaded outside the gate, destined both for the canteen and for those workers doing tasks that were dangerous to health. One day the Etzel (Irgun) bands turned up with a lorry outside the entry to the refinery, but the two tanks they unloaded were stuffed with explosives and a timing mechanism. The explosion was terrible; according to some witnesses, seven Arabs were killed there and some fifty others seriously injured. The noise of the explosion was heard inside the refinery, and news of the attack spread like wildfire among the Arab workers who started congregating with calls of 'Death to the Jews!'
>
> That was on 30 December 1947. I was working on a platform together with Arab colleagues, some of whom were friends of mine. When we heard the explosion, we didn't pay particular attention. It wasn't any-thing unusual on the site, and on top of that this was a troubled time. At a certain point I came down from the platform to look for a tool, and was surprised to see that the place was deserted, quite different from usual. At the same moment, I saw two Arabs whom I knew well come running, and they shouted at me: 'Get away as soon as you can!' I ran, but others came from both sides and I locked myself in an empty cabin together with six other Jewish workers. The Arabs broke down the door

and left us for dead. I was the only one out of the seven who survived, and I only owe my salvation to the fact that they thought I was dead. When the British police arrived, they found me under a pile of bodies, and someone noticed that I was still moving. I was taken to hospital, where I woke up five days later. I was kept there for several months, and was unable to work again at the refinery until the end of 1949, in a far less demanding job. In all, thirty-nine Jewish workers were killed during these events.

The way that the Arab workers reacted to the attack was clearly absurd, but not hard to explain. The worst was that the Etzel gangs, these terrorists of whom Begin was one of the leaders, went around afterwards explaining that they had acted preventively after learning that the Arabs were preparing a pogrom in the refinery!

According to a version very widespread in Israel, the Haganah 'kept its hands clean' during of the confrontations that marked the founding of the state of Israel, not taking part in the atrocities that the Irgun was guilty of. Yankel Taut is in a position to counter such assertions:

Following this whole business, the Haganah carried out a raid on two Arab villages situated between Haifa and the refinery, killing some of the inhabitants, driving out others, systematically murdering all the Arab workers of the refinery that it managed to locate in the surroundings. What happened at Deir Yassin was not an isolated case.

Some years later, I was eating in the refinery canteen along with some Jewish workers. They included the leader of Mapaï in the plant, and I told him what a tragic absurdity the provocation by Etzel in December 1947 had been – nearly costing me my life. His response was literally these words: 'Blessed are the hands that did it!' I was flabbergasted. 'Have you gone mad?' I asked him. 'Not at all,' he replied, 'but do you think we would have our state today if we hadn't resorted to all possible means to drive out the Arabs?'

When the Arab general strike broke out, the Palestinian Communist Party expressed its solidarity with the Arab national movement. But it failed to preserve its critical independence from the movement's leadership, and for this reason was unable to play on the contradictions that ran through the Jewish community, if only to convince a small minority of the *yishuv* of the good grounds for Arab discontent. The PKP's unreserved support for the initiatives and ideology of the Arab national movement lay at the root of the deep disagreements between the leadership inspired by Moscow and a number of its militants who were more linked to the Jewish community. The division that appeared at this time within the Palestinian communist movement was not between Jewish and Arab militants, even if the oppositionists were Jews. Leo Lev, at this time the leader of the Tel Aviv branch, was one of them. He explains the cleavages that broke out:

> The first dividing line was between those who had just returned from Moscow, cadres fresh out of the 'Middle East school' established by the Comintern, and those who had stayed in the country. The former, who included a number of Arabs, had been schooled in Moscow in the spirit of a die-hard schematism; they saw the world in black and white. One day, I said to one of them, 'You see, the difference between us is that you write reports for the Comintern and have to present things in accordance with today's credo, whereas I don't have those diplomatic considerations.'

In actual fact, those communists who sought in this difficult situation to take into account the feelings of the *yishuv*, to maintain contact with that portion of the Jewish population not completely under the thumb of the Zionist organizations, were caught between hammer and anvil. When the Zionist movement called on the Jewish population to break the Arab strike that had paralysed the port of Jaffa, all they could do was exhort Jewish workers not to spill blood and accept the role of strike breakers. In the same manner, when the PKP leadership called them to take part in certain terrorist actions, against the British but also against certain Jewish institutions, they refused. It was not long before they were expelled from the party.

'My differences with the party leadership', noted Leo Lev, who soon left for Spain, were in no way a prelude to a rapprochement with Zionism. I considered myself in solidarity with the Arab national movement; I disagreed with the slogan of 'Jewish labour' that even the most radical Zionist organizations accepted, including Hachomer Hatzaïr and Poale Zion, even if they preferred to call it 'organized labour' so as to sweeten the pill.

When he left Poland twenty-one years later to return to Tel Aviv, after travelling the world, Leo Lev found employment as a carpenter with his former boss, a party member. In this way, he avoided having to be vetted by the Histadrut in order to obtain work.

The expelled comrades were convinced that they embodied the continuity of the Palestinian communist movement against the party leadership. They appealed to the Comintern and sometimes found unexpected support, for example from Louis Gronowski, the leader of the MOE in France. But beyond these differences, the national cleavage that set in at this time would dominate the subsequent development of the Palestinian communist movement. In 1937 a Jewish section was founded within the PKP and rapidly acquired a certain autonomy. At the same time, Arab communists made their first major breakthrough among the Arab workers and intelligentsia. In 1943, in the wake of long factional debates, the party split into two groups, one Jewish and the other Arab. This is the same dividing line still found twenty-two years later within the Israeli Communist Party.[8] Today, this party, known as Rakah, is essentially composed of Arabs.

The history of the left Poale Zion movement in Palestine is dominated by an accumulation of insoluble contradictions, only swept away by this group's abandonment of any independent policy when it joined the Zionist Organization in 1937, beginning in 1946 a process of fusions and splits that would lead to its dissolution. Today the greater part of its former militants are in the Labour Party.

Most of the founders of left Poale Zion in Palestine arrived with the third *aliyah* that began in 1919. They came from Russia and Poland,

---

8   Cf. Ilan Greilsammer, *Les communistes israéliens* (Paris: Presses de la fondation nationale des sciences politiques, 1978).

and experienced the repercussions of the October Revolution on the Jewish workers' movement in their countries. Some of them fought in the ranks of the Red Army, where there were even temporary units named after Borochov, the founder of Poale Zion. Others held positions in the Bolshevik apparatus. Their political and social traditions were deeply anchored in working-class Yiddishland.

It was not so much their general programme as their practice that clearly distinguished socialist Zionist groups such as Ahdout Ha'aboda, Hapoël Hatzaïr or Hachomer Hatzaïr from the left Poale Zion. The former, in fact, were oriented above all towards a form of 'communitarian colonization' of Palestine which complemented the Rothschild-style colonization based on the purchase of land and its exploitation by cheap and thus often Arab labour. The aim of this 'labour' colonization was not immediate profit, rather the conquest of the country. A number of radical young Jews from Eastern Europe were attracted by the 'concrete' prospect of egalitarian work on the land, the plunge into manual activity in a new communitarian context, a kind of 'democracy of the elect'. A voluntarist dream of this kind, several of our informants explained, had far less of a hold on those militants who had had real experience of factory or artisanal work, trade union or political activity, than on young people from a middle-class background whose radicalization was around ideological themes such as 'rehabilitation by physical labour' or 'proletarianization' on the distant lands of Palestine.

In the event, this populist ideology of 'return to the land' encountered several obstacles from a socialist perspective: the young people carried away by this dream had to accept that they had no greater 'historic' right to occupy the land on which their kibbutz or *mochav* was built than did the Arab fellah who had cultivated it for centuries. They had to accept that the great universal socialist dream, as evoked by the Marxist classics, was reduced by the weight of facts to socialism not so much in a single country as for a single people, a single nation, even a single kibbutz.

Despite these contradictions, the perspective of this 'socialism of the elect' remained for a significant portion of the radical youth of Yiddishland more attractive than their parents' condition as

Luftmenschen. Jakob Moneta, who embarked for Haifa some months after the Nazis' seizure of power, deciding to join a kibbutz, likes to recall the attraction exerted on a young European Jewish 'leftist' by this world in which all the evils of capitalism seemed to have been abolished: the chase after money, the spirit of submission, competition between individuals, the thirst for possessions. The egalitarian spirit that prevailed on the kibbutz, the division of tasks, the collective education of children, convinced him for ever, he says, that the socialist prophecy of a world without exploitation or oppression contains an indestructible rational kernel. When the Arab revolt broke out in 1936, however, and barbed wire and watchtowers were installed around the kibbutz, along with the arrival of Haganah instructors to teach the colonists how to handle a revolver and a machine-gun, young Jakob was led to wonder whether 'our' socialism conflicted with the aspirations of others. These doubts were enough for him to be counted as an unreliable element; he was expelled from the kibbutz, along with a few others.

The Zionist 'socialism' of the pioneers – not to speak of their present-day heirs – operated a transfer of utopia and programme. By a process of alchemy, class struggle became 'construction of the country'; the *union sacrée* of all classes and vital forces of the 'nation' prevailed over the internationalism of holiday speeches, just as the dogma of 'Jewish labour' prevailed over the theme of fraternity of all working people. Strike pickets were organized to prevent Arab workers from access to orchards and factories, the more cynical not being afraid to invoke the necessity to prevent the 'exploitation' of Arab labour power. Out of necessity, subsequently made into a virtue, they allied with the British to stifle any inklings of revolt among the Arab population. In the end, the 'socialist' idealism of the pioneers agreed on all essential points with the economic interests of those who held the purse strings of the stock exchange and saw a new field for their appetites opening in Palestine.

In this context, left Poale Zion was cast in a different mould than were those groups whom the colonization of Palestine caught in a logical trap. Its militants had a harder time adapting to the new version of colonial 'socialism'. As we have seen, many of them remained faithful to their European revolutionary education, broke with Zionism and joined the communist movement in Palestine. Conversely, those who remained loyal to left Poale Zion could only find themselves marginalized, forever forced to combine fire and water. As members of the Histadrut, they asked for this to be divided in two: a trade union in the strict sense, open only to wage earners whether Jewish or Arab, and another exclusively Jewish body oriented to colonization. They opposed the slogans of the 'conquest of labour' and 'Jewish production', but with arguments that were sometimes 'nationalist'. The struggle for 'Jewish labour' had a negative effect, as it amounted to reducing the wages of Jewish workers to the level of the Arabs. While cultivating a verbal anti-imperialism, the leaders of Poale Zion in Palestine saw the Arab revolts of the years 1936–9 as no more than anti-Jewish riots. They appealed to fraternity between the two peoples, but for all that scarcely counted any Arabs in their ranks – with a single exception, bad tongues said.

David Sztokfisz, a militant of left Poale Zion in Poland, recalls how in 1936 an Arab from Jaffa, George Nasser, who was a militant of their party in Palestine, came to Poland for a lecture tour. 'He spoke Yiddish very well, and the *Folstsaytung*, the Bund's newspaper, wrote that we had disguised a Jew as an Arab.' Leo Lev likewise remembers this George: 'The militants of left Poale Zion, our great competitor, also tried to develop work among Arabs, but in vain. They just managed to recruit a single Arab, the famous George, whom they paraded about everywhere, that was their attraction.' Elkana Margalit, who has devoted an exhaustive study to the left Poale Zion in Palestine, describes its activity as that of an 'impotent sect' failing to arouse a response, a group 'frozen for decades, foreign to the majority of the Jewish community and its state of mind, whereas in its native land it was immersed among the masses, their language, their way of life'.[9]

How did the 'landscape after the battle' look for those Yiddishland militants who survived, in the wake of the Second World War? The majority of them, as we have seen, were torn between mourning for

---

9   Elkana Margalit, *Anatomia shel Smol* (Anatomy of a Left) (Tel Aviv: Lamed Peretz, 1976), p. 113.

their massacred families and ravaged culture, and the hope of a new life that had arisen from the combats of the Resistance and the new balance of forces in Europe in 1945.

For the communists, the predominant feeling was certainly that of 'history on the march', the prospect of a new combat that continued those of the past. After so many struggles in which victories alternated with defeats, after Spain and the Resistance, ghettos and camps for some, the Red Army for others, the people's war in Yugoslavia, etc., the realization of the great socialist dream seemed finally within reach. The order of the day was the building of a new society in those countries of Eastern and Central Europe liberated from fascism by the Red Army. The new hopes matched the dimensions of the nightmare that had just ended.

Hanna Lévy-Haas, freed from Bergen-Belsen, wandered for weeks across a ruined Germany, physically and morally mutilated by her experience of concentration camp. But the prospect of discovering a 'new Yugoslavia' enabled her to overcome her destitution. 'I felt that the new regime had been brought to power by the struggle of an entire people, that it was based on a collective consciousness, that the mass of the population were favourable to the abolition of capitalism.' Yet life was not easy in this devastated country, even for those like her who found appropriate work:

> I wanted to go into teaching, but I was told, 'You're over-qualified, you have political talent, you can be more use to us elsewhere.' I became a journalist and translated. We lived and worked just as in the partisan years. I didn't have my own place, but lived with a childhood friend whom I'd met up with by chance in the street. We were on call day and night. I was responsible for radio transmissions in French. It was very dangerous, you had to be sure not to deviate from the line, have a reply to everything, be responsible for everything. I was also in charge of a number of foreign-language publications, such as Tito's correspondence with Stalin.

Very often, however, these militants rapidly found themselves drawn into the apparatus of the new states being constructed. The majority of them were cadres, experienced militants, cultivated intellectuals. In a context in which the communist parties, often in a minority, were led to play an ever-growing role in the new institutions – to the point of seizing all the levers of power a few years later – cadres were the essence of the struggle. Few of our informants could resist the siren call. Though well established in France, where he lived with his family, Isaac Kotlarz agreed none the less to return to Poland; he was a disciplined militant, and the party appealed to his devotion. Adam Paszt, for his part, had already lived for some years in the USSR, and though the scales had fallen from his eyes, he still had hopes: 'I told myself that the USSR was a backward country, that in Poland, a more developed country, the way to socialism would be different.' Those who had been shattered by the defeat in Spain and the discovery of Soviet reality were freshly mobilized by the new situation; this upsurge of utopia, this summons from history, overshadowed the factors that for others were already a sufficient reason to leave their country – the Polish pogroms that greeted the country's resurrection, in an echo of 1918. Yaakov Greenstein recalls a scene when this anti-Semitism still glowing beneath the ashes flared up visibly:

> At the end of 1946 I returned to my native town, Pabianice. I walked through the streets in my Red Army uniform, decked out with medals and decorations, and saw that things had changed a lot: there were no more Jews. I reached a market that I knew very well, and before the war had been a Jewish market where *chmates* were sold – but now there were only *goyim*, Poles. And suddenly I noticed an old Jew with a beard who had in his hand a pair of rubber boots and a fleece-lined jacket. Presumably he had nothing to eat and was trying to sell these. I didn't know him, he must have just returned from Russia, but he had a striking resemblance to my father and I wanted to talk to him.
>
> At that moment, a *goy* of some forty years old, probably drunk, came up to him, grabbed the boots and went off. I was quite close, and if the old Jew had not recognized me as a Jew, the thief immediately did so. A few moments later he returned to the charge, clearly intent on provoking me. He grabbed the jacket that the old man had, but the latter, seeing a Red Army officer close by, began to resist. I had stayed

calm until then, remembering a directive of Stalin that a Red Army soldier who mistreats a citizen of a 'friendly' people would be severely punished. I couldn't contain myself and seized the man by the throat. It was just what he wanted, to provoke a brawl, and he began to ape Jewish speech: 'Well, Zydek, where did you buy your medals?' People began to gather round, hostile. That encouraged him, and he continued with his insults. I opened the case of my pistol, but without taking it out. Then he yelled, 'Look, the Jew wants to conduct a pogrom against Poles!' Three Polish policemen arrived, armed with rifles, and asked me to hand over my pistol, which I naturally refused to do. They took me to the station, where I demanded that they arrest the hooligan who had started the whole affair. The officer in charge at first struck a superior tone, but when I said that I wanted to phone Ignaz Logosovinski (who was a fellow militant before the war; we were very close), then one of the communist leaders in the region, he turned pale. Logosovinski arrived and I told him the whole business; he wanted to carry out a raid, but I dissuaded him. We left the police station together and suddenly he said to me, 'Wladzio – before the war my name was Wladek – Wladzio, do you want to leave the country?' I didn't say either yes or no, and shortly after I received a summons from the central committee. I went and was offered a responsible position in the voyvoydship of Upper Silesia. That same night, I illegally crossed the Czech frontier and made for a refugee camp in Germany. I enrolled in the Haganah, campaigned for the right of European Jews to reach Palestine, collected weapons, and conducted negotiations with the Soviets in this context. Then I myself left for Palestine, where I took an active part in the War of Independence.

What amazes some other people today is that in Poland, Jewish communist cadres were quite systematically entrusted with even the most senior positions in the army, the police, the diplomatic corps, economic management, etc. The Russians were wary of a resurgence of Polish nationalism, and so deliberately placed Jews in key positions, knowing them to be immune to this disease – so it is said. According to others, it was convenient for the Poles, in the chaotic situation that the country experienced in the wake of the war, to entrust Jews with responsibilities that had little chance of making them popular: the militia, rural collectivization, etc. Adam Paszt, for his part, stresses the particular criteria that often governed the employment of Jewish cadres:

> They knew that the population was anti-Semitic, so they tried to conceal the fact that there were Jews in leading positions. It was basically not the political apparatus that was anti-Semitic; it simply tried to cope with the anti-Semitism of the population. Jews in responsible positions were thus encouraged to change their names. Those who were blond, who looked 'right' – that's what they said – were promoted, those who spoke good Polish. The others could not fill positions of responsibility. It was under Gomulka that anti-Semitism really became systematic.

Bronia Zelmanowicz, a grassroots militant, sees the situation rather differently, mentioning the ambiguity of the relationship that developed between Jewish communists who returned to Poland and the new state power that was established:

> When I returned to Poland I joined the party. Almost all the Jews did so. Some profited from the opportunity to rise higher than their abilities or their education should have let them. This was called 'rising with a party card'. It did a great deal to tarnish the image of Jews among the Polish population. The same phenomenon was seen in the USSR. Clearly, it did not prevent both Poles and Russians from also drawing benefits from a party card.

Thus the blue heaven of utopia soon gave way to a reality with far more varied colours. The new regime, not just in Poland but also in Romania, Bulgaria, Yugoslavia, Czechoslovakia and Hungary, needed these experienced Jewish militants, who thus turned from revolutionaries into officials, privileged people in countries that had a hard time rising from their ruins. Though militants, they were also now members of the *nomenklatura* whose loyalty to the regime was based not only on conviction, but also on the material advantages that it gave. This is certainly the reason why some of our informants who took part in this episode, particularly in Poland and Romania, speak about it with great discretion. The new society that was being built obeyed the strictest canons of Stalinism, and it was with an iron broom that the new administration consolidated its power against the 'forces of the past'. If the majority of our informants held fairly modest positions, some must have agreed to 'get their hands dirty' in this new phase of history, to bend to the Stalinist precept that you do not make an omelette without breaking eggs. They are all the less willing to speak about it in that the machine that they helped to set in motion did not take long to crush them, or at least some of them, a few years later, so that today they have the sense of a great swindle.

The support of these militants for the new regime amid misunderstanding and ambiguity, the petrification of their revolutionary values into Stalin-type 'socialism', was the key to their subsequent disenchantment, which would lead the great majority of them far from communism. For the rather few representatives of other currents of the Jewish workers' movement who returned to Poland after liberation, the problem was raised in a far less complex way. The social fabric on which organizations such as the Bund or Poale Zion had been built no longer existed. The Stalinists, moreover, sought to complete the work that the Nazis had been unable to carry through: the destruction of all Jewish workers' organizations. In 1948, what was left of the Bund was dismantled by the new Polish state.

Several survivors left in search of a substitute Jewish world, concentrations of Jewish population in which they might hope to find roots. The Bundists made for France or America, but also Israel in this situation, despite their historic aversion towards Zionism. The militants of Poale Zion who left for Israel did so at the price of a far less perilous dialectic.

In 1953, Haïm Babic, a Bund veteran, was freed after spending nine years in Soviet prisons and camps. He decided to return to Poland. But his children were already in Israel, and moved heaven and earth for him to be allowed to join them. In 1956, he finally managed to leave the USSR. He mentions the state of mind in which an old Bundist made his reluctant *aliyah*:

When I arrived in Israel, it was not without pangs of conscience. I knew that the country was not empty before our settlement there. We had experienced a tragedy, but did another people have to pay the price? On the one hand, I think that after the gas chambers it was quite legitimate for Jews to have a place to live. I myself thought I had a right to my place in the sun. But I am not someone who bases his claim to the land on Abraham.

For Jewish communists, once the immediate post-war phase had passed, the time of disappointment set in again, partly on account of Stalinist policies and methods in their respective countries, as well as factors specific to their 'little difference' – their condition as Jews. The two aspects often merged, moreover, as at the time of the 1950s trials. Max Technitchek worked for the general staff of the Polish army, and later in various embassies abroad. In 1952, at the time of the Slansky trial, he was recalled and arrested. Trials were being prepared in Poland too:

> I had the ideal profile for a Slansky trial in Poland. I had been a militant in Czechoslovakia, I'd been in Spain, and the Czechs arrested in the context of the Slansky trial would certainly have given evidence that I was a Trotskyist agent before the war, a police spy, etc. That would have made a formidable dossier.

But Stalin died, the climate slightly shifted, and the investigation begun against Technitchek was abandoned. 'In any case,' he says, 'I was too small a fish to carry the weight of a trial on my shoulders. And then, when the thaw set in, I began to believe in a change: the first articles against Stalin in *Novy Mir*, the first rehabilitations.'

Adam Paszt describes the atmosphere prior to the trials:

> After 1945, I worked in the Polish diplomatic service, in particular as military attaché to the Polish embassy in London. I remember return-ing for a few weeks to Poland at the end of 1949, and already being quite shaken by the prevailing climate. Then I worked for the secret service and in the army. I saw how things were heading: there were Russians

everywhere, everyone was wary of everyone else, there was a poisonous atmosphere and trials were being prepared.

This was no accident: Yugoslav Jewish communists seem to have been from the start far more sensitive to Stalinist methods, the bureau-cratic deformations of the new state being established, than were their Polish comrades. This was because, in the one case, the revolution was based on the resistance of an entire people, and in the other, on the bayonets of the Soviet army. Léa Stein recalls an incident that was in some sense premonitory. As a militant in the French Resistance, after liberation she found herself in charge of a camp of Yugoslav refugees, in Châteauneuf-sur-Cher:

The people there were basically Slovenian peasants whom the Germans had deported from Yugoslavia to settle *Volksdeutsche* in their place. They were first of all deported to Germany, then to France. Close by, there was a camp of Ukrainians, administered by Soviet troops.

I was asked to take charge of the Slovenes, and given a uniform – which I never wore. I ate in the canteen like everyone else, though I could have eaten in the mess with the officers. That was a mistake, as I realized later on. On the evening of 8 May, I had the flag of the new Yugoslavia raised in the courtyard (we were lodged in a disused school). I knew that these peasants weren't particularly favourable to Tito, but all the same ... I told myself that I had to react. I gathered everyone in the courtyard and began to give a speech, recalling what the Germans had done in Yugoslavia, that it was Tito's partisans who had defeated them, that it was Tito who was going to give these exiled Slovenian peasants back their farms, in the new Yugoslavia. But my words did not have the effect I anticipated. Some people began shouting that they didn't under-stand anything because I was speaking Serbo-Croat and not Slovenian. Insults and threats exploded on all sides; others complained that I stole their food in the canteen. The most excited ones threw me to the ground and started hitting me. Other people stopped them: 'Perhaps what she's saying is true.'

At that moment, some Russian officers arrived, attracted by the noise. They told me that I could go back to my quarters; they would deal with this matter. This annoyed me and I told them where to get off: 'How dare you, this is a Yugoslav camp here, and I'm in charge. I can answer to Tito!' They were rather abashed, left me a pistol and went off. I didn't then know that I was applying Tito's line so early on. I put the pistol under my pillow and forgot it. I'd never touched a weapon in my life, not even in Spain.

Later on, the Yugoslav mission in Paris sent a political commissar to back me up. He had a rifle and hardly ever left it. The Slovenes boycotted him, but in the end they accepted me. That was my only satisfaction, and finally it was with them that I returned to Yugoslavia.

For the most part, however, it was above all the fact of 'being Jewish' that would pose a real crisis to their commitment. Their adherence to the new regime, and the activism they deployed in its service, did not seem totally to fill the abyss opened under their feet with the disappearance of the milieu that had been familiar to them. Hanna Lévy-Haas, despite her enthusiastic support for the new regime, well expresses this persistent unease, the sentiment of mourning that constantly divided her from her own country:

I was asked to join the party, but I felt so uneasy that I didn't do so. I translated texts, closely followed the development of the crisis with Stalin, but I had the impression that we weren't being told everything, that we weren't being shown the underside of the cards. At all events, I was very busy, and this activism helped me overcome my personal crises, my emotional fragility. My whole family had been killed during the war, in particularly atrocious conditions that were described to me. This was a wound that I carried inside me, and still do so. I have never accepted it. And so, being unable to wipe this out, I did not believe I could really make a new beginning in Yugoslavia.

Others emphasized a different aspect: the socialism constructed in Poland, Romania, etc. was above all a national one. After the break between Tito and Stalin this was not openly nationalist (the USSR kept watch) but constructivist, in other words, oriented above all to building up the country, its symbols being the builder's trowel and the peasant's sickle.

In the context of this national socialism, in which internationalism tended to be reduced to the obligatory reverence towards the guardian power, Stalin's USSR, Jewish militants very often felt out of place. If the national idea still has a future, they wondered, contrary to what we imagined, why then should we Jews be kept apart from this movement? Did not the Jewish tragedy in Europe challenge a certain conception of the universalism of our struggle, did not we cherish some illusions about the perspective of assimilation? Hadn't the Soviet leaders themselves maintained that Jews had paid for their entry ticket to the concert of nations? These were questions that these militants could not avoid facing at the time when the state of Israel was making its appearance on the historical stage.

Still today, Shlomo Shamli is categorical that the reason he decided to leave for Israel in 1948 was not because he detected any whiff of anti-Semitism in Bulgaria. 'In Bulgaria, the communists supported the creation of Israel by invoking the legitimacy of a national liberation struggle, an anti-imperialist one. Dimitrov himself said that "after all the sufferings endured by the Jews, there was now the historical opportunity for them to organize themselves as a nation, with their own state". All Bulgarian Jews who wanted to do so could leave for Israel.' Armed with this blessing, Shamli himself left.

Hanna Lévy-Hass explains her emigration to Israel in similar terms:

In 1947, Gromyko delivered his famous speech from the tribune of the UN that amounted to an official baptism of the state of Israel. I was greatly impressed by this speech, which was subsequently termed 'Zionist'. I remember having had discussions with Jewish friends in Belgrade: should we leave for Israel or not? Since Gromyko had spoken of giving a piece of land to the martyred Jewish people, I told myself that it was perhaps just as well for me to remake my life on a socialist footing in this new country.

The disappointment that led to the abandonment of a utopia was a cumulative process. For the majority of our informants, the doubts went way back, to the 1930s when the swastika seemed to have the upper hand over the hammer and sickle. But a shock was needed for unease to be transformed into revolt or refusal: the direct discovery, at their own expense, not only that socialism did not put an end forever to anti-Semitism, but also that it could even make it, if not into a state religion, then at least into an effective instrument of domination. This cruel discovery began with incidents in everyday life, 'unimportant little things', and culminated in the horror of anti-Semitic campaigns that, like that of 1968 in Poland, fully matched those of the prewar Endecy.

Léa Stein recalls these 'little incidents' that eventually weighed heavily in the balance of major decisions:

> I remember the words that a Serb member of the central committee said to me one day, during a trip we made to Poland in the company of a commercial delegation: 'How is it that there are so many Jews in the Polish party leadership?' I was petrified and, noticing this, his wife tried to put things right: 'You know, Léa, he doesn't have you in mind, "they" aren't all like you!' I was annoyed, and slammed the door in their faces. I was so scandalized that I tried to raise the problem in my party cell, but I was prevented from doing so. I felt that people were drawing away from me. A high official whom I had known from the first days of my party membership told me, 'Be careful, many people are going to pay for their opinions, be a bit discreet!'

Bronia Zelmanowicz tells a similar story:

> One day, when my daughter Ilana was still very young, I left her in her cradle to go shopping – queuing up for meat. Some people arrived and didn't join the queue. I protested and they shouted back: 'You wanted this regime, didn't you?' They had seen by my face that I was Jewish. For them the old equation 'Jew = communist' was perfectly valid.

What happened in Poland in 1968 was on a different level. It was the authorities themselves, a faction of the communist apparatus, certain leaders and not the least senior among them, who conjured up the old demons, seeking to channel a major crisis by arousing familiar spectres. This unbridled campaign against 'Zionists' on Polish radio and television poisoned public life, with Jewish cadres being silently dismissed, and a glacis forming in only a few days around the few tens of thousands of Jews that Poland still had at that date, leading to hasty departures. For several of our informants, this cold pogrom in Polish institutions and society was more of a confirmation than a revelation. It was already years since they'd stopped 'believing', practising towards the regime a form of silent conscientious objection. Some had sought to leave but not been authorized to do so, as they knew too much about the functioning of the apparatus and its secrets. Their names were placed on 'ten-year' and even 'fifteen-year' lists (the time until they might be allowed to leave the country), leaving them trapped. Finally, in 1968, the restrictions on emigration were abolished. One central committee member replied to a Jewish militant who handed in her party card in protest at the anti-Semitic campaign, 'If it's a question of anti-Semitism, why only resign now?'

Jonas Brodkin expresses the disgust of those who left Poland at this time:

> Gomulka's anti-Semitic propaganda, echoed everywhere in the newspapers, on the radio and television, disheartened me. I abandoned everything, even the substantial military pension to which my service in Spain entitled me. I told myself that I was at bottom a Jew, and at 68 years old I started work here, with just one leg.

David Szarfharc, for his part, is an exception among those who experienced this testing time, the only person we met who still defines himself as a communist. In 1969, he was expelled from the Polish party not as a 'Zionist' but as an 'anti-party element', having been so bold as to denounce the anti-Semitic campaign of the previous year as 'counterrevolutionary, anti-Leninist and directed against the workers':

> I didn't think that the party leaders were personally anti-Semites; they were simply reactionaries in general … When I was asked why thousands of Jews had emigrated to Israel after the restrictions were lifted

in 1968, I replied that five minutes of a certain speech by Gomulka had done more for that than decades of Zionist propaganda.

The Polish case was certainly extreme, but if the specifically Jewish aspect of disillusion and rupture holds a central place here, it was never negligible for former communists elsewhere in Yiddishland: in Czechoslovakia, Hungary and Romania, the trials and liquidations of the 1950s also had an anti-Jewish connotation, sharper or less so as the case might be. In the USSR, the campaign of 1952–3 left indelible traces. Pierre Sherf, a Romanian former communist, indicates very well how in this country, which today has excellent relations with Israel, Jewish cadres were encouraged to 'Romanize' themselves, and how he experienced the slow path of disillusion:

I returned to Romania with my wife in December 1945. We were at the same time naive and fanatical. We had a deep sense of coming home, finally leaving behind our condition of wandering Jew. I was appointed to a high position in the foreign ministry, but after the foundation of the state of Israel one of my brothers became a minister in the Israeli government, and I was suddenly removed and transferred to another ministry. When Ana Pauker was dismissed in 1952, I felt the net tighten around me. My superior in the hierarchy was arrested and a case against me was opened. As in Czechoslovakia, Hungary and the USSR, veterans of Spain were fingered as 'spies'. When some of my friends were brought to trial, they appealed to me as a witness. I remember one significant incident in the court, when the prosecutor asked me, 'Do you have any criminal convictions?' 'Yes, two,' I replied. The judge rubbed his hands, seeing the kind of witness that the defendants had. I quickly added: 'Once in 1933 and again in 1935, for communist activity.' He was dumbstruck.

I never hid the fact that I was Jewish, and the party needed us, as it needed cadres belonging to other national minorities living in Romania. But it was afraid that the population would resent the large number of Jews in the party leadership. Like many others, I had therefore to 'Romanize' my name. I now called myself Petre Sutchu instead of Pierre Sherf. During the trials of the 1950s, the spectre of 'Jewish nationalism' was brandished, as in other countries. This suspicion was scarcely belied by future events. Later, a member of the political bureau was eliminated because his daughter had asked to emigrate to Israel. In Spain, in the Brigades, there was an artillery unit named after Anna Pauker, but when she was dismissed, it was given a different name in the official history museums.

Basically, there had never been real popular support for the project of constructing a socialist society in Romania. After 1945, in an essentially peasant country, old mentalities continued to prevail: 'I pretend to work, and the state pretends to pay me' is how Romanians define this situation. We arrived with our dreams of justice and freedom, but we soon understood that it wouldn't work. There were not many communists who were really genuine, like us. We wanted to leave, but in Romania you couldn't say, 'I've had enough, I'm handing in my party card and leaving.' As soon as you gave the impression of no longer playing the game, you rapidly felt the consequences, and your family as well. That's why we stayed in Romania for thirty years until finally the conditions came into being for us to ask for an emigration visa.

When these militants once again took the road of exile, they were in a quite different frame of mind than when they had left Poland or Romania for the first time, fleeing from repression or misery. They were no longer bearers of a message, a programme destined to overthrow the world; no longer heralds of the future, rather wanderers into the void. Their life as militants was a summation of defeats. The paths they took for this new exile were often the same as before, but led intellectually in a quite different direction. The sky of politics and ideology had collapsed on their heads, and the majority of them were no longer interested in pursuing a cause of any kind, seeing the world through the spectacles of a faith or a credo. Having awoken from so many dreams, they most often turned to a 'realism' that made the best of their situation, were wary of any extremism or prophetism, and judged more often in the name of a moral humanism than a political programme.

What pressed them to come and lead a 'normal' and peaceful life as retirees from politics in a modest suburb of Tel Aviv was not a spectacular ideological U-turn but rather this conversion to 'realism'. First of all, there were children and grandchildren living there, the powerful need to rebuild the fabric of family and society in the wake of genocide and the collapse of values. There was also a basically negative aspect: the European workers' movement and socialism had failed to resolve the Jewish question in its national dimension – not just in Europe but in the whole world. It was not just the great universal utopia of communism that had been trampled underfoot, turned into its opposite by those who proclaimed themselves its champions. More modestly, it was the ideas that the Bund tirelessly defended, a national and cultural identity for the Jews, which had failed to find even a beginning of realization. From this point of view, after the Nazis and after Stalin, Jewish history seemed to present itself as an eternal recurrence founded on the permanence of anti-Semitism. Historical optimism gave way to a cultural and moral pessimism that highlighted fugitive values. In this field of ideological ruins, Israel appeared, for want of anything else, as one of those fugitive values, a shelter, a place where at least, as one of our informants put it, 'I can be sure not to be treated as a Yid' – a little Jewish homeland which, in the absence of a world without exploitation and oppression, spares the former Jewish revolutionary the most humiliating discrimination, that based on 'race' or national identity. Since other peoples continue to live in national narrowness and egotism, our informants often repeat, what else can we do except assert ourselves as a nation, a state? And then, while it is a long way from the narrow alleys of a *shtetl* to the concrete avenues of Tel Aviv (from Sholem Aleichem to Begin likewise), the fact remains that every Israeli who has lived in pre-war Yiddishland carries something of it on the soles of his shoes; so that, despite everything, it is easier for these men and women, at the end of the day, to feel Israeli than it would be to feel Swedish or American.

Based on defeats and basically negative factors, the conversion to the reality of Israel rather than to the Zionist credo was rarely enthusiastic or uncritical. From this point of view, Pierre Sherf's confession of faith is more of an exception among former communists:

In Romania, we lived in fear for thirty years, fear of a knock on the door in the early morning. Here it's different, we feel really at home. It may seem strange that someone who was a party member for forty-nine years should express himself in this way; but here, for the first time, when I see a policeman in the street I look on him as a friend, I don't feel any distance between him and me.

Far more common are the words of those who, despite maintaining the historical legitimacy of the existence of the Jewish state, nonetheless regard its social reality and political orientation with a critical eye. Ordinary citizens, rarely engaged in political activity, they none the less assert a kind of continuity between the moral values in the name of which they were mobilized in the past and those in whose name they assume their condition as Jews and Israelis. Max Technitchek:

This country exists, it has a right to exist. Whether the politics of its government are good or bad is something else, and from that point of view there are many things that I don't like. For my part, I have all the rights of a citizen, but the way in which those whom they call a minority, the Arabs, are treated, is detestable. The very word 'minority' is detestable, as I well know, having belonged to a minority for decades, Jews. So, let them find another word and stop borrowing the vocabulary of reactionary *goyim*. I well understand that you wouldn't give an Arab a position in the army general staff; after all, we're at war. But all the same, when I hear the country's rulers – and not just Begin – most often I'm bothered.

Or again Adam Paszt:

What worries me here is the hatred that has developed between the two communities, between the Jews of the Arab countries and those of Central Europe. The expressions you hear in the street, which one community use to denigrate the other, often remind me of the worst expressions of anti-Semitism in Poland. It's even worse, as in Poland people wouldn't dare speak openly in that way.

It's two worlds that face and confront each other here. One of them was already established when the other arrived. That generates a form of jealousy, which also reminds me of Poland. It's a scourge that you find everywhere, at work, in public and political life …

Despite all these worries, I feel fully Israeli; this is my country and I don't have another one. In Sweden I would never have felt Swedish. But when I came here I expected to find a modern, progressive, secular country. And I see this country increasingly becoming a medieval ghetto. That's why I'm pessimistic about the future. It's not just a political question, but above all a social one. The Jews from Europe are increasingly in a minority, and they include a large proportion of religious fanatics who have heaps of children. The greatest danger for Israel, therefore, is being undermined by its internal contradictions. In the long run, the external contradictions between Israel and the Arab countries will decline. The international situation will force Israel to make concessions. Even someone like Begin will have to make concessions!

But the internal contradictions, those between secular and religious, and above all between Ashkenazi and Sephardic, are becoming increasingly explosive. It's the second generation of Sephardis who are rebelling, young people who have never known the conditions of existence of Jews in the Arab countries. They are the majority here and want power; they'll get it. That's what worries me, I'm afraid that this country will become a second Lebanon, that there'll be no more tolerance or democracy.

Finally, it is deeply moving to see the surviving nucleus of Israeli Bundists diligently administering the tokens of a problematic historical continuity. In their small office on Kalisher Street, Tel Aviv, between shelves full of books in Yiddish and faded photos of great forerunners, a few men in their seventies are at work, men who experienced the yoke of Piłsudski's prisons or Stalin's camps – if not both. From classes in Yiddish to revolutionary choirs for young people, they stubbornly continue their extinguished dream; in the full sense, they are witnesses of the past. The gaping contradiction of their presence in Israel is something that they bear with dignity and detachment, without ever denying the traditions of the Bund. Like Haïm Babic or Moshe Green:

I never was so sure of my non-Zionism as I am today, both in terms of politics and that of language and culture. Besides, is it our fault, that of the Bundists, that so many people are leaving the country today? That the great majority of Algerian Jews went to France and not Israel? It doesn't gladden me, on the contrary …

Basically, my dream is that one day the state of Israel will cease to be a Zionist state, that there will be a Jewish state, but without the Zionist ideology that is an obstacle to peace. It is true that one of our mistakes was to underestimate the need for a sovereign Jewish state. We thought that socialism was the universal panacea. But it is also true that the communists and socialists did not help us at all in our struggle to assert the rights of the Jewish nation, and so the necessity of this state imposed itself. But as I see it, in less than a generation there could be a sovereign Jewish state freed from Zionist ideology.

Here, the Bund has the reputation of having been an inveterate enemy of Israel. But that does not correspond at all to the truth. I did not become a Zionist by moving to this country. But I accept and support the reality of this state. On the other hand, this is far from being reciprocated.

In a general sense, the Zionist establishment is not ready to recognize the positive achievements of other currents. In the schools, in Israel, you never hear anything about the historical role of the Bund. And yet, didn't the Bund play a part in the Warsaw ghetto insurrection?

People here act as if the Bund had never existed. Yet, when it was founded, Jewish workers lived like slaves: working ten or twelve hours or more, humiliated by the Russians, confined to the Pale of Settlement. They lived with bent backs, and it's the Bund that enabled them to stand up straight, to be aware that they were men. It's the Bund that led their struggle in 1905, even against the Jewish bosses who exploited them. It's thanks to it that they acquired consciousness; it's the Bund that rehabilitated and developed their language and culture. Today, in the retirement home where I live, close to Tel Aviv, I act as librarian. I'm in charge of some 1,700 books in Yiddish that we possess.

Whether they work in the field of memory and commemoration, like these veterans of the Bund in Israel, or take up the position of critical observer like the majority of former communists whom we met; whether, like the majority of the former militants of Poale Zion, they have rallied to a Zionism that has little in common with that of Borochov, all these veteran revolutionaries from Yiddishland crossed a new Rubicon by coming to live in Israel. In their political trajectory, this transition marks an irrevocable caesura. 'What can an old revolutionary Jew living in Israel do?' Elija Rosijanski asks ironically, a former Trotskyist activist in France, former militiaman in the POUM, who at the time of liberation 'searched in broad daylight, with a lantern, for Jews in the streets of Paris'. The idea of coming to end his existence in Israel, as a low-ranking employee for the social security, would never have entered his mind if, in the early 1950s, the French Republic had not brusquely refused him naturalization.

This sense of not having a grip on the reality of their adopted country, of being cut off from the field of action, is widely shared by the majority of our informants. There is, to be sure, the weight of failures and defeats, fatigue and age, the scepticism in the wake of lost illusions. But there is also the unease that necessarily affects those who rallied de facto to the reality of Israel in being faced with this reality, the dominant ideas that cement its consensus, its powerful mechanisms of self-justification. Hence the constant oscillation of our informants when they talk about Israel – however critically – between homage to an idea that triumphed, the Zionist utopia become reality, and the deep unease they express about the elements of crisis that pervade this society, the actions and exactions of those who preside over its destiny.

All the more remarkable in this context is the minority position taken by those who, after making this transition, continue active in the same camp, in the name of the same values – more than ever against the grain of their environment. Communists such as Hanna Lévy-Hass, Shlomo Shamli and David Szarfharc who, despite the countless vicissitudes of the Israeli communist movement, weakened by the major split of 1965, 'hold their course' in the name of loyalty to their own past, but also in the name of the unshakeable conviction that the conquering Zionism of Begin and Dayan is a historical impasse pregnant with immense tragedies. In the name, therefore, of a historical imagination that returns to the original dream of the first communist generations in Palestine, and does not renounce the perspective of coexistence between reconciled national communities, in a Middle East where the hatred that plays into the hands of the great powers will no longer prevail. For them, as for Yankel Taut, who, after years in the wilderness, found himself comforted in his convictions by the appearance of young 'leftists' in the late 1960s, there is in Israeli reality one irrepressible dimension: the presence in the Middle East of a Jewish national community, a Jewish society of several million who are now irreversibly rooted in this land. But, in contrast to the apostles of conquering Zionism, they continue to believe in history and not mythology. For them, this reality in no way implies the undivided domination of a Jewish state to the detriment of the other people that have a legitimate right to the land that they seek to assert – precisely because they do not despair of history, do not believe that the present forward flight of the Zionist leaders (which does not open a radiant future for the Jews of Israel, but rather the perspective of an endless state of war, an interminable suicide) is the only prospect for the community of which they feel themselves full members. And since hundreds of thousands of Israelis demonstrated in summer 1982 against the war in Lebanon, they feel far less alone.

Epilogue

All the dead are really dead, but so are the living
who flee my sight like blackened smoke.
With pained look I try to pursue them
but I know that in my heart they cannot return to life.

Avrom Liessin

The Yiddishland revolutionary is the archetypically tragic character of our history. He or she paid double tribute to the horrors of
the century. In relation to both the workers' movement and Judaism,
they experienced absolute negation, the sense of the end of the world
without a redeeming beyond; their existence was trampled by the
passage of the Four Horsemen of the Apocalypse.

Even if they survived the convulsions of this history, even if the
reality principle prevailed in them over the dizzying sense of nothingness, they can never dismiss the spectres that come to meet them,
from Warsaw to Kolyma, Albacete to Auschwitz. They have themselves joined these ranks. They survive, mentally, in the ruins of
Yiddishland and the revolution. The human community from which
these men and women came is destroyed; the great utopia that set
them in movement turned into a demoniacal farce.

'There are living men among us', wrote Richard Marienstras,

who do not end up dying, either because they cannot detach their
gaze – the gaze of their being – from the past moments in which their
world was destroyed and which they constantly relive, or because they

turned their gaze to a new project that required a clean break with the completely abolished past, and by accepting this break, they lost their being ...[1]

The heroes – or anti-heroes – of this book bear within them a double death. In their mental universe, the spirits of this buried world incessantly come to life; but between the past and their everyday life an abyss has opened up, and they live the obligatory triumph of the new reality with a divided self. Their existence is dominated by the conflictual coexistence of two times, that of the past and that of the present. The past has become for them a mystery over which the angel of death hovers, their role being that of wanderers into the void. And yet this past is history, and they cannot prevent themselves yet again from seeking to understand, from bearing within them the shadow of the old utopia. For the Yiddishland revolutionaries, the clock of history stopped most often at the time when the world turned cannibal and expelled them to the ranks of unwanted and banished. Often, then, history is reinterpreted mythologically in terms of a world of sphinxes and demons. This tragic perception of a world grown obscure can only be reinforced today, with the endless continuation of a macabre farce in the Israel of Begin and Sharon.

In certain countries of the diaspora, France above all, the 'new Jewish identity' leaves no stone unturned in its tireless search for sources and roots, sometimes encountering there the Jewish workers' movement and the revolutionaries of Yiddishland. But the image that this 'new Jewish identity' sees there is that of the loser, the retiree from the revolution, who has most often abandoned the illusions of youth. What it sympathizes with here is not so much their utopia and action of a former time as their disillusions and present 'realism', their return to certain 'refuge values', in particular their re-evaluation of their Jewish 'being-in-the-world'.

Most often, the movement for a 'new Jewish identity' develops in an opposite direction to its own inspiration before the history of the century swept the militant of the Bund or of left Poale Zion, or the

---

1   Marienstras, *Être un peuple en diaspora*, p. 11.

communist, into its bloody whirlwind. The Jewish specificity is no longer a springboard from which it is possible to reach the universality and infinity of a world in fusion; it has become a search for what distinguishes and divides, a never-ending confirmation of the tragic fate of the Jews. Narcissistic contemplation of the 'little difference' swells to the dimensions of an essential and irreducible alterity. As in the preachings of rabbis, the non-Jewish world, the universe of the *goyim*, tends once more to become a perpetually threatening other and elsewhere.

It is easy to understand, then, the ambiguous relationship between the master-thinkers of this current of renewal of diasporic culture and the state of Israel. They assert their 'right' to live in the diaspora, not feeling obliged to support unconditionally the orientations of those who preside over the destiny of this state, but they also avoid 'washing dirty linen' in public, essentially reserving their objections and criticisms for the 'tribe', and when the mass media allow perplexity or indignation to show through, as with the bombing of Beirut, they attack this as an intolerable interference into 'their' problems. Faced with the forward flight of the Jewish state, challenged by the massacres of Sabra and Shatila, they interrogate their unease of being a 'left-wing Jew' in these difficult times, redouble their efforts in terms of conferences and round tables, most often simply forget to go and cry their indignation and disgust outside the Israeli embassy: Beirut is a long way from the Marais.

There are only a few today who, despite this 'unease', break radically with the rules of good and bad conscience imposed by the resistible triumph of Zionism; those who, after the model of the Yiddishland revolutionaries, act against the communitarian consensus. But against the current, they perpetuate a legacy that is already being lost in the mists of time.

Selected Biographies

Haïm Babic

Born 1908 in Nowy Dwor, near Warsaw, son of a pedlar. Joined the Zukunft ('Future'), the Bund's youth organization, in 1924. Started work as a carpenter at the age of fifteen, became a Bund cadre and trade union militant first in his home town and then in Warsaw. In September 1939, he managed to reach the eastern part of Poland occupied by the Soviet army. Moved to the Urals, worked in a factory in Astrakhan and subsequently on a *kolkhoz* (collective farm). Arrested in 1945, accused of 'counterrevolutionary activity' and condemned to six years in a labour camp, then exiled to Kolyma, not returning until 1953. Left the USSR for Israel in 1956. Still active in the Bund, in Tel Aviv.

Leo Lev

Born in Ostrowiecz, near Radom, in 1905. Learned the trade of carpenter and joined the Young Communists. In the early 1920s he left to join his brother in Palestine, where he worked on a kibbutz. In 1924 he moved to Tel Aviv, worked again as a carpenter and was active in the Palestinian Communist Party (PKP). Became head of the party's Tel Aviv branch. Expelled in 1936 for having criticized the way in which 'Arabization' was being carried out. Left for France, then joined the International Brigades in Spain. Took part in the defence of Madrid and the battle of Malaga. Returned wounded to France. Interned in the camps of Gurs and Le Vernet, transferred to the Djelfa camp in Algeria. Travelled to the USSR in 1943, joined the Polish army of Wanda Wasilewska, and returned to Poland at the end of the war. Active there in the Communist Party and the Jewish Committee. Emigrated to Israel in 1957, and resumed his work as a carpenter.

Hanna Levy-Haas

Born 1914 in Sarajevo. Her father owned a small shop in the city market, but soon went bankrupt. Attracted by communism at the age of fifteen. At the University of Belgrade, became an organized sympathizer of the illegal Communist Party and took part in street demonstrations. Became a high school teacher, constantly moved from one school to another on account of her Jewish origin and political convictions. Was in Montenegro when the war broke out, and organized medical care for wounded partisans. Continued her Resistance activity under the Italian occupation. Arrested by the Gestapo in the wake of the German invasion of Yugoslavia, she was deported to Bergen-Belsen in August 1944. Returned to Yugoslavia after liberation, worked in government services as a journalist and translator. Emigrated to Israel in 1948 and joined the Communist Party there. Took the Maki side when the Israeli Communist Party split. Subsequently active in the women's movement, against the war in Lebanon, and in the association of anti-Nazi veterans.

Yehoshua Rojanski

Born 1896 in Slonim (Byelorussia) in a trading family. Joined Poale Zion in 1913. Worked in a tannery. Arrested by the Okhrana in 1914, on account of his activities as a political and trade union militant. Fled to the Caucasus in 1915 to escape conscription. Built up a section of Poale Zion in Tsaritsyn (subsequently Stalingrad, now Volgograd). In 1917 moved close to the Bolsheviks while remaining a member of Poale Zion. Arrested by the Whites in Rostov-on-Don during the civil war. Managed to escape, active in Azerbaijan and Armenia, where he took part in the establishment of Soviet power. As leader of the Poale Zion in Minsk in 1920, came into conflict with the Bolsheviks. Resigned from left Poale Zion when it decided to dissolve and merge into the Communist Party. Underground socialist Zionist activist from 1923. Arrested in 1955 for Zionist activities and condemned with his wife to ten years in prison. Emigrated to Israel in 1974, now a member of the Labour Party.

Yankel Taut

Born 1913 in Galicia. Shortly afterward his family emigrated to Berlin, where he grew up in the Scheunenviertel, where Jews from the East congregated. His father was extremely pious and lived from odd jobs.

At the age of fourteen, Yankel became an apprentice in an engineering business, joined the Young Communists and was active in the trade union. Expelled from the Communist Party in the early 1930s for having criticized its ultra-left orientation. Active in the Brandlerite opposition and sympathetic to Trotskyism. Left for Denmark in 1934, then Palestine. Worked in the orange plantations. Active in a small Brandlerite group, then formed a nucleus of Trotskyist militants. Became a skilled worker at the Haifa oil refinery after the Second World War, and again a trade union activist. Now retired and still active in the anti-Zionist Marxist Matzpen.

Max Technitchek

Born in Galicia, the son of a bank official. Sympathized with the Ukrainian national movement, then moved towards communism. Left for Czechoslovakia in the early 1930s, where he was very active in the communist movement. Enlisted in the International Brigades when the civil war broke out in Spain. Temporarily secretary of the Balkan brigade. In 1939, joined the French army as a volunteer. Prisoner of war in Germany, escaped and recaptured twice. Returned to Poland after liberation, worked in the army general staff then in various embassies. Arrested in 1952 at the time of the Slansky trial, then released and rehabilitated. Emigrated to Israel in 1968.

Glossary

aliyah   Literally 'ascension' or 'spiritual elevation', referring to Jewish immigration to Eretz Israel

chalutz (pl. *chalutzim*)   Zionist pioneer

chmates   Literally 'rags', by extension the 'fringes' or *tzitzit* that orthodox Jewish men are required to wear as an undergarment

galut   The 'exile' resulting from the dispersion (diaspora) of the Jewish people

goy (f. *goya*, pl. *goyim*)   A non-Jew

Hassid (pl. *Hassidim*)   Adherent of Hassidism, a religious movement founded in Ukraine and Byelorussia in the eighteenth century by Israel Ben Eliezer, known as Baal Shem Tov, in reaction to scholarly Judaism. Hassidim place particular stress on joyous communion with God, principally by way of song and dance

kosher   Foodstuffs permitted by the *kashrout*, the Judaic alimentary code

mamelosh   Literally 'mother tongue', meaning Yiddish

matzo (pl. matzot)   Unleavened bread consumed for Pesach (Passover)

Ostjude   An 'eastern Jew' as opposed to a German Jew or French Israelite

pletzl   'Little place' in Yiddish, referring to the Saint-Gervais neighbourhood in the fourth arrondissement of Paris, which from 1881 to the Second World War received tens of thousands of Jews from Yiddishland and was the centre of Jewish life

Sabra   A term for all Jews born on Israeli soil

Shabbat   The weekly day of rest observed from before sunset on Friday to Saturday after dark

shtetl   The extended village typical of Jewish settlements in Eastern Europe before the Second World War

shtreimel   The fur cap worn particularly but not exclusively by Hassidim

teffilin (or phylacteries)   Two leather boxes containing parchment scrolls with verses from the Torah, which orthodox Jews wear on the head and the left arm for weekday morning prayers

treife   Not kosher

yeshiva   Centre for studying the Torah and Talmud, generally run by a rabbi

Yiddishkeit   The cultural heritage of Yiddishland, and by extension a way of living

Bibliography

Works Cited

Arendt, Hannah (1961), *Eichmann in Jerusalem*, New York: Schocken.

Berman, Adolf Avraham (1978), *Bamakom asher ya'ad Li Hagoral* (Where Fate Has Placed Me), Tel Aviv: Hakibbutz Hameuchad.

Böhm, Adolf (1935), *Die zionistische Bewegung*, 2 vols., Berlin: Jüdischer Verlag.

Bunzl, John (1975), *Klassenkampf in der Diaspora*, Vienna: Europaverlag.

Deutscher, Isaac (1968), *The Non-Jewish Jew*, London: Merlin Press.

Deutscher, Isaac (1971), 'The Tragedy of Polish Communism between the Two Wars', in *Marxism in Our Time*, London: Jonathan Cape.

Diamant, David (1971), *Les juifs dans la Résistance française*, Paris: Le Pavillon.

Diamant, David (1979), *Combattants juifs dans l'armée républicaine espagnole*, Paris: Éditions Renouveau.

Elek, Hélène (1977), *La mémoire d'Hélène*, Paris: Maspero.

Ertel, Rachel (1982), *Le shtetl*, Paris: Payot.

Grayek, Chalom Stéphane (1978), *L'insurrection du ghetto de Varsovie*, Paris: Foyer ouvrier juif.

Greenstein, Yaakov (1968), *Oud Mikikar-Hayovel* (A Firebrand from Hayovel Square), Tel Aviv: Hakibbutz Hameukhad.

Greilsammer, Ilan (1978), *Les communistes israéliens*, Paris: Presses de la fondation nationale des sciences politiques.

Gronowski, Louis (1980), *Le dernier grand soir*, Paris: Éditions du Seuil.

Hemingway, Ernest (1994), *For Whom the Bell Tolls*, New York: Arrow.

Kochan, Lionel, ed. (1971), *Les juifs en Union soviétique depuis 1917*, Paris: Calmann-Lévy.

Korzec, Pawel (1980), *Juifs en Pologne*, Paris: Presses de la Fondation nationale des sciences politiques.

Krall, Hanna (1981), *Lekhadim et Elohim* (Going before God), Tel Aviv: Adam.

Krall, Hanna (1983), *Mémoires du ghetto de Varsovie*, Paris: Éditions du Scribe.

Lévy-Hass, Hanna (1989), *Journal de Bergen-Belsen 1944–45*, Paris: Éditions du Seuil.

London, Artur (1971), *The Confession*, New York: Ballantine.

Margalit, Elkana (1976), *Anatomia shel Smol* (Anatomy of a Left), Tel Aviv: Lamed Peretz.

Marienstras, Richard (1975), *Être un peuple en diaspora*, Paris: Maspero.

Medem, Vladimir (1979), *The Memoirs of Vladimir Medem*, New York: KTAV.

Mendel, Hersh (1988), *Memoirs of a Jewish Revolutionary*, London: Pluto Press.

Minczelès, Henri (2010), *Le mouvement ouvrier juif*, Paris: Syllepse.

Picon-Valin, Béatrice (1973), *Le théâtre juif soviétique pendant les années 20*, Lausanne: L'âge d'homme.

Poliakov, Léon (1951), *Le bréviare de la haine: Le 3e Reich et les juifs*, with a preface by François Mauriac, Paris: Calmann-Lévy.

Rajsfus, Maurice (1990), *Sois juif et tais-toi!*, Paris: EDI.

Rodinson, Maxime (1997), *Peuple juif ou problem juif?*, Paris: La Découverte.

Rodinson, Maxime (1983), *Cult, Ghetto and State*, London: Al Saqi Books.

Rosenthal-Schneidermann, Esther (1970), *Naftoulei Derakhim* (Turns and Detours), vol. 1, Tel Aviv: Hakibbutz Hameukhad.

Slovès, Henri (1982), *L'Etat juif de l'Union soviétique*, Paris: Les presses d'aujourd'hui.

Smolar, Hersh (1973), *Heichan ata khaver Sidorov* (Where Are You, Comrade Sidorov?), Tel Aviv: Am Oved.

Smolar, Hersh (1979), *Tokhelet veshivra: Zichronot shel 'yevsek' leshéavar* (Memoirs of a Former 'Yevsek'), Tel Aviv: University of Tel Aviv.

Sperber, Manès (1952), *Qu'une larme dans l'océan*, Paris: Calmann-Lévy.

Steinberg, Lucien (1970), *La révolte des justes: Les juifs contre Hitler 1933–1945*, Paris: Fayard.

Strauss-Marko, Shlomo (1978), *Dam Tahor* (Pure Blood), Tel Aviv: Or-am.

Trepper, Leopold (1983), *The Great Game*, New York: McGraw Hill.

Tucholsky, Kurt (1982), *Bonsoir révolution allemande!*, Grenoble: PUG.

Tucholsky, Kurt (1982), *Chroniques allemandes*, Paris: Balland.

Vidal-Naquet, Pierre (1996), *The Jews: History, Memory, and Present*, New York: Columbia University Press.

Weinberg, David (1974), *Les juifs à Paris de 1933 à 1939*, Paris: Calmann-Lévy.

Weinstock, Nathan (1987) *Zionism: False Messiah*, translated by Alan Adler, London: Pluto.

Wiesel, Elie (1999), *The Testament*, New York: Schocken.

Zalcman, Moshe (1977), *Histoire véridique de Moshe, ouvrier juif et communiste au temps de Staline*, Paris: Édition recherches.

Further Sources

Altshuler, Mordechai (1980), *Hayevsektia bebrit hamoatsot 1918–1930* (The Yevsektia in the Soviet Union 1918–1930), Tel Aviv: Sifriat Poalim.

Auty, Phyllis (1972), *Tito*, Paris: Éditions du Seuil.

Berger-Barzilia, Joseph (1968), *Hatragedia shel hamahapecha hasovietit* (The Tragedy of the Soviet Revolution), Tel Aviv: Am Oved.

Berger-Barzilai, Joseph (1974), *Le naufrage d'une génération*, Paris: Denoël.

Bolloten, Burnett (2015), *The Spanish Civil War: Revolution and Counter-revolution*, Chapel Hill: University of North Carolina Press.

Broué, Pierre (1964), *Les procès de Moscou*, Paris: Julliard.

Broué, Pierre (2006), *The German Revolution, 1917–1923*, Leiden: Brill.

Carr, Edward H. (1970), *A History of Soviet Russia*, London: Penguin.

Carrère d'Encausse, Hélène (1981), *Decline of an Empire*, New York: HarperCollins.

Caute, David (1973), *The Fellow Travellers*, Worthing: Littlehampton Book Services.

Centner, Israël (1966), *MiMadrid ad Berlin* (From Madrid to Berlin), Tel Aviv, privately printed.

Copfermann, Émile (1982), *Les patries buissonnières*, Lausanne: L'âge d'homme.

Fejtö, François (1971), *A History of the People's Democracies*, New York: Praeger.

Frank, Pierre (1979), *Histoire de l'Internationale communiste*, Paris: La Brèche.

Garnier-Raymond, Philippe (1975), *L'affiche rouge*, Paris: Fayard.

Gorkin, Julian (1978), *Les communistes contre la révolution espagnole*, Paris: Belfond.

Gross, Sidonie (2008), *Tant pis si la lutte est crulle*, Paris: Syllepse.

Halevi, Ilan (1987), *A History of the Jews: Ancient and Modern*, London: Zed Books.

Haupt, Georges, Michael Löwy and Claudie Weill (1974), *Les marxistes et la question nationale, 1848–1914*, Paris: Maspero.

Haupt, George and Jean-Jacques Marie (1969), *Les bolcheviks par eux-mêmes*, Paris: Maspero.

Joffe, Maria (1978), *One Long Night*, London: New Park Publications.

Kantor, Levi (1969), *Méa shnot ma'avak 1865–1965* (A Hundred Years of Struggle 1865–1965), Tel Aviv: Yahad.

Klingberg, Marcus and Michael Sfard (2007), *Hameragel ha'akharon* (The Last Spy), Tel Aviv: Ma'ariv Book Guild.

Léon, Abraham (1969), *La conception matérialiste de la question juive*, Paris: EDI. (also available as Abram Leon, *The Jewish Question*, at marxists.org)

Lerner, Warren (1970), *Karl Radek: The Last Internationalist*, Stanford: Stanford University Press.

Levin, Nora (1977), *While Messiah Tarried: Jewish Socialist Movements, 1871–1917*, New York: Schocken Books.

Markish, Esther (1974), *Le long retour*, Paris: Robert Lafont.

Marrus, Michael R. and Robert O. Paxton (1995), *Vichy France and the Jews*, Stanford: Stanford University Press.

Meyer-Leviné, Rosa (1977), *Inside German Communism*, London: Pluto Press.

Michkinski, Moshe (1981), *Reshit tenouat hapoalim hayehoudit beroussia* (The Emergence of the Jewish Workers' Movement in Russia), Tel Aviv: Hakibbutz Hameukhad.

Morrow, Felix (1974), *Revolution and Counter-revolution in Spain*, Atlanta: Pathfinder Press.

Orwell, George, *Homage to Catalonia* [1939] (2001), London: Penguin.

Poretski, Elisabeth K. (1969), *Les nôtres*, Paris: Denoël.

Rajsfus, Maurice (1980), *Les juifs dans la collaboration: l'UGIF 1941–1944*, Paris: EDI.

Robin, Régine (1979), *Le cheval blanc de Lénine ou l'histoire autre*, Brussels: Complexe.

Schramm, Hanna and Barbara Vormeier (1979), *Vivre à Gurs: Un camp de concentration français 1940–1941*, Paris: Maspero.

Slanska, Josefa (1969), *Rapport sur mon mari*, Paris: Mercure de France.

Suchecky, Bernard (1979–80), *'Socialistes-Sionistes', Sejmistes et 'Poaley-Tsiyon' en Russia: les premières années, 1901–1906*, DEA dissertation, Paris: EHESS (mimeographed).

Trotsky, Leon (1970), *On the Jewish Question*, Atlanta: Pathfinder Press.

Trotsky, Leon (1973), *The Spanish Revolution (1931–39)*, Atlanta: Pathfinder Press.

Weinstock, Nathan (1969), *Le sionisme contre Israël*, Paris: Maspero.

Index